be fully alive. After I read this book - I felt compelled to... do life even better as both a person and a leader!!!"

Tarina W | #1 international bestselling author of The Deliberate Effect **and** More Life Please**, global corporate speaker and master life strategist**

"This is a must read for any entrepreneur. In today's world of business, the idea of being 'too busy' to take care of ourselves, and the ones we love is permeating organizations around the world. *The Happy Leader* is not only a reminder of the fundamentals required for our own success, but also a guide to getting back to our self so we can create the strength we all need to serve the ones we love, happily."

Robert Murray | Co-Founder of Intrigue Media, Growth 500 list for 4 years in a row

"*The Happy Leader*, I must say, is a modern masterpiece, and it expressly addresses the ills of today—alienation, depression, deep-seated anger and guilt, self-destructiveness, lack of empathy and drive, and more— and reveals to us how to deal with them. Mr. Johal has woven a brilliant, poignant tale of downward spiral and recovery and forgiveness— toward exquisite happiness and self-realization or what you may call enlightenment. A great reminder of how real Karma is; there are no coincidences in life. The tools provided at the end of the book are very good and can be put to immediate use by the reader. I venture to say that this will be a classic someday."

Tom Fedro | Co-Founder, Paragon Software Group Corp.; bestselling author of Next Level Selling

"To me, this book has a certain meditative quality that settles me down whenever I feel lost or anxious. I owe that to Mr. Johal's elegant, sharp writing, which is such a joy to read because I can vividly see both places and characters! I even began bringing this book along in my early morning jogs. It has become a great friend to me. I'm highly recommending this book to everyone."

Rick Orford | Co-Founder & Executive Producer at Travel Addicts Life, and bestselling author of The Financially Independent Millennial

PRAISE

"Shawn understands the true essence of Leadership, Happiness and Change. It is a must-read for every leader looking to grow both personally and professionally!"

Verne Harnish | Author of Scaling Up **and Founder of the Entrepreneur's Organization (EO)**

"Shawn Johal's first book is an instant classic, I read it in one evening. Through his brilliant storytelling, we can see ourselves, the decisions we make and the choices that impact our happiness. We also understand deeply that it is in our own power and control to change as we gain a window into how to begin that process."

Robert Glazer | Bestselling author of Friday Forward, Elevate and Performance Partnerships

"*The Happy Leader* is a must read for those who want a fun look at leadership and happiness. The fable is a wonderful tale about growing, leading and finding happiness. It is learning, once again, that the three are not mutually exclusive. This is a tale of truth and happiness. Shawn has done a wonderful job of making this for compelling reading. I highly recommend *The Happy Leader*!"

Warren Rustand | Dean of the EO (Entrepreneurs Organization) Leadership Academy, CEO of Summit Capital Consulting

"In his creative story-telling style, Johal teaches us how to break self-limiting beliefs and strive for more in our lives. Be prepared for a truly transformative experience!"

Spencer Sheinin, CPA, CA | CEO of Shift Financial Insights and #1 bestselling author of Entreprenumbers

"Do not walk .... RUN to get this amazingly simple but super powerful book. Shawn articulates in his beautiful writing what it means to

"All the characters in *The Happy Leader* are unique, compelling, and real, especially Ethan and Ravi, whose friendship was the heart and soul of this book. The characters suffer from the troubles—family, health, relationships, business, dreams, careers—brought on by the rapid, demanding pace of the modern world. However, each character helps us find a way through it—by showing us that transformation is not only possible but also inevitable, for it is a choice we can make at any time! Don't miss out on reading this one. I guarantee *The Happy Leader* won't leave you unchanged."

Chris Magnone | Co-Founder & CEO of Buddha Brands

"*The Happy Leader* is unputdownable! I read it from cover to cover in a single sitting. It's an adventure story of self-discovery, self-recovery, and self-reconciliation—toward the inner path of happiness. It also showcases a set of striking concepts on psychology, business, mentorship, and leadership. But what sets this book apart from hundreds of books is that it clearly and effectively shows us the concepts rather than just telling us about them. *The Happy Leader* is an astounding performance—a highly recommended reading!"

Cléo Maheux | Entrepreneur & Visionary Scaling Up Coach

"Shawn Johal's book, *The Happy Leader*, stands among the few books that have thoroughly changed my life. It has impacted hugely the way I live and work every day. It's no exaggeration to say that I learned something from every single chapter. It's such a magnificent story. Just read it and be floored."

Vicken Kanadjian | Co-Founder of Cesium

"After reading *The Happy Leader*, I came out a changed man. There are wonderful long passages, which were such a pleasure to read. There are many unforgettable, powerful scenes too, which I have not read from any other stories but here. There was not a single part of this story that I didn't enjoy reading. Reading *The Happy Leader* was a momentous experience for me."

Jebb Nucci | CEO of iCubic

"Nearly all the scenes in this book are moving and revealing. They don't leave you unchanged, and that's why this book is so powerful. The characters are so real, it's like I've known them for a long time. *The Happy Leader* has stirred me awake. Now I wake up every day incurably happy and filled with the zest for life. I've no doubt this book will do the same for you."

Ali Razi | Founder & CEO of Banc Certified Merchant Services

"One can read *The Happy Leader* as a novel or a self-help book. It's a hybrid of both genres. In adversity, an unhappy individual identifies deep insights for a happy journey in life. The very moving story immerses you into the ideas the author introduces, like *time-anger gap*, *spinning positivity*, and *circular reciprocation*, which are simple yet profound, a blend of philosophy and modern neuroscience. Many more life-changing ideas await you here, so don't waste any more time not reading this book."

Bill Bierce | award-winning international business and technology attorney; best-selling author of Smart Business Exits

"While this is a 'leadership book,' many lovers of stories will also appreciate this wonderful tale. It's not often that we come across a story that blends well with the complex ideas the author introduces without being preachy. Mr. Johal has done that remarkably in *The Happy Leader*. The story is good enough to stand alone, but the ideas (a great mix of Zen, psychology, and neuroscience) infused within the story just made it even more outstanding! This is one of those powerful, life-changing reads everybody needs."

Sanjay Jaybhay | bestselling author of Invest and Grow Rich

"I've already read *The Happy Leader* a couple of times—in fact, I lost count—it seems exhaustible as I learn more and more things each time. The book is so rich in concepts, situations, and characters, and what I do is flip to the pages and go back to certain passages and reflect on them. Then I'd apply what I learned in my daily life. This book has grown so dear to me now, and I couldn't thank Shawn enough for writing this amazing, life-affirming story."

Tamara Nall | President and CEO at The Leading Niche

"*The Happy Leader* is such a great pleasure to read from start to end. Never a dull moment. No words wasted. All scenes and characters add up to the mounting tension—until boom! It's like I never knew what had hit me, but I began crying at how the story turned out. The story is just so wonderful and heartwarming. I suggest that everyone from all walks of life read it and learn the invaluable lessons in the story."

Kristin Cripps | self-made millionaire, bestselling author
of Shepreneur

"Storytelling is recognized as one of the most powerful tools for communicating key messages. Shawn Johal has accomplished that and more by weaving an absorbing tale that you will read from start to finish because it is truly interesting. Along the way the lessons are given and bound to be absorbed. A true life and business primer that can change your effectiveness and happiness."

Tony White | CEO and Founder of enChoice, Inc.

THE HAPPY LEADER

A Leadership Fable about Transformation in Business and in Life

SHAWN SUKHRAJ JOHAL

Leaders
Press

ISBN 978-1-63735-051-5 (hardcover)
ISBN 978-1-63735-085-0 (paperback)
ISBN 978-1-943386-93-2 (ebook)

SIMON &
SCHUSTER

Print Book Distributed by Simon & Schuster
1230 Avenue of the Americas
New York, NY 10020

Library of Congress Control Number: 2021905973

GO BEHIND
THE SCENES WITH
20+ WORLD CLASS
LEADERSHIP EXPERTS

DISCOVER HOW TO BUILD
A BUSINESS AND LIFE YOU LOVE.

THIS EVENT BRINGS TOGETHER
SOME OF THE TOP EXPERTS
IN LEADERSHIP
TO HELP YOU GROW
YOUR BUSINESS
AND YOUR HAPPINESS AND

IT IS FREE

FOR A LIMITED TIME

WWW.HAPPYLEADERSUMMIT.COM

Dedicated to Sarah, Chloe, and Tristan,
for believing in me unconditionally

To my parents, for showing me the
power of hard work and dedication

CONTENTS

PROLOGUE

*T*he beating of his heart vibrates wildly throughout his entire being. Oxygen refuses to enter his lungs. Each muscle in his body gives in slowly, forcing him to the ground onto a patch of sleek, wet grass. A cramp seizes his left calf, then his right thigh, causing an explosion of unbearable pain. He knows he should keep walking forward. Nausea twists his stomach into knots while dizziness grips his mind with unforgiving tenacity. His vision seems blurred, out of focus. Sweat streams down his cheeks, mixing with tears. It does not seem real, as if his body belongs to another person.

He gazes up at the grey skyline, unable to think straight. He cannot grasp the feeling and does not understand the sensation coursing through his body and blood. His abdominal muscles suddenly lock viciously. He immediately stretches his arms over his head to bring urgent relief. He takes a very deep breath, attempting to calm down.

A few seconds later, his children are rushing to his side.

Lying there, paralyzed, he remembers reading about this experience. The article was titled "When the End Arrives." Still, it has not prepared him in the least. Words could never have prepared him for this moment.

He has learned many important things on this journey. Faith, courage, and determination all come to mind. Above all, however, belief tops the list. A belief he never imagined possible.

He asks for some water. Sipping gingerly, he wills his body to stand. Something in him has changed on this day, which he barely survived. Despite his physical agony and mental fatigue, he has just achieved a goal he considered unattainable. He now knows, without a sliver of doubt, that he will have the confidence to tackle any challenge life throws at him.

PART I

DISCOVERY

PART 1

DISCOVERY

LIFE AS I KNOW IT

Life is not a problem to be solved, but a reality to be experienced.
—Soren Kierkegaard, founder of existentialism

*W*atching the light stream in through the window, Ethan felt the familiar knot of dread twisting through his thoughts. His body ached all over, as if he had gone ten rounds with a professional boxer the night before. It was an all-too-familiar feeling he experienced most mornings. His doctor had identified stress as the main culprit. Ethan demanded a better diagnosis, one ideally remedied with a magical pill or three. He knew he should have found a more mainstream medical expert instead of some holistic voodoo master. He forced his legs out of bed, slipped on his crumbling slippers, and made his way downstairs.

As he entered the kitchen, Eva kept her eyes on a *Women's Health* magazine. He couldn't remember exactly when they had stopped greeting each other with a warm kiss in the morning, but it had certainly been a very long while. Come to think of it, he couldn't even recall the last time they had shared a simple smile at breakfast.

He poured his coffee and sat down in his usual spot. He never liked this spot. It was the worst spot at the table.

"Will you be home on time tonight?" Eva asked without looking up.

"Why?" answered Ethan. *Going out again*, he thought to himself.

"I told you last week I planned a dinner downtown with Claudia and Anne. We're meeting at seven sharp."

"I'll be here," he answered.

"I'm serious, Ethan. The last time I had to cancel because of your apparent emergency meeting. Remember, the night you got home at God knows what time with some lame excuse."

Ethan got up and walked straight for the den. "I said I'll be here!" he yelled. He needed space, and he needed it now.

As he walked into the room, he tripped over a toy truck and landed flat on the floor. It wasn't so much the stabbing pain in his foot that angered him; it was his constant need to remind his children that toys should be put away. He took one look at Luca, his blood boiling to the surface.

"How many times! How many times before you listen to a word I say? I told you and Kayla to clean up after yourselves! Is that too much to ask?"

Luca just stared at his father. Kayla continued watching her show.

"Well," probed Ethan.

"It wasn't me, it was Kayla!"

"I don't care!" screamed Ethan. "I want it cleaned up!"

"I'll do it after the show."

With that, Luca returned his attention to the television screen. That was enough to send Ethan into one of his many furies.

"That's it! You're both done here. Go to your room. If you're not going to listen to me, you'll have to deal with the consequences!"

"But, Dad!" cried Luca and Kayla simultaneously.

"Not another word!"

They stood, hesitating. Neither took a step. Ethan clenched his fists. "Now!" he shouted and gave both children a small shove. Kayla lost her balance, a yelp escaping her mouth, as she tumbled onto the floor. Teary-eyed, she quickly disappeared up the stairs.

Luca tried to swat his father's hand away as he backed up. Defiance oozed from his pores. "I hate you!" he yelled as he scrambled to his room.

Ethan stared at the empty staircase. The storm of emotions slowly faded away, his heart rate slowing back to normal. He paced the room, searching for an answer. Every fiber in his being told him he had crossed the line. Screaming was one thing, but laying a hand on his children was another. He loved them dearly. They meant the world to him. But once his anger took control, he was no longer in charge. A dark, impenetrable haze filled his mind. Try as he may, it could not be defeated. He often dreamed of the day he would speak calmly to his children and treat them with the patience of a Buddhist monk. He had little confidence this could ever become a reality.

Ethan blamed his father for the explosive personality bestowed upon him. Growing up, Ethan and his sisters often referred to their father, Francis Stone, as "Jekyll and Hyde." They would be playing in the yard, enjoying a sunny day, when the back door would fly open, and their father would enter a fit of rage. It could be for any reason, often irrational and inexplicable. He would bellow at the top of his lungs, throwing insults as if they were darts meant to sting deep. Strangely, the bulk of his frustration was reserved for his son. Ethan's two younger sisters were spared, for the most part. These fits would last for hours, and Ethan did his best to avoid eye contact, knowing the slightest sign of defiance would cost him a hard slap or worse. Ethan lived in constant fear of these moments. He had often felt completely helpless, never quite knowing what he had done wrong. Generally calm and obedient, Ethan spent his days hiding from his father. Eventually, all the tension would fade away for the day, and a certain tranquility would return to their home.

His father's calamitous moods wrecked a special sort of havoc on Ethan's poor mother. Sweet and serene, she showered her three children with boundless love and affection. She protected them whenever she could. She was not immune to Francis's anger. Most often he used the same verbal attacks on her. On one occasion, however, Ethan remembered his father pushing his mother hard into the wall. She had held her ground, which had shocked Ethan, who was secretly watching the scene unfold from a crack in the bedroom door. He vividly remembered a tear escaping her eye, but she had not given in. This had made Ethan proud. He admired her for the strong woman she was. His mother was the glue keeping their family together. All for naught in the end, when Francis had made the unforgivable decision to throw it all away.

Ethan knew his dad issues came down to trust. He had lost all trust in his father long ago. It had started when Ethan was just seven years old. At the time, their family lived on the wrong side of the tracks. The neighborhood was rough and shoddy. On the first day of second grade, as he walked to school, Ethan was quickly surrounded by a gang of boys. All four were much bigger than him. After a few insults were thrown his way, they proceeded to dump his lunch and books on the ground. Then they pushed Ethan around, including some sneaky, well-timed punches to the gut. This would go on until the bus arrived. As much as Ethan tried to avoid the senseless gang of brutes, they always managed to get him one way or another.

Being at his wits' end, Ethan devised a plan. He made some rough calculations and figured if he took the back street from their small apartment, hid, and sprinted to the stop as the bus arrived, he could make it without being victimized. His plan worked for three days, and he started feeling better.

On the third day, when he walked through the door after school, Francis was waiting for him. Eyes shining with vehemence, Ethan knew something bad was about to happen. Francis grabbed his son by the collar and dragged him into the living room. He interrogated his son, wanting to know exactly why he was taking the back road to the bus stop. Ethan explained his predicament, hoping his father would see the fear he was living through. Maybe his father could help him. But Francis had other plans. Never would his son grow up being the laughingstock of their neighborhood. Never would his son be weak and helpless.

On that day, Francis decided seven-year-old Ethan was going to grow up. He hit his son several times, shaking his little body. He yelled with deep anger, as if his own rage would enter his son's spirit and make him fight these bullies with pride. They spent two hours going over self-defense techniques, all while tears streamed down Ethan's face. With every tear shed, Francis grew more frustrated by the frail being he perceived in front of him. He was relentless, oblivious to the fact he was essentially breaking the sacred fatherly bond of trust. All Ethan wanted was help. He never stood a chance. The days continued much as before until eventually the bullies found another poor soul to harass.

Had the timing been different, his mother might have been able to rescue him. She spent odd hours as the head nurse at the Montreal General Hospital, regularly working into the evening. He never told her what happened, fearing the potential consequences of betraying his father. He knew it would cause another fight, and he didn't dare put his mother at risk.

That was the day Ethan decided he would never trust his father again. As it turned out, Francis would do something far worse to their family, sealing his fate.

As he sat there in his home, thrust into his role as the family patriarch, he could witness the depths of his delusion. He deeply loved both his children, but understanding and patience were not part of his DNA. He tried listening to them and being a better role model than Francis, but he felt unable to connect with them, often letting his growing temper poison their relationship. It pained him to see the look on their little faces, much how he must have looked upon his own father. He knew they did not trust him. He did not blame them.

He drew the smallest sense of solace from the fact that his guilt always surfaced after these frustrating encounters. He wanted to change. It could be the only solution to his growing problem. But Ethan had no clue how to be a better man. Whenever he took one step forward, something would send his emotions into a tailspin, and he would unequivocally take two steps back. He was pushing his children further away each day.

As for his unquestionably gorgeous wife, Eva, the same downward spiral of hopelessness could be seen with her. She had lost interest in their relationship. He couldn't figure out exactly when it had happened. There were a couple of experiences he could look back on as the cause, but he surmised that the sum of endless screaming matches and broken promises were the true reason for their predicament.

He no longer made any effort. He knew they were headed toward a worst-case scenario. The pressure was building, much like a dam about to overflow. Tension could be felt at every turn. Ethan never thought of cheating on his wife. He could never do that. Taking that dark path would make him just like his father—the family betrayer. Nor did he think Eva capable of making such a dangerous decision. She was, at her core, the most genuine, sincere person he had ever met. Neither of them would dare cause such direct harm to the other. Instead, they just let their bond dissipate with time, until they were incapable of making it whole again.

In his younger days, he had dreamt of the moment his family would look exactly like this: a beautiful wife, an athletic son, and an independent, strong-willed daughter. He knew it fit every cliché imaginable, but it represented his view of happiness. From an outsider's perspective, Ethan had it all. Even his career as a successful sales executive at Premier Marketing was envied by his entourage of friends and family.

Yet his misery had reached new heights in the past months. He felt hollow, demotivated, moping around in a pointless routine day after day. Every time he tried to connect with his children, his temper got in the way. Every time he looked at Eva, he knew he would regret letting her slip from his grasp. He wondered if she felt the same.

Ethan made his way upstairs to shave and shower. As he washed his face, he glanced up at the mirror. For the first time in his life, he felt old. His once-smooth skin sagged under his eyes. His hairline was receding fast. His muscles held none of the firmness from his younger days. Throughout high school, Ethan had tried various sports, finally choosing basketball, given the lack of players on the team. He never climbed the ladder of success the way some of his teammates had, but he certainly put his heart and soul into the sport. His fitness and ability to stay slim had been taken for granted in those days, even as a benchwarmer. Then he made the track team. It wasn't a popular sport, but Ethan had the ability to break out in a sprint like no other. He won several races in his age group, blowing by competitors at will. He remembered those days, feeling invincible, at the top of his game.

The past ten years of exaggerated office hours, having children, and simple laziness had taken their toll quite succinctly. His once-ripped abs resembled cookie dough, which made sense considering his daily cookie intake. He wasn't exactly large, but rather busting at the seams. His piercing blue eyes could still attract some flattering attention, although the ever-growing patch of baldness on the top of his head did not.

He threw on his navy suit jacket, made his way downstairs, yelled goodbye from the doorway without waiting for the deafening silence he was accustomed to, and climbed into the car. After a few moments alone, he started the engine and escaped out of the driveway.

WONDERFUL

This society is driven by neurotic speed and force accelerated by greed and frustration of not being able to live up to the image of men and women we have created ourselves; the image has nothing to do with the reality of people.
—Yoko Ono, singer and peace activist

E very morning, as Ethan walked through the mahogany doors of Premier Marketing, he came face-to-face with a large portrait of Vincent Massa. In 1976, this talented, young entrepreneur founded the company from an idea scribbled on a paper napkin. Everyone knew the story. Vincent had been a true philosopher, an innovator. His vision had left most business owners astonished. Legend had it that Vincent could listen to a customer's business challenges and within hours, despite the depths of complexity involved, define a solid marketing strategy that would be embraced, implemented, and successfully launched only weeks later.

Vincent also gave back to the community in many ways. He had written four successful business books, the proceeds of which he used to fund various charities helping children in need around the world. Through all this, he had remained one of the most sincere and level-headed visionaries Ethan had ever met. In fact, Vincent's core values were the reason Ethan had aggressively pursued a career at Premier Marketing. It all seemed so perfect—and actually was for a time—until Vincent's sudden death. That moment could easily be described as the beginning of the end for Ethan and many others at the company. Vincent developed a brain aneurysm and passed away two weeks later, to the chagrin of thousands.

Since that unfortunate moment, the Massa Family had abruptly taken over all decision-making duties. Their new strategies rarely made sense, and the glue that held the precious pieces of the company together disappeared with Vincent. With two of his brothers and six cousins struggling for power within the business, company vision was an afterthought to those immediate, urgent fires. Ethan was hanging on by a thread, sticking around for the loyal customers he loved, but the sheer effort was taking a clear toll on his happiness.

Although Ethan lost patience often at home—a reality he blamed equally on the new Premier Marketing ownership team and his father's dark character—he still cared deeply for his clients' best interests. And this showed in his work. Yet he knew his honest business philosophy could not last in the tornado of distrust Premier Marketing had become.

Ethan arrived at his desk with his briefcase in one hand, his mental baggage in the other. He tried to remember the last time he had enjoyed a day at the office. Turning on his computer, he decided more coffee could potentially change his negative mindset. He was aware it was his personal responsibility to muster up more positive vibes to get his attitude back on track. He also realized he drank too much coffee. He still chose the path of least resistance to the nearby kitchen.

Diana was waiting for him at his desk when he made his way back. Of all the executive assistants in the building—and there were many—Diana was the only one armed with intelligence, efficiency, and the perfect amount of sarcasm required to succeed at Premier Marketing. Ethan greeted her warmly.

"What a wonderful smile! One I wish I could keep on your face this morning."

Ethan sighed heavily, accustomed to negative situations these days. "Give it to me straight. It makes things easier."

"Well," Diana continued, "accounting didn't agree with your assessment of the hours worked on the Thomas Lumber marketing project."

"What you mean to say is that Sylvia Massa didn't agree."

"Correct you are."

"And pray tell me exactly how far off we can possibly be."

Diana looked down. "You won't be impressed."

"It can't be that bad, Diana. I know one hundred seventy hours is the right number. We only revamped one of their smaller brands. Thomas Lumber seriously invested on this one. I can't even be sure it will work out in the long run for them, as it was their newest division we worked with."

"You know you're preaching to the choir," said Diana.

Ethan stared at her. "Well, given the facts and your tone of voice, I will venture to say Sylvia wants to bill them for two hundred hours?"

Diana shook her head.

"Two hundred twenty hours," said Ethan nervously.

Diana barely whispered the number.

"What was that, Diana?"

"Two hundred ninety hours."

Ethan stared at his assistant in disbelief. Thomas Lumber, a long-standing customer opened by Vincent Massa himself in the early '80s, was being taken to the cleaners by his niece Sylvia Massa. This was a typical maneuver by the new Premier Marketing management team. But never at such an exaggeration. Ethan had personally handled the entire project. And he was a very thorough man. In his view, this could only be defined as actual theft. Thomas Lumber controlled most of the North American wood market, and their monthly payroll represented more income than some small countries, but that did not matter in the least to Ethan. Integrity, passion, and belief were the three cornerstone values at Premier Marketing, as created by Vincent himself. Not one was being respected by Sylvia Massa today.

"I'm going up," said Ethan. Diana could only stare sympathetically at him as he rushed away, impressed by his will to confront a member of the Massa family.

Entering the elevator, he slammed the button for the twenty-eighth floor and started preparing for Sylvia. He was visualizing the many incredibly powerful arguments he was about to make. He was determined to get his point across.

The elevator doors opened, and he gunned straight for her office. As he arrived, fuming, he found Sylvia with her head in a massive pile of paperwork.

Sylvia Massa ran the accounting department for the entire $118-million company. At thirty-one years of age, she had become the youngest person to hold such a prestigious title. The daughter of Joseph Massa, Vincent's youngest brother, she was one of the six famous cousins constantly lobbying for power and control of the organization. Sylvia's important position in the company had been handed to her on a silver platter. A sense of pure entitlement embraced her being from head to toe. Ethan had little respect for her, knowing full well she was unqualified for the role.

Ethan entered her office without knocking. "Sylvia, we need to talk." He closed her door.

She barely moved her head. "Yes, Ethan."

"The billed hours for the Thomas Lumber Project are wrong. Clearly, there's been a mistake." Ethan used the confident tone he had practiced in his mind.

"Is that so?" She kept her eyes on her paperwork.

"I covered the entire marketing plan beginning to end. As you know, I am quite meticulous when it comes to hours billed, and I can assure you the total is one hundred seventy."

She finally graced him with eye contact. "And what do you know about accounting?" The question seemed rhetorical, but Ethan answered anyway.

"I have enough experience to determine the time we spend on a client's marketing plan."

"What is your title, Ethan?"

"Excuse me?"

"Your business card. What is written on it?"

Ethan could sense the conversation heading in the wrong direction. "It says, 'Director of Sales and Marketing.'"

"So why are you here, in my office, worrying about billed hours? You must have many other important things to tend to right now." She did not attempt to hide her sarcasm.

"Sylvia, clearly you do not understand my explanation here. We are treating Thomas Lumber like second-class citizens. We can't—"

She swiftly cut him off and vaulted into a furious personal attack. "You know what I think, Ethan? I think you haven't the slightest clue how accounting works!" she yelled. "In fact, I know you don't. This is way above your pay scale, and I strongly suggest you back off. I have reviewed the project, and my numbers show two hundred ninety hours! There is no more discussion here. You need to get back down to your office and start focusing on sales and marketing, not accounting!"

Ethan was speechless. He had never been one for confrontation; he simply didn't handle it well. Still, he felt so embarrassed being scolded like a schoolchild by Sylvia that he tried one last time:

"Please try to hear me out. We are going to lose this account, Sylvia." He was pleading desperately.

"We're done here. This discussion is over." And with that, she got up from her desk, picked up a stack of files, and left Ethan alone in her office. He could only watch her leave, his stomach churning, his forehead sweating. After some time sitting in a daze, he slowly convinced his legs to move, and he went down to sulk.

***

The one place where Ethan could always find some time for himself was his office. He had spent hours decorating his humble space. Pictures of his favorite athletes lined the walls. Photos from cool cities he had yet to visit gave him hope. And a few drawings from Luca and Kayla reminded him work was not everything. He had more.

He had always wanted to build something in his life, to make a real difference. He knew it sounded cheesy. Everyone says they want to make a difference. But for Ethan, this desire fluttered constantly in his mind. He often found himself staring out of his window at the "For Rent" signs on some of the buildings in the area, debating the idea of marching in one day and putting pen to paper on his own space. There he could start a meaningful endeavor, take a chance with life. *Pipe dreams* was the term his colleagues used as soon as anyone tried to be truly original nowadays. He didn't even know what he wanted. It kept nagging at him. He felt destined for bigger and better things. His fear of risk-taking held him back. He knew the game and felt safer on the team that paid him well enough, even if it meant dealing with selfish people. He told himself things would change.

He had been at Premier Marketing for twelve years, right out of business school with the highest of expectations. It had started wonderfully. His time as a junior sales executive had been well spent, learning the ropes from some of the greatest minds he had ever met. In those days, Ethan could turn to one of ten people in the Premier Marketing Leadership team and get great advice from any of them. With Vincent's unexpected departure, most had been pushed out by the family or had left on their own terms. Ethan's decision to stay made sense at the time. Once the family realized they were losing most of their best players, they needed others to pick up the slack. They gave Ethan more responsibility, more money, a better title, and the apparent freedom to go out there and conquer the world. With two young children and a new home, it was all the convincing he needed. He wondered where he would be had he left at that moment.

The phone rang and snapped him back to reality.

"Let's hit lunch, Stone." Finally, the voice of reason.

"Already that time? This wonderful day sure is flying."

"Yeah, sure, Stone. Give it a rest. My treat today. We're hitting up that new sushi joint!"

"I thought you'd never ask."

Ethan had two people at the office he could always turn to for great advice and sincere laughs—Diana, his awesome assistant, and Sasha Mikos, a woman who could light up any room in seconds. An almost visible circle of energy surrounded her being at all times. Ethan could not remember a time when Sasha looked upset or frustrated. She lived the daily struggles just like the other employees at Premier Marketing, but her positivity kept her above the noise. Ethan had much to learn from her.

They met outside and walked down Notre Dame Street, with Sasha's high heels battling the cobbled streets of the Old Port of Montreal. They passed the Montreal Culinary Institute, then City Hall, and continued toward their destination. The overcast sky threw a grey cloak of darkness on the city, as if day were turning to night before their eyes. It captured how Ethan felt about his entire life at that exact moment. A few minutes later, they arrived at the new sushi shop. A hip, eclectic crowd filled the small restaurant, and Ethan suddenly felt very old. He had never seen himself as a grown-up. He still clung to the belief that he could mix it up with the next generation. But standing there, he realized he hadn't seen time pass by, and things had changed in a hurry.

The host sat them down at a window table. They barely fit, but Sasha was clearly enjoying every minute of it.

Given his state of mind, it would have been so simple for Ethan to jump into a soliloquy of depressing statements meant to dampen the best of spirits. Sasha, being part of that exclusive, rarified group of great listeners on the planet, could bear his frustrations. He wanted to talk to her. He needed to. He could tell her how his life was spinning out of control like a tornado. He could explain how he was no longer able to drum up even an ounce of patience with his children. He could admit his relationship with Eva was on the fritz. He could confide that every passing day brought an enormous weight to bear on his shoulders, one that threatened to derail him for good.

He hesitated, knowing it wasn't fair for him to act that way with a coworker (and more importantly a close friend). They shared a lot of stories, but Ethan kept most of it about business. He had never been comfortable talking about his personal life. Instead, he decided to show interest in Sasha's life. And he knew how. All he had to do was mention a name.

"How is Andrew?"

Her smile could have caused permanent stretch marks around her eyes. After falling in love several times with a bunch of hapless losers, Sasha had finally met her match in the strangest of places—a baby shower. It took place at her sister's house, and Andrew just happened to be the flower guy. He owned a quaint, highly successful flower shop on the South Shore. It was love at first sight. Sasha still told the story today, over a year after that chance meeting. What made Ethan most envious was their deep passion for each other. They had only been together fourteen months, but the connection was impressive. He vaguely remembered something of that sort in his own life some distant time ago.

"He is wonderful! This weekend he surprised me with a night out when he was supposed to be preparing a wedding engagement. He got Marty to handle the grunt work, picked me up, and whisked me away. We went to eat at Milos!"

"What a guy."

"Honestly, Ethan, after the crap I dealt with for so many years, with so many idiots, I still don't believe I deserve this royal treatment."

"Sasha, if one person deserves it, it's you. Besides, Andrew is the lucky one here."

She smiled, but that was enough small talk for Sasha. She had known Ethan for five years and had a clear understanding of his growing discontent at Premier Marketing. She could easily sense Ethan's foul mood. Even the most profoundly egotistical, self-absorbed narcissist could have detected his frustration. She trod softly, knowing he needed to vent. "So…what happened today?"

Ethan, still determined to avoid the start of his whining, continued his non-Emmy Award–winning performance. Sasha always listened carefully to his issues, which actually made him feel quite vulnerable.

"What do you mean?" he replied.

"Come on, Stone, cut the act. You've never been good at hiding your frustrations. I can read you like a book, you know that."

"Seriously, everything is fine."

"Right," answered Sasha.

"Simply an accounting mix-up. No big deal."

Sasha stared at Ethan curiously, forcing him to make eye contact. She had a way of easily extorting information from him. She smiled warmly, inviting him to open up. But on this day, Ethan truly had no agenda or hidden desire to bash the Massa Family. He felt too exhausted to even begin that hopeless journey.

"Honestly, Sasha, I'm tired. I make such an effort, day in, day out, attempting to get Premier back on the right track. I care deeply about our clients, and I thoroughly enjoy working with great colleagues like you and Diana, but enough is enough. Something has to change, and soon. I have been taking the stress of this job home with me the past few months, forcing Eva and the kids to deal with my horrible attitude. Worst of all, I don't see what will change."

Sasha took a few thoughtful seconds before responding. "I hear you, Ethan. I know it can get really frustrating, but stay strong. At its base, this is a solid organization that needs people like you. You are a difference maker. It will get better. It has to."

Ethan loved her optimism, but could not bring himself to agree. "Sasha, I have been waiting four years now. We both have. Actually, *waiting* isn't the right word. I have tried and tried to help this company succeed. I don't see the light. Perhaps moving on makes more sense."

"That's a big decision, Ethan. Have you looked at your options?"

"Not yet, but I'm going to start soon."

"Well, make sure you remember to take me with you!"

He laughed. "That will be my first demand at the job interview. I'll just explain I have a nonnegotiable request. I need another office with full benefits for Sasha Mikos, no questions asked! No sane person could refuse you anyway."

"Always the charmer. You know I hate seeing you like this. Just be sure before doing anything drastic. The grass isn't always greener."

They finished their sushi and talked about the horrible weather among other lighter subjects. They paid up and went back to Premier.

At the office, Ethan busied himself with sales reports and fulfilling customer requests. He needed an organized desk and inbox, and neither looked too appealing right now. Within a few hours, he managed to invoke some semblance of organizational integrity. He looked at his watch and noticed the time. Late. He was late. Eva would not be impressed. He immediately closed up and sprinted for the door.

In the parking lot, the rain pricked at his clothes with a vengeance. Only thirty feet to his car, yet his weight had doubled under the thick wetness of his being.

He started the car and made his way to the highway. The traffic had somewhat calmed after the madness of Montreal rush hour. He eyed his watch and felt he could still be close to making it on time for Eva's outing. His iPhone buzzed with a new message: a text from his friend Reza asking about the best gift to buy Luca for his birthday. Ethan started responding to the message, glancing up at the traffic every few seconds. The rain continued pounding the windshield incessantly.

As he finished typing a ridiculous response about Luca wanting new golf clubs for Daddy, he glanced up and saw two red lights much too close. He tried slamming the breaks but was a fraction too late. His car skidded wildly across the wet pavement.

The sound of crushed metal filled his ears. In the split second it took him to realize his mistake, the airbag came flying at his face and slammed his head backward. He didn't move for a few seconds, stunned by the impact. Gathering himself, Ethan forced his way out of the car to regain his composure. *The other driver*. He immediately went to check on the car he had hit. A woman, at least seventy years of age, sat in silence in a state of shock.

"Ma'am, are you all right?"

The woman slowly turned her head and nodded ever so slightly.

"Let me help you out," offered Ethan.

He carefully opened the door and took her by the arm. Although she seemed quite fragile, Ethan didn't believe she was hurt.

After speaking with her for a few minutes, he could thankfully confirm she had no serious injuries. A few scratches, but nothing requiring surgery.

In truth, he knew the situation could have been so much worse. His desperate reaction had been enough to soften some of the impact. And then a thought struck him. He had been texting and almost caused a fatal crash. *How completely stupid and immature!* To jeopardize not only his own well-being but also that of a total stranger could only be described as utterly selfish.

The police arrived several minutes later to take their statements. The tow trucks only made their appearance some time thereafter. His bumper lay uselessly on the side of the highway, and his headlights no longer served their purpose, being smashed to pieces.

Once the details had been sorted through, Ethan realized he had completely forgotten to call Eva. Considering his iPhone had shattered during the accident, he had to borrow the tow truck driver's cell. He dialed his home number. Kayla answered.

"Helloooooo!" Kayla enjoyed extending words with a melodic twist.

"Hi, sweetheart, you doing okay?"

"Yes, Daddy. Where are you?"

Ethan felt a deep longing to see his family.

"I'll be home very soon, honey. Is Mommy there?"

"Ya."

After what felt like an eternity, Eva took the receiver. "Ethan?"

"Hi, babe. I'm so sorry, I know I ruined your night. But listen, there was an accident. Well, I caused it. I am so ridiculous. I was typing a text, not paying attention, and the next thing I knew, bang! I hit this poor woman. She's fine, but you know, how horrible. The airbag hit me in the face. That was a first. Car is being towed…only a fender bender really!" He blurted all this in a barely comprehensible flash without taking a breath.

Eva answered flatly, "I'm happy no one got hurt. You should be more careful, Ethan, and you know better. I'm putting the kids to sleep, and I'll be in bed by the time you get home." And with that, she hung up.

He just stared at the phone that wasn't his. He had secretly hoped for more sympathy, knowing deep down it made no sense given the circumstances. He felt worse after their short conversation. Eva had missed her dinner, and Ethan was the reason. His guilt kicked in. There was nothing he could do but make his way home and hope for a better day.

TIMING IS
EVERYTHING

*Observe due measure, for right timing is in all things the most
important factor.*
—Hesiod, ancient Greek poet

*T*he following morning, Ethan made every conceivable effort
to treat his family right. He knew this drive born from guilt
would only last so long, but he also understood Eva and the
kids didn't deserve a grumpy husband/father after the previous night's
events. He put on the charm and smiled in quite an exaggerated fashion. Unfortunately, he looked like a used car salesman.

"So, kids, what's going on at school today?"

Luca looked up from his cereal, surprised his father had time for
questions. He didn't know if he should answer. Kayla continued playing with her backpack.

"Well, I'd love to hear about the fun stuff you have planned," continued Ethan.

Luca finally took the bait. "It's our outing today!"

"Where are you going?" asked Ethan.

"It's the place with stars and planets and suns and moons and solar
sectoriums!"

"You mean solar systems, right, buddy?" Ethan asked, sincerely
interested at this point.

Eva jumped in. "The Planetarium, remember the name, Luca?"

"Yeah, that's it. And the whole class is going!" Luca's eyes glittered.

"Well, that is truly awesome, my boy. I hope you have a good time,
and I can't wait to hear all about it tonight."

Luca's smile beamed through the entire kitchen. *Why is this so hard for
me? I should be more involved. Look at that face.* Ethan had quite obviously

and unfortunately drifted further into his own responsibilities and issues in the past months. He hardly recognized his son. *Growing up very fast.*

At Eva's cue, the kids picked up their lunch boxes and ran out to catch the bus. Ethan dearly wanted to smooth things over with Eva.

"I'm sorry about last night," he said with a detectable tone of sincerity. Not something Eva remembered recently. Not quite enough for her though.

"Okay."

"I mean it, Eva. It was my fault, and I screwed up your plans."

"Yes, those are the facts." Eva kept her guard up.

"I'll find a way to make it up to you."

Ethan leaned in for a kiss. Eva turned her head at the last second, giving Ethan access to her ear and hair.

With that as his final, triumphant moment, he left for the office—or rather his four walls of doom and gloom.

***

The week passed uneventfully, and Ethan felt relieved. After the fiasco with Sylvia, he didn't need any more issues. TGIF had arrived, and it was time to enjoy the weekend. He spent several hours that week trying to figure out the best way to treat Eva to a special evening. Her coldness had not thawed in the least. She seemed to have one goal in mind—prolonging his guilt. Ethan didn't know what to make of it, so he kept on his solitary path and tried not to worry. He buried his growing despair as deep as possible, hoping it would disappear. It rarely did.

He could hear a continuous vibration and realized a few seconds later his cell phone was buzzing. He looked at the caller ID and saw the familiar and comforting name of Mike May.

Mike believed in three things in life: being single, living single, and staying single. He cared only superficially about his friends' way of life, a noticeable problem considering all of them had moved on from their bachelor days and had multiple children running around. With Mike, you always knew what you were getting. You didn't invite Mike to family BBQs or zoo outings. Mike was the first call you made when you wanted to golf, fish, or hit the town. And Ethan needed that kind of distraction right now.

Ethan answered in his most serious voice: "Ethan Stone, here to serve your every need."

"Hey, loser, stop pretending to work and cancel your boring, useless, dreaded afternoon plans."

Ethan knew the meaning of that wonderful sentence. "We golfing?" This was said at a whisper as the door to his office stood wide-open.

"Damn right we are! And not just anywhere, my good man. I got us a tee off at Royal Montreal!"

Ethan couldn't believe his luck. He had been wanting to play the historic golf course for years. Needing a private membership, it took the best of connections to have any chance. He had only been there once, to watch the President's Cup with Vincent Massa. He had vowed that one day he would find a way on. The one and only Mike May had found a way to make his dream come true. "I'm definitely in, but pray tell how you pulled that off?"

"Long story, immensely interesting, one I will recount in the greatest of details at three o'clock sharp when we meet at the Clubhouse." Mike May hung up without saying goodbye.

Now all Ethan needed was a solid exit plan.

Years ago, when Premier Marketing functioned like a well-oiled machine, Ethan wouldn't have thought twice about catching a round of golf on Friday afternoon. If the work was done, no one worried about schedules. In the aftermath of the numerous changes that had taken place after Vincent's death, the balance of power had shifted. The unwelcome changes gave many unprepared individuals significant management roles within the organization. Ethan had learned by experience that a title does not make a leader.

Ethan looked carefully at his watch. It read 1:15 p.m. He had one hour to gather his wits, figure a quiet way out of the office, and hit the road to pure golfing bliss.

Over recent months, Ethan had spoken to many industry colleagues. He wanted to understand the state of other businesses out there, specifically regarding the abuse of power. It was in such deep prevalence at Premier that he decided to research it for himself. He discovered certain inconvenient truths. Within many companies, there existed a person of power who seemed to thrive on his subordinates' unhappiness. An individual so focused on negativity, their only pleasure came from causing frustration to others. A manager so deeply rooted into their own self-created cave of nauseating repression, their only answer was to steal the glory of another's success. At Premier, this man existed and happened to be Ethan's boss.

Ethan made his way to the cafeteria to grab a coffee. He didn't want a coffee, but he needed to stake out his boss's whereabouts. He poured, nervously looking left and right, and burned his finger in the process. Annoyed, he carefully walked back toward his office. Taking an unnecessary detour through the design department, he glanced at the window to his manager's office. No sign of him. All looked very still. The lights were off, and the desk appeared clean. Ethan could hardly contain his joy. *Finally, a good break*, he thought to himself. He deserved to have some fun.

As he turned the corner back toward his own office, his legs weakened, almost sending his hot beverage flying. Robert Samuels stood menacingly in his doorway, his stocky 240 pounds blocking Ethan's path to happiness. He forced a smile and greeted his dictator. "Hi, Robert, thought you had left for the day!"

"You kidding, Stone? It's not even two o'clock. Where would I be, playing golf?"

"I just assumed…"

"You know what I think about assumptions."

With tree trunks for legs, Robert Samuels preferred stomping his way from one place to the next. Loud and ferocious, he cared little for the niceties of life. A hunter since birth, his only vacation each year consisted of spending two weeks in the wilderness with other alpha males. Their singular goal—killing, eating, and drinking. Ethan was terrified of this man. Robert had deep connections to the entire Massa family. Ethan didn't know the full story, but it involved long-lasting friendships spanning decades. Robert climbed through the ranks at warp speed after Vincent's death.

Robert Samuels did not golf. He openly hated the sport and considered it a foolish waste of time. A heavy contrast to Ethan's life philosophy, although he kept that part quiet to avoid any unnecessary ill will with his boss. Everyone at Premier knew the toughest part about having Robert as an immediate supervisor was his Friday afternoon routine. Robert Samuels had no children, wife, or presumably any real friends. He didn't have any interesting commitments outside of work and therefore didn't see the need for people to get out on time for the weekend. Robert enjoyed scheduling meetings or customer progress reports at four o'clock on Friday afternoons, often keeping his employees past dinnertime. There was no way Ethan could deal with that now. He had a date with destiny, or rather, Mike May.

"We're wasting valuable time here," said Robert. "I wanted to sit down with you this afternoon to review next month's sales strategies."

Ethan's heart plummeted at the mere thought.

"But it's not to be, Stone. Something has come up."

Ethan's sliver of hope returned.

"I have an assignment for you."

And with those few words, the potential glory of his afternoon plans evaporated. He could sense it now, feeling the precious opportunity slipping away.

"I got an interesting call from a new potential customer. He is the president over at the Elevation Leadership Institute. You heard of it? I gave Diana his name. Foreign fellow, it would seem from the accent. British, Australian, heck if I know."

Ethan tried to think of a million excuses to avoid making a customer call on a Friday afternoon. His mediocre golf game needed some attention. Ethan desperately wanted to get away from this conversation. He needed to figure something out that made sense.

"He specifically requested you, Stone. I don't know how he knows you. He said something about a referral. He wants you there at three. It's actually pretty close to here. Don't be late. I want you to call me when you're done so we can discuss how it went."

His boss loved micromanaging everyone and everything and truly enjoyed controlling Ethan's every moment. His world, which just minutes earlier held that wonderful excitement of adventure, crashed into a wave of frustration.

He politely thanked Robert for the lead without betraying his immense disappointment. He snatched his iPhone and texted Mike May: "No go, stuck working, cannot believe it. Have fun without me."

Ethan grabbed his briefcase and made his way down the escalator, though he had already reached rock-bottom.

Man with a Plan

*The best way to look back at life fondly is to meet it—and those
along your journey—warmly, kindly and mindfully.*
—Rasheed Ogunlaru, author of *Soul Trader*

he meeting place took fifteen minutes to reach on foot. Ethan
decided to walk. He thought about the last time he went to
the gym. He had no recollection. He pictured the treadmill at
home, which had become an efficient clothing stand to dry his shirts
on. Self-justification crept in as he analyzed the past few days, and he
decided to hail a cab. After all, he was having a rough week, he thought
to himself. The driver listened to the address request, stared at him
incredulously, and brought him to his desired location in five minutes
flat.

Still fuming from his ruined afternoon, his mind went back to
Robert Samuels and Premier Marketing. How had he managed to find
himself in such a dire situation? His daily work life had taken on such
a calculated monotony, he wondered why he was still doing it. Dealing
with the "Roberts" and the "Sylvias" of this world did not bring him
an ounce of satisfaction or happiness. He needed to think about an
alternate career path.

He debated skipping the meeting and trying to make the golf game
with Mike. After all, it was only a quarter to three. Perhaps he had
time. He knew it made no sense. There was no chance he could get
out of the downtown core and cover the distance needed in Friday
afternoon traffic.

More importantly, Ethan realized his pettiness. *This isn't me. I don't
skip out on my future clients. I treat them with respect and fairness. I will
not let myself sink to that level of amateurism.* Little did he know this
decision would alter the course of his life.

He composed himself and looked up at the address. The window lettering read, "The Elevation Leadership Institute." He opened the glass doors and walked in.

The smell immediately engulfed his senses. The sleek, well-designed lobby was filled with beautiful flowers. He knew literally nothing about flowers, but the colors and fragrances brightened his mood instantaneously. Vibrant white and yellow ones, warm violet and red ones, comforting peach and rose ones, and especially the bright orange ones. He had never visited any office with this type of entrance. And despite the impressive number of flowers, the stylish lobby somehow kept its significant design flair intact.

After what seemed to be several minutes in wonderland, his eyes focused on the person sitting at the half-moon-shaped glass desk. He introduced himself, "Hi, I'm Ethan Stone from Premier Marketing, I'm here to see…" He paused, dumbfounded. In his distracted mood, he had completely forgotten to ask Diana for the name of the person he was to meet, and all he could remember was Robert mentioning the person had asked for Ethan by name. This was very embarrassing since Ethan normally thrived in these types of situations.

The woman smiled warmly. "You're not sure who you are here to see?"

"I'm so sorry," Ethan admitted, his face blushing. "I ran out of the office without the details. I'll make a quick call and sort it out." Ethan fumbled for his iPhone.

"No worries, Mr. Stone, I have all the information right here." She pointed to her head and winked, amused yet working hard to eliminate Ethan's clear discomfort.

"Thank you so much," Ethan replied, embarrassed.

"Feel free to relax and enjoy the scenery." She picked up the phone and made a quick call. "Ravi, Ethan Stone is here."

At least part of the mystery is solved. Ethan sat, immediately feeling his body mold into the leather sofa. Immense cushions surrounded and embraced his body. *Strange place*, he thought to himself. The entire experience up to now resembled a five-star resort more than a place of professional business. He realized after a few moments of reflection that it did embody the type of setting Ethan wished he had dreamed up himself. It felt right.

Still frustrated by his lack of professionalism, another thought struck him. He still had no clue why he was meeting this Ravi character. Ethan always prepared for customer calls. He researched the company thoroughly, verified their history from sales tactics to marketing strategies, and made sure to understand their vision and goals in advance. Today, he had done none of it. His anger had clearly derailed his reliable attention to detail. He was completely off today.

The brilliant idea of pulling out his iPhone and simply searching for the desired information arrived two minutes too late. The main door opened. He jumped out of the sofa, determined to get back to his A game. Out strode the infamous man of mystery.

Tall, dark, and handsome were the first words to pop into Ethan's head. The man in question stood at six feet, looking extremely fit for his forty or so years. His wavy hair and dark eyes gave him a sophisticated look, which radiated both confidence and warmth. Ethan could also detect an elusive familiarity. He knew this man from some hidden place in his memory. One of Ethan's strongest qualities was his ability to remember names and faces. He wished it were the case today.

The man greeted Ethan with the friendliest of handshakes. "How are you, Ethan? I can call you Ethan, right?" It was less a question than a statement, yet stated with genuine curiosity.

"Of course, no problem," answered Ethan, nervously. He tried to dissect Ravi's smooth accent. He detected British as the main ingredient, melted with a few ounces of Indian, topped nicely with local North American flair. It added further to Ravi's suave demeanor. Ethan often wished he had more of an exotic flavor.

"You can call me Ravi. No Mr. Channa nonsense, even though I am a potential client. That makes me feel old. And I see you have met our executive director, Julia Everhart. She is truly our CHO—Chief Happiness Officer!"

"It's truly nice to meet both of you," said Ethan.

Ravi smiled, directing Ethan back the same way he had just come. "First and foremost, let me give you a tour of our facilities."

They walked side by side through the frosted glass doors and entered a large open area. As the sight hit Ethan's eyes, he could barely contain his surprise.

"Different setup than you've seen before, I imagine?"

Ethan just stared, gaping, attempting to understand the concept before him. There were so many things happening at once that his brain couldn't grasp whether this was a consulting business, a fitness center, a meditation sanctuary, or a school.

Finally, he looked at Ravi and asked the obvious question: "What is this place?"

Ravi grinned, thoroughly enjoying himself. "Well, Ethan, that is the million-dollar question. Let me walk you through our vision, and the pieces of the puzzle will come together."

He led Ethan toward the first conference room delineated by clear glass walls. On each wall hung beautiful double-sided portraits of the world's many inspirational leaders—Nelson Mandela, Mahatma Gandhi, Winston Churchill, Michael Jordan, Martin Luther King Jr., and still others. Therein sat six people on colorful cushions, dressed professionally yet comfortably, having a calm discussion among themselves.

"This is a very special room we refer to as THE SELF," said Ravi proudly. "We believe for an individual to have any type of success in their life, whether personal or professional, there must be a cleansing of sorts. You see, we train our brains and bodies to follow society's guidelines. We allow our peers to dictate our own worth, constantly comparing our achievements against those around us. And yet, what is the norm? There are billions of people on this planet, and we all live in our own bubble, trying to impress people just to fulfill our own need for self-worth. This type of longing cannot be satiated as any victory is only temporary. Possessions and titles mean nothing in the end. Our first goal at the Leadership Institute is to assist every individual in discovering their true potential. This can be accomplished through three steps: "Self-renewal to Self-acceptance to Self-confidence.

"This is the room where that first step to happiness takes place. Those executives from a pharmaceutical firm are actually learning to meditate right now. We believe meditation is the true foundation of renewal and eventually accepting oneself. It therefore must be the beginning of the process."

Ethan listened carefully to Ravi's explanation. He tried judging if there was something solid here or if these ideas were spiritual mumbo jumbo. Perhaps this new way of thinking could refresh his own way of life. But to Ethan, meditation was reserved for hippies.

"Any questions?" asked Ravi.

Ethan stared, a smile creeping up his face. Of course, he had questions, but he wanted to understand the whole concept first. He simply shook his head.

"Great, let's keep moving. There is more to it, but we'll go over the details later."

They continued onward and reached another glass-walled room. Within this space, several modern individual work desks were occupied by probable students concentrating on some type of test. Peculiarly, the two apparent teachers stood in full fitness gear. They seemed ready to either scale a mountain or bench-press each other. Written in perfect white lettering, Ethan read the words CHALLENGE & CONQUER. His curiosity peaked once again. He stared at Ravi, waiting for the answer. Words were not flowing as easily as usual today. In this environment, he felt much more induced to listen, something rare for Ethan in recent weeks.

"Once a person feels completely comfortable and confident with their core being through our first steps to Self-renewal, they find themselves in this place. In the quest for understanding and achieving success on a higher level, one must first fuel their own being. This is accomplished by challenging the body and mind through a physical challenge beyond their current self-imposed scope of reality." Ravi's enthusiasm was visibly growing with every word.

Ethan did not follow. "I'm sorry, I don't quite grasp the idea." Normally, he never allowed his vulnerability to surface, especially not with a new potential client. He couldn't help it as he already felt completely at ease with Ravi.

"Let me break it down for you. What physical activity do you participate in, or have you done in the past? It can be anything."

Ethan knew all too well the unfortunate answer to his present non-existent activity schedule, so he pulled out some old-school exercise. "I ran short-track distances in high school."

"All right, that is an excellent example, Ethan. Now, tell me the longest training run you ever did."

"Well, considering I ran mostly between one hundred and eight hundred meters, I would say maybe seven miles."

"Great. Now, in this room, there would be some of those types of questions but taken much further. Our mind-and-body experts design specific tests to understand the level of physical ability of each individual. Working with that person's skill set, they come up with a very specific stretch goal challenge. This must be something the person in question absolutely could not attain if he or she tried it today. In fact, they should not be able to accomplish this challenge after even a full month's training. Our team then creates fitness workouts, nutrition plans, and uses psychological tools to help each person achieve their stretch goal challenge."

"And what about my challenge? What would that be with the information you have?" asked Ethan curiously.

"Well, if I told you, I'd have to kill you." Ravi laughed and grabbed Ethan by the arm. "That's for another day. It's important to trust the process."

He walked Ethan to the next section of the Elevation Leadership Institute. They arrived at five offices, aligned next to each other, quite similar in size, but incredibly unique in personality. Again, the impressive theme of using glass as the main design element worked wonders. These rooms sported colorful, vibrant furniture. The most surprising to Ethan was the setup. He slowly walked from one end of the hall to the next, taking in the details. These were much fewer offices than cool lounges to hang out in. Each had its own set of designer sofas, cool accessories, and, to Ethan's delight, awesome architectural flair.

The first room resembled a modern Miami condo. Two matching Zen-inspired white tables with chrome legs stood in the center, adorned by large cream-colored seashells. On each side, impressive chaise longues connected intricately, forming an uneven rectangular shape filling the balance of the space. Many photos depicting the oceans and beaches of the world hung from the ceiling in contemporary brushed nickel frames, individually lit by silver LED spotlights.

Room 2 had clearly been created for F1 racing enthusiasts. Being a fanatic, Ethan immediately recognized six exclusive Ferrari Scuderia seats. Unbelievably, each had been transformed into a chair on wheels. On the black, shiny desk along the wall, several model race cars were exposed. An autographed Michael Schumacher Marlboro Team jersey had been suspended from the ceiling—an item Ethan profoundly desired.

Now completely mesmerized, Ethan strolled dreamily to his right for a better view of room 3. "This is my favorite," Ravi said with a grin. A spectacular and realistic handcrafted replica of the Taj Mahal stood dead center at six feet tall. It seemed to be constructed from polycarbonate and acrylic materials. In front of the unbelievable structure were four spacious royal armchairs, each with its own vibrant color: orange, red, blue, and violet. A beautiful Persian rug added the final touch of class to the space.

Ethan could only stare, speechless. He greatly appreciated the creativity and heart put into these spaces. He started to understand the concept, but wanted to see the final two rooms before discussing more with Ravi. Looking up, his eyes focused on a quote written in deep blue letters: "To accomplish great things, we must not only act, but also dream; not only plan, but also believe. (Anatole France)"

Time for room 4. Ethan could hardly contain his curiosity. As he looked through the glass walls, he could see a person relaxing in an actual hammock, presumably recounting a story of some sort. He couldn't believe his eyes. There were also mini palm trees in each corner, with bamboo style chairs completing the space. Water streamed from a small fountain filled with tiny grey and brown rocks. He imagined the soothing sound it must offer to guests.

Without saying a word, Ethan walked over to the final space. The simple, classical room surprised him. Nothing flashy, but he could readily recognize the touch of authentic luxury flair. Three dark burgundy sofas were positioned in a triangular layout, with a coffee table as their center point. A stylish Tiffany chandelier with matching table lamps lit the space.

"Based on your vast career experience, Ethan, I assume you have read a number of interesting business books?"

Ethan nodded, trying to detect if Ravi was being serious or sarcastic.

"Have you read *The Dream Manager* by Mathew Kelly?"

Ethan vaguely remembered someone bringing it up, but could not pinpoint the exact time or place. "It does ring a bell."

Ravi continued, "You must go out today and pick up a copy. It will blow your mind! Let me give you our adapted version of his incredibly inspiring concepts."

Ravi stretched his arm across, introducing the rooms to Ethan again in his own debonair fashion. "In this area, we practice the art of dream facilitation. The idea has two distinct parts.

"First, we teach people how to assist their significant others and close friends in achieving their dreams. For example, let us imagine your sister is miserable in her daily employment. She confides in you and wants to change direction but has no clue how to go about it. We would give you the tools necessary to make this happen for her.

"Second, we work with each individual's dreams. We take time to understand their wants and needs. We help them focus, truly pinpointing their goals for the short, medium, and long term. And we diligently follow their progress. 'We' actually means our five trained dream facilitators."

Ethan had rarely been this impressed by a person or a company. Ravi's vision seemed to be unique and continuous. He questioned the viability of this business, yet the place just happened to be swarmed on a Friday afternoon. He realized he never knew it existed, and he had no clue what type of revenue Ravi could be bringing in. *Good questions for later*, he noted.

They walked along another hallway and made their way to a final conference room, again made up of glass walls. There seemed to be no secrets or privacy here, only full transparency. Ethan was not sure how he felt about the wide-open feel of the Elevation Leadership Institute.

As they approached the large double glass doors, the letters simply spelled out LEADERSHIP. Ethan could see several executives working with a large smartboard located on the farthest wall. Every person seemed fully engaged in sharing ideas and using animated hand gestures to communicate their messages.

"Every company needs a strategic angle, wouldn't you agree?" Ravi's energy filled the air. "We partner closely with firms and companies across North America to teach them the value of leadership, goal setting, public speaking, mentorship, succession planning, social media marketing, and every other aspect necessary to running a highly productive business. A type of executive coaching division, if you will."

"I can see how that would tie in nicely to every other division in your institute," responded Ethan.

"We try, indeed we try. Come, Ethan, let's go to my office and discuss a few things."

Ravi led Ethan back to his space. There were four offices, connected to each other in a square shape. Ethan followed Ravi into one of them. They each took a seat in wonderfully comfortable white leather armchairs, designer enough to merit a second glance, yet comfortable enough to eliminate any possible hint of pompousness.

Ravi jumped in immediately. "Ethan, I'm looking for a marketing firm to spread my message. We have been going in the right direction for many years, yet something is missing."

Ethan nodded, understanding it was finally his chance to prove his worth.

Ravi continued, "I have many creative ideas I want to try. I'm confused on the best way to implement them on a grander scale without throwing away our funds."

"Well, I'm sure Premier Marketing can provide you with the necessary tools to gain many more clients, and quickly. We have an excellent creative team for the branding piece and an exceptional design team for the finishing touches. We can tailor a complete program for the Elevation Leadership Institute, starting with market research of your brand equity. This will tell us if we need to pursue your current path or possibly take another direction completely."

Ethan was talking, but not believing. He put so much effort into his spiel, yet he knew there were deeper problems right now at Premier. The in-fighting at the Massa family level had become unbearable, the creative and design teams had no direction, and he himself felt incapable of succeeding at Premier. If anything, it seemed the entire company needed to spend a few days here with Ravi. However, he didn't feel this was the time or place to spill his guts.

Ravi stared at Ethan curiously, seemingly reading his thoughts. "Tell me, Ethan, why should I work with Premier? You've given me some valid points, although most large marketing firms can offer the same. Tell me, why I should go with your company?"

Ethan took a few seconds. He prepared to answer the question with an amazing speech about unparalleled dedication, unsurpassable customer service, and guaranteed results. He knew he couldn't. Ravi had truly inspired Ethan with a vision he wished were his own. He was impressed beyond belief. It struck him how Ravi's company was, in fact, the polar opposite of Premier. Here, they worked with transparency and honesty. At Premier, you had to watch your back at every moment. Ethan worked for a company that cared solely for the results printed on the financial statements. Yet even after all the discord and disappointment, Ethan felt compelled to do his job to the highest of his abilities. He looked Ravi directly in the eyes. "There are many reasons you could choose or pass on Premier Marketing, Ravi, but if you do choose us, I promise you I will do the very best I can."

Ravi smiled affectionately. "Well, wasn't that an honest answer. Tell you what, Ethan, give me a few weeks. I am meeting other firms. This is quite a big leap of faith and an investment for us, so we have to be sure of our final decision." He got up and shook Ethan's hand.

"Thank you for your time, Ravi. It was honestly an invigorating experience." Ethan squeezed Ravi's hand a little harder than necessary and left the office. He walked out of the main doors, thanking the wonderful receptionist who could easily have embarrassed him for his lack of professionalism. And as he made his way onto the sunlit street, he looked up at the blue sky and tried accepting the fact he was putting an important potential customer at risk. He had little faith Premier could do right by Ravi, even if he gave his all.

He decided to walk back to the office, wanting to appreciate the moment. Ravi Channa was already having an impact on him.

ONLY THY SELF

*We lead our lives so poorly because we arrive in the present always
unprepared, incapable, and too distracted for everything.*
—Rainer Maria Rilke, Bohemian-Austrian poet

*E*very car in the city seemed to have converged in front of him,
as though to make sure his travel would take as long as possible.
It didn't matter; he was almost home. Although he could have
been on the fifteenth hole of one of the most prestigious golf courses in
North America, Ethan felt elated and rejuvenated. Things could have
gone smoother today, but he had learned so much from Ravi's vision
and he promised himself he would get in touch with him soon.

At the very same time, another thought crept into his mind. He
remembered a conversation from earlier in the day. He had promised
his kids that morning he would pick them up with Eva and take them
for ice cream after school. He hadn't even turned his cell phone back
on after the meeting. Either way, Ethan realized, he would have been
on a golf course. But surely, Eva would have understood his unique
opportunity to play Royal Montreal.

He pressed the power button, knowing all too well the discom-
forting message that would appear. After a few seconds, nothing happened. *That is even more depressing. They expected me to forget them.* He
called home, and there was no answer. He called Eva's cell, and it went
straight to her voicemail. He decided to make his way home and deal
with the fallout.

As he arrived in the driveway, Eva pulled up beside him. He smiled
apologetically and opened her door. She did not make eye contact,
simply stepping out and walking straight for the house. The kids
shouted their excitement at seeing him, although Kayla immediately
complained about her daddy not picking her up. Ethan's renewed guilt
felt raw and deserved.

"I'm so sorry, sweethearts, I had a late meeting."

"That's okay, Dad," replied Luca. "We're used to it."

A dagger through his eye socket would not have caused a deeper stab of pain. The realization that his kids no longer had any expectations threw Ethan back into the long, forgettable childhood he had experienced with his father. *I am following his pattern.* He helped his children out of the car, and they went inside the house.

After setting the kids up with their favorite television show, he made his way upstairs. Eva had her eyes glued to the computer screen in their home office. He attempted a discussion. "Hey, honey, sorry about this afternoon."

She ignored him.

"Seriously, I feel terrible," he continued. "A work thing came up. You know how Robert Samuels can be. At the very last minute, he sent me to see a new potential client. I couldn't say no, considering how things have been lately at the office. But I met the most interesting man..." He stopped, understanding this was not the time or place. Eva typed away.

He tried changing the subject. "What do you feel like for dinner? I could pick up some pizza from Lino's?"

No response.

"Please, love, I said I'm sorry. I'll make it up to you. We'll bring in a babysitter next week and go out for a date night. It will be fun, I promise."

Eva didn't acknowledge any of his words. Ethan made his final reconciliation attempt.

"Babe, you know my work is demanding. I had no choice. I should have called, I admit, but it happened so fast, and I was late."

Eva finally glanced at him for a split second and, just as quickly, returned her attention to her screen.

"You wouldn't understand anyway." The ridiculous statement left Ethan's mouth unexpectedly, and he knew the mistake could not be taken back. Eva launched her attack.

"Understand? You don't think I get that you choose work before your family? You know, Ethan, the funny thing is that I am not affected by your empty promises anymore. I am a grown woman, and I can deal with your nonsense. But the kids are being shaped, or rather shattered, by their lack of a father. You constantly break their hearts, and I am at a loss. You walk around the house, forever moping in a terrible mood. The kids are terrified to make the slightest noise, expecting you to blow up at them!"

"Don't exaggerate. You're being overly dramatic."

Eva shouted louder. "Wake up, Ethan! You are really lost. You are going to regret every missed moment, you'll see. I can't fathom how blinded you are by your egotistical, selfish attitude. The kids need you. This can't continue."

The door to the office slowly nudged open. Both Kayla and Luca were standing there, eyes watering, with that questioning look only found on a child's innocent face.

"Why are you screaming?" Luca asked quietly. His voice quivered.

Ethan jumped in. "It's nothing, don't worry, sweet peas! Let's go downstairs and play."

As he grabbed both his kids and exited the room, he gave Eva one last look. From the corner of his eye, he could see tears streaming down her cheeks.

He tried playing board games with his kids, but his mind kept drifting back to Eva. Luca had to remind him three times to take his turn. All he could think about was the state of his relationship. He knew some blame must go his way, but why did she not realize he worked hard for his family? He didn't spend money on cool gadgets, fancy clothes, or crazy golf trips to California like some of his friends. He provided for the household day in and day out. But he also understood his unplanned absences and broken promises could not continue. Even now, he was not giving his children the attention they deserved. After a few minutes, he hugged them both and took them upstairs.

He put Luca to bed first. Given his two years of brotherly superiority, he always went to bed later than Kayla. Things were different tonight. Ethan clearly saw the evening's unfortunate events had affected his seven-year-old more than he wanted to admit. He held him for several seconds. He could feel his son shaking ever so slightly. This worried Ethan. He stayed a few more minutes, rubbing Luca's forehead. He then kissed Luca on the cheek and closed the light. "Sweet dreams, I love you."

"Me too."

Ethan found his daughter drawing at her small desk. Kayla often asked her father to sit with her and partake in some coloring. He couldn't remember the last time he had indulged her.

As he picked up a purple marker, he stared at her for several seconds, appreciating the moment. She seemed intensely focused on every detail of her masterpiece. Ethan couldn't determine the result of her work from where he stood, so he decided to move in for a closer look. "What are you working on, sweetheart?"

"I made a picture."

"Can I see it?"

"Sure, Daddy."

Kayla handed her father the colorful paper. As his brain registered the image, his heart sank. Depicted quite realistically, despite his daughter's five tender years of age, was a drawing he would remember for many years to come. Mommy, Luca, and Kayla playing at the park. Ethan was nowhere to be found.

For good measure, with the innocence of a child, Kayla smiled and said, "Daddy, you're at work."

He kissed her, hiding his embarrassment, holding back his emotions, and helped her under the covers.

He walked toward the bedroom and found Eva fast asleep with the reading light still on. There were tissue papers crowding the bedside table. Turning the lamp off, he walked over to his side of the room, threw off his clothes, and stared into the darkness. In the last eight hours, he had managed to meet a true visionary—the type of man Ethan aspired his entire life to become—while simultaneously alienating his entire family.

He had a wonderful, caring family unit he treated disrespectfully. His job no longer brought him any real satisfaction. His physical health was spiraling out of control, and ironically, he could see it all with crystal-clear clarity. *What is wrong with me? I've lost my way, and I can't get back on track.*

He climbed out of bed and went to sit on the front steps. For the first time in twenty years, Ethan wept. He cried fully and unguardedly, his head submerged into his palms, feeling completely alone and confused. He had always been a strong man, never willing to show weakness. It had caught up to him on this night, and a plethora of dark emotions entered his being.

He thought about his wonderful mother, Nora. Seeing Eva distraught, having fallen asleep in tears, brought back a flood of unfortunate memories of his childhood. When his father would lose control and tear into his mother, an eerily similar scene would occur. In those moments, Ethan would sneak into bed with his mother and try his best to comfort her. He never realized the pain she must have felt. He wanted to bring her joy and make her forget—and she always did. She always found a way to move on and love Francis despite his flaws. Reality unfolded right in front of his eyes. Ethan was becoming his father. He would lose Eva if this continued. It absolutely terrified him.

After an eternity lost in thought, he managed to calm himself and stop the tears. Change. Change was the only way forward he saw possible. Ethan knew not what to change, or how to change it, but he inherently understood the need to sweepingly alter the course of his life. He could only think of one way, or rather one person who could help him accomplish this:

Ravi Channa.

RETROSPECTION

*One of the greatest regrets in life is being what others would want
you to be, rather than being yourself.*
—Shannon L. Alder, author

$\smile$

he smell of cooked brown sugar filled the air. She threw in
walnuts, eggs, and squashed ripe bananas to complete the rec-
ipe. As the scent rose from the pan, Eva felt a stab of resentment flush through her. She pictured Luca and Kayla, disappointed yet
unsurprised their father had broken another promise. She remembered
falling in love with Ethan. He always knew how to love her and make
her feel like the only person that mattered in the world. Stirring the
pan, frustration flooded her thoughts. Such loving and healthy children. A nice home, financial security. But as she cooked, the void dark-
ened her mood. She couldn't deny the feeling anymore. It took over
her every moment, paralyzing her, leading to further anger. An endless
loop.

Most weekends, Eva whipped up delectable desserts for her family
and friends. She loved playing with ingredients, trying combinations
of flavors to create a new masterpiece. She had learned her art at the
Montreal Culinary Institute, what seemed like ions ago. She had graduated top of her class. Her teachers constantly praised her for the dedication and creativity she exemplified. The future looked bright, and
more importantly, she knew she was following her dream. Until her
plans were derailed.

She turned off the stove and sat at the kitchen table with a steaming
cup of tea, letting the heat burn her hands. Her memory floated back
to the fork in the road, when life took an unexpected turn. She stared
through the window as raindrops multiplied on the pane. She could
barely hear Luca and Kayla playing in the basement.

She had been with Ethan for three years. They had decided to travel
Europe together, backpacking and blending in with the students they

met. They were past that stage in their lives, but wanted to experience the world from a local perspective. Italy to Spain, France to Portugal—there were no boundaries. It was at that time inspiration hit her. At every corner, in every country, she found baked goods that made her heart skip a beat. So simple, so fresh. She realized she could not resist walking into every bakery that crossed their path. Ethan could only laugh, but he saw her passion and had no problem partaking in taste tests with her. The idea came together, and she decided to open her own place as soon as they got back home.

As she began the formal financing steps, locking down a location, and preparing her menu, an accident occurred. A miracle really, although the timing left room for debate. Luca appeared in her belly. It had happened during their trip, based on the dates. It had not been planned.

They wanted children. They had discussed it on several occasions. But the plan had a specific schedule—a few successful years with her new business first and not the other way around.

She tried finding solutions, new ways to follow her dream during pregnancy. It wasn't meant to be considering the necessary commitments her new life of parenting had brought to the table. Her exciting venture took a back seat, but only for a short period of time, she had told herself.

Several years later, with regret on her mind, she sat alone with no purpose. She loved Luca and Kayla unconditionally. She had created a deep bond with each of them no one could ever break. Her kids meant everything to her and more, considering her increasingly unbearable relationship with Ethan. They needed her, as children always need the warm touch of their mother. And she needed them. But she needed more, too. It made guilt well up within her. She felt judged by her family and her friends, as if they expected her to be satisfied with her life as it was. Ethan told her it was in her mind. But she was still the ambitious woman from her past. Her desire to accomplish something bigger never left her.

Her cherished idea had come up a few times in the past years. Of course, the timing never made sense. As soon as Luca escaped diapers, they decided they wanted another child. Once both kids were at daycare and she saw a new chance to pursue her passion, Vincent

Massa died, throwing Ethan's stable employment into limbo. And then they lost their way. It happened slowly, day by day, minute by minute. Ethan worked longer hours, putting business before family. She grew frustrated and stopped communicating her feelings. Their relationship floundered, making it impossible for her to follow her heart.

The doorbell rang, startling her. The kids sprinted up the stairs. Eva didn't move.

"Well, hello, my munchkins!" boomed her father's voice.

"Come give me a hug!" shouted Grandma.

Eva listened. The kids always enjoyed time with their grandparents. She quickly wiped away her tears and got busy in the kitchen again.

Her father came in and greeted her with a hug. "You doing all right, honey?"

She nodded, avoiding eye contact.

Her father stared at Eva for a few seconds. Rubbing her back, he shifted his attention back to Kayla and Luca, chasing them outside to the backyard at an impressive speed for his age. His little trick gave Eva some time and space to discuss things with her mother in private.

Eva greatly appreciated her mother and father and everything they did for their family. In her circle of close friends, she was the only person with healthy, energetic parents. This allowed for several advantages, most notably her attempt at having a life outside of the home. Considering Ethan's excessive hours at the office and his golf outings, she had a mutually beneficial option for the kids. Everyone involved found great happiness in the arrangement.

Eva often laughed at her parents for treating her with such overbearing love. When she was born, her little heart had several complications. She spent her first three months of life surrounded by doctors and nurses at the children's hospital. Apparently, for a few worrisome days, there had even been talk about a life-threatening condition. The incredible staff took great care of her, and by her six-month anniversary, Eva resembled every other healthy child. Her parents always referred to those days as a "living hell" and "the most stressful time of their lives."

It certainly explained their strong attachment, one they openly showed in every circumstance without exception. Eva remembered her teenage years when it annoyed and embarrassed her. Now, years later, she did not take it for granted, specifically in the years since her own kids were born. *You can never truly understand a parent's love until you have your own children.* Her mother and father gave so much in time, love, and energy. It made such a difference in her life, more than she could ever tell them.

"I see you are making one of those wonderful banana breads. I hope you have a few slices for your father."

"His version with chocolate chips is already in the oven. My kids get enough sugar, no thanks to the both of you." She didn't meet her mother's gaze.

"How are you?"

"I'm good, I mean, fine, all things considered."

"And Ethan, how is he?"

"I wouldn't know," answered Eva. "We haven't spoken."

Her mother looked at her. She never judged Eva. She had an uncanny ability to ask the right questions and listen carefully to the responses, always refraining from giving her opinion. Eva considered this to be her mother's greatest quality.

"Where is he?" her mother inquired.

"He's playing golf. Although I suspect they may have been rained out."

"When is he expected back?"

"I'm not sure. Soon, I guess. Maybe not. Who knows?"

"I suppose we'll miss him," said her mother. Despite all their issues, Ethan maintained a highly positive relationship with his in-laws. He cared deeply for them and made every effort to make them feel welcome. This small fact gave Eva a glimmer of hope for their future. *Don't most men despise their in-laws?* For this much she was thankful. It made everything easier for her and the kids.

"Mom, I've been thinking a great deal lately, and I have decided I should go back to work. Luca is seven, Kayla is five, and quite honestly, the repetition of daily life in this house is driving me crazy. I can only bake so much for family and friends."

"That's interesting, sweetie. What would you do?"

"There are many places I could work," said Eva. "Perhaps in retail or real estate?"

"I'm sure you would be excellent at both."

"Estelle has that clothing boutique in Rockland, and she is constantly nagging about having me run the place. She wants to expand but needs help."

"That could be just perfect for you. You have always respected her abilities and business sense."

"I have."

"I wonder," continued her mother, "about your passion for food. You are incredibly talented. Wouldn't there be a way for you to find something in your field?"

Eva expected the conversation to lead back to this subject. Her mother, forever encouraging her.

"I don't know, honestly, Mom. I dreamt so vividly about the pastry shop. The fact it didn't happen for me…perhaps faith is telling me the project had no legs. Now I can't see myself pursuing any other career in the food industry. It all seems lost."

Her mother stared into her eyes. "Perhaps, or maybe time has allowed for a better perspective."

"What do you mean?" asked Eva.

"I understand it did not work out as planned. I can feel your regret and disappointment. I have constantly thought about the way it happened, or rather, didn't happen for you. But let me tell you something as your mother, and more importantly, as someone who has great taste. I see such happiness when you are focused on your cooking. Your recipes are exceptional. What if your time is *right now?*"

"It can't work anymore, Mom. That is why I feel it is time to get on with life. I can't dwell on the past. I have been dwelling for eight years. Life goes on." Eva's voice quivered.

"I want you to be happy. That is all I have ever cared about." Her mother walked over and embraced Eva, holding her for several seconds.

A few more tears fell down her cheeks. Eva quickly wiped them away. She did not want her children seeing her in such a state.

"I know, Mom, I know. And thanks for always being here for me." She composed herself and straightened her blouse. "I'm nervous and confused, every day, all the time. I have no idea where Ethan and I are headed. The kids are seeing all of it, they are living our arguments. I can't stand putting them through such a negative experience." She could sense the tears coming back, but she held herself firm. "That is why I want to go back to some type of job. I need to find some independence, some self-confidence."

Her mother nodded. "It makes total sense."

The back door flew open and both kids came rushing in, Kayla embracing her grandmother, Luca hugging his mom. Her father followed several steps behind, visibly panting.

Eva shared one last look with her mother, silently conveying her gratitude for having such an amazing presence in her life. She opened the oven to take out the banana bread that could have pleased even the most impossible critic.

PART II
THE CLEANSING

A New Perspective

From a motivation perspective, helping others enriches the meaning and purpose of our own lives, showing us that our contributions matter and energizing us to work harder, longer and smarter.
—Adam Grant, author of *Originals*

unlight snuck into the room, bringing proof of a new day. Something hard landed on his ribs. The bed shook violently. Confusion clouded his thoughts as he realized his children had opened the blinds and decided to use him as a human punching bag. He tried to cover his face with the pillows, not accepting the morning's arrival. However, his kids had other plans, jumping uncontrollably until he finally had no other choice but to drag himself out of bed and make his way downstairs with them. Despite his fatigue, he welcomed their enthusiasm and energy. He hoped it could change his mood.

Arriving in the kitchen, he gave them each a bowl of cereal and cut some peaches. As he poured the milk, Eva came dashing in from her morning jog. They stared at each other awkwardly, both unsure if a smile or frown was in order. Nothing felt natural these days. Eva kissed both kids and made her way upstairs to shower without saying a word. Ethan ate his breakfast with Luca and Kayla as he flicked through the morning paper. His mind began to wander.

The last week—since his breakdown on the front steps—had passed fitfully. Ethan wanted to call Ravi and make amends for what he perceived was a failed meeting. He had not been his best that day. Ethan had rarely been so impressed by a person. Ravi had incredible vision and a certain inexplicable mystique about him. He couldn't explain it, but Ethan knew he must pursue their relationship in some way.

As he heard Eva descending the stairs, Ethan stood up, wanting to get ready for work. He hesitated as they crossed paths in the kitchen door and he brushed against her ever so slightly. Eva's long golden-brown hair fell softly to her bare shoulders. She wore a simple white tank top with light-blue jeans and flats. Her natural beauty struck Ethan to his core. He hadn't felt that kind of sensation in months. If Eva noticed his reaction, she gave nothing away. They continued their separate ways.

Freshly groomed, he announced his departure to deafening silence. He walked out and entered the car. His phone rang. He didn't recognize the number. "Hello?"

"Ethan, how are you today?"

"Mr. Channa, so great to hear from you," answered Ethan. He looked at his phone in disbelief. "I was just thinking of calling you."

"Is that so? Funny how our infinite universe sometimes works in small coincidences. I must, however, admit my frustration at being called by my given name. Much too formal for me."

"I apologize," continued Ethan. "I get swamped by formality in my daily life."

Ravi laughed. "So why were you going to call me?"

"Well, to be completely honest, I didn't provide you with my highest level of service when we last met. That day, I have to admit my personal agenda trumped the importance of our meeting. I should have been more present." Ethan waited for Ravi's response.

"I appreciate your sincerity, and I did sense a certain level of hesitation on your behalf. We all live through days where we'd rather be someplace else. But you're being too harsh."

"Perhaps, but I strongly believe you deserved more focus and a better strategy for your needs."

"Let's not dwell on the details. Can I assume you want to meet again?"

"Absolutely, if you'll have me."

"Of course, in fact, I am still in my decision-making process. I have a suggestion that may be different from your typical meetings."

Ethan's curiosity was piqued. "What do you have in mind?"

"Where do you live?" asked Ravi.

"In the beautiful western suburbs of Montreal. Beaconsfield to be exact. Do you know the area?"

"Oh, quite well. I lived in Hudson for many years. I have since moved slightly closer to the city in a comfortable spot near the water on Lakeshore Drive. Very close to you. I want you to meet me at my house. Be there at seven o'clock sharp tomorrow morning. The address is 2448 McConnell Avenue."

This surprised Ethan. He couldn't quite grasp the concept of meeting at Ravi's house, and that early. "Sure, no problem. I'll prepare some numbers and show you a few ideas I believe can make a real difference for the Elevation Leadership Institute."

"We are not quite there yet."

"Okay, so we will go over more details regarding your business and the desired direction?"

"Wrong again." Ravi sounded amused.

Ethan had no idea what to respond. "What did you have in mind?"

"Bring your running shoes and a warm sweatshirt. See you tomorrow!" Ravi hung up the phone and left Ethan completely confused. *Running shoes and a sweatshirt. Is he serious?* Perhaps he simply wanted them to walk and talk, get some fresh air, and allow their brains the freedom of inhaling great ideas. Ethan could make that work. As his mind processed the information, another thought struck him. *Ravi seems super fit.* Did Ravi actually want them to run along the waterfront? *It can't be, he would have told me, right?* He truly had no clue.

***

Ethan loved watching football and took lessons from the greatest coaches in the game. That is where he learned about "Lombardi Time"—the concept of arriving fifteen minutes early to every meeting. The famed Green Bay Packers coach Vince Lombardi demanded this from his players, and Ethan loved the idea. With this in mind, he arrived at Ravi's house with time to spare. He found Ravi stretching in his driveway, dressed with the flair of an Olympic marathoner. *Oh boy, we are going running.*

Ethan slowly opened his car door, soaking in the beauty of the home. A combination of rich chocolate-coloured bricks and dark grey panels made up the façade. The style exuded modernism with the faintest touch of traditional class. A majestic deck hung over the lake, suspended in the shimmering light. Ethan imagined the incredible BBQs that must take place there in the height of summer. He could have used the heat right now, considering the chill of a Canadian October morning entering his bones.

Ravi's grin ran from ear to ear. "Early, I see. I must say that bodes well for our run. You better get stretching!"

Ethan couldn't recall the last time he had stretched out his increasingly tight muscles. He decided to follow Ravi's lead and made a futile attempt at looking like a runner. He had been a runner once, many, many years ago. *I wonder if running is like riding a bicycle. Does it simply come back naturally?* Unfortunately, Ethan realized his legs would be doing the work, not a machine.

"Tell me, Ethan, what's going on in your life?"

Ethan hesitated, knowing there were many answers to that loaded question. "Well, everything is good. Work is busy, several projects happening right now. Our company is continuing to grow and expand." He left out the part about upper management treating customers with arrogance and dishonesty to make an extra dollar.

Ravi reached down and touched his toes in a deceptively flexible manner. "I am more interested in your personal perspective, Ethan. I want to know how you perceive your environment altogether."

He had stumped Ethan. *What is he looking for? Are we talking business or personal? My perception of the company or my world vision?* As he prepared to answer, Ravi started jogging away from him toward the path on the waterfront. Ethan took this as an obvious sign their mysterious run had begun. The pace seemed acceptable, in essence a fast walk.

Ravi sensed Ethan's confusion. "As I started my business several years ago, life became hectic. I had no time for my family or my friends. I stopped taking care of myself and those around me. I essentially lived at the office and cared little for anything else. Despite all of it, do you know what the single most difficult thing was for me to deal with?"

"What was it?"

"The seclusion. I had turned so far inward, focusing only on my business and corporate goals, I forgot to connect with others."

Ethan could relate. Although he didn't run Premier Marketing, he did manage his small department and most often felt alone. Except for Sasha, of course, but he made every effort not to tell her too much for fear of sounding selfish.

Ravi continued, "In many ways, I regret that part of my life. It's easy to look back with remorse—many of us do it daily. And yet, although I am at a point now where I have found some balance, I made significant choices then that caused much pain to my loved ones. I don't presume to know you well, Ethan. But one thing is certain—you are not happy."

The statement left Ethan's mind reeling. With any other person, Ethan would have regressed into his primal state of fight or flight, either lashing out or going dark and silent. He may even have rudely ended the conversation. But with Ravi, he felt at ease. He sensed the message had a deeper meaning, a more defined direction. He didn't answer, allowing Ravi to continue his thought process.

"Let me be clear, Ethan, I am not judging you in any way. I am stating what I see as your current mindset. I sense something amiss, as though you are being held back by a heavy emotional weight. As a business acquaintance, you could just ignore me. But as my running partner, you now have a more difficult situation to deal with as we must talk about something during the next five miles."

Ethan laughed and then stopped dead in his tracks. "Are you serious, Ravi? You will kill me. I can't make it five miles! I can't make it a half mile!"

Ravi simply smiled. "With me, you'll make it. No need to worry, I will keep you in check. We'll take it nice and slow."

They continued several steps in silence. Ethan spoke first.

"I have to admit I am quite surprised. I'm not sure how you figured it out, and the fact you did deeply concerns me. Am I projecting my unhappiness so obviously?"

"Not at all. It is quite subtle, but I spend my days with people working toward a better life. I can definitely tell when the stars are not aligned."

Ethan took a few seconds to compose his thoughts. His panting and increasingly labored breathing distracted him. "You are right. I am not currently at my personal peak of happiness. There are several issues plaguing me." Ethan let loose, having an excess of built-up frustration to shed. "Let me break it down for you. I don't want to sound ungrateful, but work has become unbearable at Premier. I know, it is an awful thing to say in the presence of a potential client. But if I'm being honest, ever since the founder died a few years ago, everything has changed in the most negative way."

"I understand. I knew Vincent and admired his ambition."

"You knew Vincent? How?" Another surprise Ethan had not expected.

"That's a story for another day," said Ravi. "Please continue."

"We no longer treat our clients with respect. To be clear, many individuals at Premier still do, but the organization has lost the essence of why it exists. And my boss—that, in itself, could take one hundred miles to discuss. I cannot begin to describe the way he treats me."

"Try anyway."

Ethan's typically reliable social barriers were dissolving by the second. "Robert Samuels represents every myth, all the negative clichés heard in large corporations around the world, about horrible bosses. He cares only for personal advancement and destroying anything or anyone in his path. The most important goal in his life is to be feared. He enjoys keeping people at the office well past reasonable hours, constantly disrupting personal commitments. He passes on blame without a semblance of guilt. All in all, I can say, with some certainty, that he cares nothing for those around him and will go to any length to succeed in his own twisted way!"

"I see," said Ravi. "But tell me how you really feel."

Ethan laughed. "Scariest part is that Robert has deep, mysterious connections to the Massa family, which explains his position of power, as far as I am concerned."

"I've seen and heard of many managers that fit the picture you have painted of this man. I have also known many individuals to have acted in a self-preserving manner in various life situations. It happens every day, all around us." Ravi slowed down to a walk, seeing Ethan struggling to keep up. "Do you believe you have somehow provoked this person?"

"Absolutely not," responded Ethan defensively. "I have made every effort to remain courteous and professional."

"I would expect nothing less from you, Ethan. Then you believe this is Robert's personality, the man he is deep at his core."

"Yes."

"And how do you react to Robert? What is your personal strategy for dealing with such an aggressive manager?"

Ethan thought for a few seconds. "I shut down, I try to hide in my office, and I avoid him. I basically act like a schoolchild running from a bully!" He realized the ridiculousness of the statement as it left his mouth.

"Have you ever tried any other approach?"

"Well, to be completely honest, not really. He is so obviously jacked up on authoritative adrenaline. I see there is no changing him."

"Do you think you must change him for your work life to improve?"

"I'm not sure I follow."

Ravi picked up the pace again, just enough to keep Ethan sweating. "In my experience, when a vicious circle is created, one of the players must break the pattern for a resolution to occur. From the perspective you are presenting, Robert will not be that person. Therefore, the only logical answer is for you to make that decision."

"How can I accomplish that?" asked Ethan incredulously. "Robert Samuels is impossible to deal with."

"There comes a time when a completely different philosophy may be necessary. It requires incredible patience and tremendous self-awareness. Those two qualities must be cultivated over time."

Ethan listened intently to every word. "I certainly agree if I were blessed with those traits, I could probably improve my situation. But I haven't been very patient lately, and I can't say I even understand the concept of self-awareness."

They stopped at a much-needed drinking fountain, and Ethan took a few rehydrating sips. Ravi looked fresh as day, as if he had just exited the shower. The morning sun shone brightly now, lighting up the rippling waves of the lake.

"We will come back to that idea. If I may ask, how is your personal life?"

This conversation is getting deep. Am I ready to go there with Ravi? Ethan thought back to his front steps and the disconcerting moment he had recently experienced. It had occurred to him at that moment Ravi may be able to help him in some way. And now he found himself confessing his most personal life problems.

"Why am I doing all the talking? You're the customer here!"

"The last time we met you couldn't get in too many words. I have a tendency to talk endlessly when it comes to my life projects. Today, I am here with the goal of listening to Ethan Stone, to learn about the man behind the man."

Ethan almost fell over after hearing the famous line from one of his favourite movies—*Swingers*.

"What? I really enjoy Vince Vaughan!" exclaimed Ravi.

"That makes two of us!"

They passed a group of rowdy high school students on the way to school who, to Ravi and Ethan's surprise, cheered them on enthusiastically.

Ethan continued, "When I'm home, I tend to let my emotions get the better of me. The kids are constantly running around screaming and fighting. I usually react too quickly and often brashly. It certainly causes discomfort for all of us. In truth, I spend much more time at the office and not enough time with my family. There isn't much balance, which is something I accept, considering my personal goal of providing my children with the best life possible. And yet, when I'm home, I'm not a great father. I know that. I'm never truly present."

"And how does your life partner feel?" As he asked the question, Ravi slowed down allowing Ethan much-needed respite.

"Eva?" Ethan wiped the sweat from his brow. *How does she feel?* He sensed such a plethora of emotions from Eva these days, ranging anywhere from frustration to isolation. "We have lost that special connection in recent months. My schedule hasn't helped, but she doesn't understand the difficulties I am facing at Premier. We're not on the same page right now."

"Can you give me a few examples, perhaps specific situations?"

Ethan took a few seconds to think it through. "Well, just the other day, I got home late from work after a fairly stressful day. I needed a few minutes to settle in and relieve some of my tension. Before I even sit down, she has her jacket on and announces she made plans for the evening and not to wait up for her."

"And why did this bother you?"

"There are several reasons why this got to me. The kids were still up and needed my immediate attention. I know she does a great deal for them, but I also have major responsibilities all day and could use some time to cool down. On top of that, she never tells me her plans in advance. Most often, she simply leaves without notice. And worst of all, she won't even tell me who she is meeting or where she is going. She could at least give me that courtesy in case something happens."

"Do you believe you give her that same respect?"

"I try to. I mean, depending on the situation, I'll call her and let her know my commitments." He didn't feel comfortable lying to Ravi, yet he still did. Perhaps a small part of him actually believed he communicated openly with his wife. The truth could not be farther from reality. He constantly used his employment as the scapegoat for his own need to stay out of the house. He complained about Eva's attitude but knew deep down he carried as much blame. Probably more. He found distractions to compensate for the solitude.

"I see," said Ravi.

They continued walking at a brisk trot, arriving at the yacht club. There were only a few boats left, considering the season had recently ended. Suddenly, Ravi turned around and began jogging back toward their original direction. "Ethan, I am pleased to announce we have just covered two and a half miles. The first half of our run is over. You should be proud considering the utter disbelief you clearly expressed earlier." Ravi smiled, and Ethan shook his head with a grin. He actually was surprised.

They carried on quietly for several minutes. To ensure Ethan remained alive and kicking, Ravi kept the pace reasonable. As an avid runner, Ravi knew all about the thin line separating motivation from overextension. He knew Ethan had not run in several months, maybe even years. The very last thing he wanted was to alienate or injure him.

After several hundred strides, Ravi slowed down once again, allowing Ethan to recuperate. Every such moment seemed a blessing to Ethan.

"You mentioned your children. How many do you have?"

"Two. An energetic seven-year-old boy and a very smart five-year-old daughter."

"And what about your children? How have they been throughout these circumstances?"

"My children are amazing creatures," responded Ethan, "and despite our difficulties, they have remained fairly upbeat. There have been times where they witnessed us fighting and arguing, but which couples don't?"

"From what you told me, you don't have the opportunity to spend much time with them."

"I certainly don't. Between work commitments and a general lack of hours in a day, our moments together are very limited."

"Do you think that is reality or a situation of your own creation?" asked Ravi.

"How do you mean?"

"You have briefly explained the way your life is structured today. Try taking a step back and looking at it from a distance, as a spectator. Do you think life simply happened that way, or were you the catalyst, writing the book of Ethan's life through your own actions?"

Ethan breathed in the fresh air as he contemplated the question. "I would say a healthy combination of both. Certain events popped up in my life, and I reacted accordingly. In other cases, I took the bull by the horns and shaped my own destiny." He liked the sound of the latter part much better.

Ravi seemed to be taking in all of this information, storing it in some deep vault to be analyzed at a later time. In reality, he was simply listening and questioning without judgement.

Ethan spoke again, "I have often wondered about the idea of faith. I guess I prefer cheating the system. When something positive happens, I enjoy taking credit. When things turn in the wrong direction, it's easiest to blame the unexpected consequences of the world around me. Sounds terribly self-justifying, doesn't it?"

"Perhaps it could to some, but personally, I appreciate your honesty. I meet many different people, and I most often praise those individuals able to take responsibility for their actions."

"I'm not sure I am taking much responsibility," answered Ethan, "but I will state the obvious!"

Ethan found himself seriously struggling for oxygen, even at their slow pace. Thankfully, Ravi kept an eye on his new running victim and immediately slowed to a quick walk. "Keep it up, Ethan. I can see the pain in your eyes, the aching in your legs. I can assure you I will only push you to the point of needing an ice bath followed by a week of physiotherapy."

They crossed an older couple jogging on the waterfront. Despite their advanced years, they were moving at an impressive speed. Ethan felt amateurish. He realized both husband and wife could have been his parents, and both would easily have destroyed him in a race. He suddenly felt ridiculous, but he knew being out with Ravi represented an important milestone given his current physical state. *Something to build on.*

They jogged a few more minutes, keeping quiet and focused. As they turned a sharp bend in the path, Ravi's house came into view. "How far is your house from here?" asked Ethan.

"Less than half a mile away."

"You know, Ravi, I am barely keeping up at this point. I can see you are still full of youthful energy, so why don't you go ahead, and I will meet you there shortly?"

"I can't just leave you here, Ethan. You're my running guest."

"Honestly, I insist. I can tell you are itching to let those legs loose, and I want to see you at full stride. Consider it a lesson in motivation for the next time."

Ravi glanced at him. "You seem pretty sure about this, so I will take your invitation. I'll see you in a few minutes." With that, he rocketed away at warp speed. At least it seemed that way to Ethan. Ravi already impressed him in so many ways. He could now add "super athlete" to the growing list.

As he approached the house, Ethan decided to go all out and really make the most of this first running workout in years. He turned the burners on and ran full tilt for the remaining three hundred yards. He huffed and puffed his way to the unofficial finish line. He finally made it and desperately threw himself on the grass, thanking the universe for allowing him to still have the ability to breathe. Ravi stood legs apart, touching the ground in front of him with both hands flat on the ground. "You better start stretching, my friend. I have that strange feeling a cramp is much too close!"

Ethan gathered himself after a few seconds and started imitating his newfound running coach. His flexibility had also paid the price of his laziness, allowing his fingers to barely make it past the shin area as he attempted to stretch his hamstrings. He moved slowly and deliberately, sensing one wrong movement could launch a bout of excruciating pain throughout his body.

"How long have you been running, Ravi?" asked Ethan, still sweating profusely.

"To be honest, I only took up the sport more seriously in the past five years. You can say I had an epiphany of sorts."

Ravi switched to a more yoga-like position, holding his right foot in his hand, balanced on one leg. Ethan attempted the pose but lost balance several times before finally staying in place for a few seconds.

"Please do elaborate for me. I am very curious."

"Well, the story is none too unique. Many years ago, I found myself spending excessive time working late, eating out, and drinking to my heart's delight. As an obvious result, my health took the back seat. One day, my heart gave in, literally. They called it a very mild heart attack. I got lucky. I only spent a few days in the hospital. Once I made it back home safely, I dramatically changed my entire life. My eating habits and physical fitness became my highest priority. To this day, I have stuck closely to my new regime and feel absolutely excellent."

"Wow, that is unbelievable! You were able to change things that quickly?"

"I had no choice, Ethan. My body sent the clearest of messages, and I could only listen. Anything less and I would have lost this gift we so often take for granted."

Ethan nodded. It made complete sense. At the same time, he realized he did not want to wait for a physical wake-up call to change his own direction.

"You know, Ethan, I have truly enjoyed our morning together. Just being here with me says a great deal about your character. I sense you are searching for something more from life. In no way am I presuming to know your every desire, nor am I making any judgement. From our conversation, the way you describe both your professional and personal life indicates as much. Am I way off right now? Please stop me if I am out of line."

Ethan shook his head. "Please continue, Ravi. I appreciate your honesty." Rarely did he accept being questioned, yet it felt strangely liberating coming from Ravi.

"Apart from the physical improvements I made in my everyday lifestyle, I learned a very simple new vision that greatly improved my mental well-being. It also made a world of difference to those around me. It can easily be summed up in three distinct steps."

Ethan listened intently.

"Tell me, what do you know about *meditation*?"

"Meditation? I've heard a few things about it, such as deep breathing exercises and extreme focus. Oh, and the part about hiding in the Himalayan mountains for several weeks secluded from the entire world!"

Ravi laughed. "Very interesting, but perhaps we can skip that last part. In its essence, it does require a combination of concentration and rhythmic breathing. To start, you simply find a very comfortable position. Sitting is fine, as long as the back is straight and the eyes remain ever so slightly closed. You then inhale and exhale deeply through your nose, calming every muscle. Easy enough so far?"

Ethan nodded, holding his arms behind his back and stretching his weak pectoral muscles.

"The simple goal is to focus on your breathing. When you start, your brain will be all over the place. Work situations will creep in, followed by family concerns. You'll think about anything and everything, from important responsibilities to daily tasks like picking up your dry-cleaning. This is what the experts call 'chatter.' It is completely normal and should be accepted."

"I can definitely see how that could happen," said Ethan. "What is the solution?"

"You work through it. Every time it happens, you reset and go back to the breathing. You do not want to fight it. After a few minutes, your mind will definitely trust you, and clarity will become reality. Always remember that the very act of realizing your mind has drifted and going back to the breathing is a step in the right direction. It is a mental bicep curl. You are training your mind."

"That seems easy enough."

"It is simple in theory, but not easy. It takes time, like anything in life. With practice, you will find it essential to your routine."

"I've heard it takes hours."

"I can assure you, Ethan, it doesn't take hours in a day. I'd say fifteen minutes each morning and night will work wonders for those who try."

"That can't be enough?"

"But it is, I can promise you. It would be nice to have more time, but in today's fast-paced environment, it allows for much-needed peace of mind."

"I think I get it. If meditation is step one, what is step two?" asked Ethan.

"Have you ever heard the quote from Epictetus? 'We have two ears and one mouth so we that we can listen twice as much as we talk.' True words of wisdom!"

"I have heard that, although I have never practiced it," answered Ethan with a grin.

"*The art of listening* is quite impactful and virtually ignored by many of us. Often when we claim to be listening, we are actually preparing our thoughts with the goal of getting in our own point of view. If we consciously make an effort to stop talking and clearly listen to those around us, it serves as quite the experience."

"I am sometimes guilty of not listening, but so are many of my coworkers and even friends," answered Ethan defensively.

"It happens in many situations," continued Ravi. "I have an interesting way of gauging a person's ability to listen. Let's say you are having an interesting conversation with a colleague, and you are speaking when her phone rings. She answers and speaks for two minutes. When she hangs up, will she ask you to continue your thought, to pick the conversation back up where she left it? In my experience, rarely do people have this ability. Even the smallest of distractions often gives us great knowledge of a person's listening skills."

"I never really thought about that. In fact, I haven't ever consciously acknowledged my lack of listening ability. My mother, Nora, was an exceptional listener. In many ways, she was the center of our family. Everyone wanted to speak with her, to confide in her. I wish I had her skills."

"Ethan, I am not pointing any fingers at you. We're talking about a very common occurrence. Let's take the last few minutes. I have been talking away endlessly. You have been listening and asking pertinent questions. That, in itself, is impressive."

"I can't take much credit here, Ravi. The subject matter has been of great interest to me. I am much more concerned with my personal life and my work environment. Looking back, I can't say with confidence there has been an amazing track record of actual listening. It is definitely an area requiring much improvement."

"Only you know the truth of that statement. It is great to see you are able to openly discuss something you feel you could be better at. Which brings me to the second part of this equation. Listening is not enough. It is a hugely important step in the right direction, but another component completes the cycle."

"What is that?"

"Judgement. Or rather the lack of it."

"I don't understand?"

"In my experience, listening only goes so far. As we become good listeners, we must also learn to respect opinions and understand the world is full of different perspectives. You cannot control what a person thinks or how they act. What you can decide is how you will interpret what you see and then react to others and their way of thinking. The only way to accomplish this is to refrain from judgement."

"Are you saying we just let others speak their mind, and if we don't agree, we simply keep it to ourselves? I can't see how that works?"

"Let me clarify by asking you a few simple questions. But first, let's go inside and grab a drink."

Ravi led Ethan through the front door. They walked to the kitchen area. Flowers lined the counter, and it reminded Ethan of the Elevation Leadership Institute. Fresh fruit sat in a metal bowl, causing Ethan's mouth to water. Ravi noticed and pushed the green grapes toward him. He poured them two glasses of water.

"Where were we? Oh, you were telling me that I can't speak my mind." Ethan smiled.

"Nice job picking up our conversation. I promise it wasn't a test. I was really thirsty!" They each took hefty sips from the cold glasses.

"Allow me to clarify," continued Ravi, "as you must be wondering where all of this is going. Essentially, refraining from judgement doesn't require a person to stop speaking. It involves a change in philosophy.

Judging is the easiest thing to do. A person gives an opinion, we decide if we agree, and when we don't agree, the judging begins. Does this make sense?"

"I think I see your point. The goal would be to respect others' opinions regardless of our own point of view. But what comes next?"

"You acknowledge, accept, and move on. Let me give you an example. The other day, my wife Daniella felt justifiably annoyed by my recent business trips. I spent nearly three weeks away visiting potential customers in Europe and Asia. She let me know how this made her feel and the way it impacted our family life. On my end, I believe these trips were very necessary to successfully expand our international marketing division. In my younger days, I would have lost my cool and defended my actions vigorously. A fight would inevitably have ensued, leading to more anger."

Ethan jumped in. "You were working hard to provide for your family."

"Perhaps," continued Ravi, "but try seeing her point of view. Our kids are young teenagers and still live at home. They have all kinds of activities going on and need rides everywhere. Daniella and I are also very close, and we don't usually spend this kind of time apart. I would have loved to bring her on the trip, but she teaches Italian classes and could not get away. Those weeks were tough on her. We sat down, and I listened carefully as she vented. When she finished, I acknowledged her frustrations, promised to plan my travel more efficiently in the future, and hugged her. We proceeded to enjoy an amazing evening together."

Ethan looked surprised. "That is interesting. But if you didn't agree, why not say the real facts?"

"There are always two sides to every issue. To be true to oneself, all perspectives must be considered. By doing so, we open up the lines of communication and allow for complete honesty. By refraining from judgement, we can create much stronger bonds."

Ethan thought about his own way of dealing with disagreements or differences in opinion. He wasn't bad at work, but with Eva and the kids, all hell broke loose. Perhaps he could try changing his approach with his family.

"We've covered steps one and two, and I am definitely curious about step three."

Ethan could tell Ravi was enjoying this conversation. His entire being exuded excitement and passion.

"Before I start explaining another simple step, have some more grapes. You need a full stomach to hear this." He pushed the bowl further toward Ethan. "I am going to divulge my secret weapon. It has helped me in more ways than I can describe. Be prepared for the unpredictable. It will shake your world. Is that enough hype for you?"

Ethan almost choked on a grape.

"Here it is. The final piece of the puzzle. Are you sure you're ready for this?"

Ethan smiled and nodded slowly. "I am. I am ready."

Ravi took a deep breath and waited a few seconds to hold the suspense. "I refer to it as *circular reciprocation*. In simple terms, be excessively nice to everyone around you. And by doing so, the universe will return the favor."

Ethan just stared. "That's it?"

"Yes."

"That is really too simple."

"Simple, but not easy."

"I just need to be nice. What if I am not a nice person?"

"Everyone is nice when they are born. Sure, circumstances can cause a person to take on a different attitude. And yet we are all able to make our own decisions. We are not born indifferent, Ethan. We get to choose how we act out there in the world."

"Sometimes I'm just tired and not willing to make that extra effort."

"I understand what you are saying, but like anything in this life, effort is necessary if we want to make a difference. And I am talking about the little things. Do you hold the door open for the person behind you? When you order a coffee, is the person in front of you a number, or is eye contact made and a sincere thank you passed on? When was the last time you told a colleague how their work is appreciated? With time, there is no effort. It will make those around you feel fantastic, and in turn, you will feel the same."

"I am fairly nice with most people," Ethan said with little conviction. He did treat his closest friends well, and his acquaintances acceptably, but strangers were an afterthought.

Ravi continued, "It may not feel natural at first to treat every single person you encounter with genuine care. It takes time to develop. It also requires a willingness to connect with others, even in everyday situations. Make eye contact with that salesclerk. Ask your waitress about her day. Tell the dry-cleaning cashier how much you appreciate his work. Oh, and treat your family as the center of your universe."

Did he read my mind again? "Basically, I treat everyone like gold, at all times."

"That is the idea."

Ethan took a few seconds to digest the philosophy they had discussed over the past two hours. It all seemed very straightforward, but deep down, he knew it required a major shift in his behaviour and habits. His schedule revolved around sports watching and work, not meditation and deep, intensive listening. In fact, he tried not listening most of the time. *That sounds so wrong, even in my own head.*

"For the sake of clarity, and more importantly, my personal well-being, here is how I understand the steps of your suggested philosophy:

"Meditate morning and night. Engage in the art of listening intently without judgement. Practice circular reciprocation by being genuinely nice to every person I meet, which the universe will return my way."

"That is exactly correct," said Ravi. "I strongly believe any person able to follow these three steps will see a significant difference in the quality of their life. Those around you will immediately notice a new Ethan. Other qualities such as patience and understanding will infiltrate your mindset quickly and surprisingly. Before long, you won't be able to remember your old habits. An aura of positivity shall grow from within and eventually take over your being." Ravi's face glowed as he conveyed his thoughts. "Very spiritual stuff, right? I hope it doesn't come across as too mystical!"

"I can honestly say I have never thought about life that way," answered Ethan, "and yet I have been searching for a fresh start for several weeks now. I'm ready to take a leap of faith."

"That is wonderful to hear, and I am going to help you as much as I can. I want to show you something." He led Ethan out of the kitchen into a large study at the back of the house. A very spacious area, books filled the walls from end to end. A massive canvas painting covered the farthest wall, depicting two runners crossing a finish line. Ravi opened the drawer of a small desk and removed a letter.

"We have spent the last two hours discussing a number of ideas. I want to read you a short letter that changed the course of my life. It serves as the cornerstone of my entire philosophy. It is my reason for being."

Ethan eagerly awaited the words. Ravi began to read:

"My dear son, I have not seen you now in over six months. I'm afraid to admit we may never have the chance to share a conversation in person again. My health is leaving me in a state of physical weakness, but there is no pain. You have been a blessing, a true angel sent from above. You have created a wonderful life, and the love your family shares has no limit. Please give Sofie, Olivia, and Liam kisses for me, and don't forget to hug Daniella.

"I have learned so much from you, more than I ever gave. As I lay in my bed alone, missing you and your mother—God rest her soul—I want to share the one true lesson this world has taught me. No one can understand how short life is until it is almost over. Please don't waste one minute arguing, one second in a dark mood ever again. The minutes are disappearing as I write these words, the seconds ticking away. The same holds true for you. Before you know it, you will be looking back at the years as I am today. What will be your legacy? Money doesn't matter; fancy cars and clothes don't make it to the grave. Only your character persists, only the impact you made on others will be valued and cherished. Promise me you will remember that the next time your ego wants to make an appearance. Take this advice to heart. Love those around you unconditionally, as it won't last forever. Ravi, may you fulfill your every dream."

Ravi breathed deeply as he finished, holding back his emotions. Ethan felt overwhelmed, his heart pounding intensely.

"My father wrote me this letter from India, three days before his death. That was four years ago. I spoke to him on the phone when he had already mailed it, but he never mentioned its existence. He never told me that day how bad his health had become. I would have flown there immediately, but my father knew this and did not want to burden me. A completely selfless man, always there for me. And I can truthfully tell you I took his words as my mantra. I changed the way

I lived, and it has been such a rewarding experience. And I encourage you do to the same. I don't waste any moment, ever anymore. We easily lose the sense of time, and only later do we realize the shortness of it all. Remember this and recognize how precious your life is and how lucky you are to have so many wonderful people around you."

The letter, and specifically Ravi's openness, gave Ethan a deep sense of responsibility. He wanted to be a better person, to have a much stronger relationship with his kids. And Eva, of course. "I will try. I definitely will try." Ethan meant it.

Suddenly, a memory flashed in his mind. Long-hidden thoughts of a moment so intense, it had caused him to completely sever ties with his own father. Ethan had never been close to his dad. How could he be? Francis Stone stood emotionless in the face of every important moment of his son's life. His inability to express his feelings had brought deep loneliness to their family. But his actions from that terrible day sealed their fate. Ethan had vowed over nine years ago to never speak with his father again. It happened on the day of his engagement to Eva. He had proposed during breakfast, taking her to the Ritz for brunch on her birthday. Romantic setting, perfect mood, an incredible morning neither would forget. They had planned on having dinner that night with his and Eva's parents to announce their wonderful decision.

Everyone arrived on time except for Francis Stone. They were having problems, his parents. That much he knew. Constant fighting, repeated disagreements. But that evening, his father crossed a line, causing irreparable damage to the family. He had taken to drinking excessively months earlier, a very nasty habit ingrained in the Stone family lineage. Thankfully, Ethan had never felt that devastating urge to intoxicate himself. Francis missed dinner without a word to anyone. He was nowhere to be found. During dessert, with the mood already in a fragile state, Francis made his grand entrance. Seriously wasted, with a strange, shady-looking woman by his side, he declared his plan to divorce his wife to the entire restaurant. He then proceeded to knock over a tray of food, fall over his chair, and twist his ankle. Ethan's mother had raced out in tears, Ethan quickly behind her. It had changed her, that hurtful and profoundly embarrassing event. She never moved on. As for Ethan, he could not stand the sight of his father any longer and decided it just wasn't worth it. The saddest part was that

Francis Stone only made a few weak attempts at reconciliation. He hadn't fought for his family.

As he thought about his past and reflected on Ravi's story, Ethan realized he wanted to be a great father and husband. He needed to be. He decided to focus on his immediate opportunity to improve his relationships with his wife and children. He knew if he didn't make changes now, he too would find himself alone.

"Can I ask you one last thing before I leave, Ravi?"

"Of course."

"Why are you helping me? I am unbelievably grateful. This morning has been an exceptional experience. But you do this for a living. I certainly can't be good for business! And I thought this meeting was to discuss your marketing initiatives. But that doesn't seem to have been the goal."

Ravi looked at Ethan, giving nothing away. "One day, I promise I will explain my reasons. For now, I trust you want to change, and I connect with that."

They shook hands, and Ethan walked out of the house ready for a new beginning. He understood an important shift had occurred that morning. He felt different, able to see his life with clarity, something he needed desperately. He planned on making the most of this opportunity.

A SMALL STEP

Be not afraid of growing slowly, be afraid only of standing still.
—Chinese proverb

Ethan pulled into the driveway. He felt completely invigorated after his run with Ravi. He needed to see his wife and share his thoughts with her. It seemed obvious now, all the inspiring ideas Ravi had explained. He wanted to try this new direction immediately. He needed Eva for that.

Suddenly, an idea sprung into his head. He grabbed the phone and called Eva's mom. She answered after five long rings: "Hello."

"Hi, Robin, it's Ethan."

"Why, Ethan, how nice to hear from you! It's been too long. We missed you last time we came over."

"I wish I could have been there. I was caught up with work stuff."

"To what do I owe the pleasure?"

"I have a big favour to ask you."

"Of course, anything."

"Can you pick up the kids today? I was hoping to surprise Eva with a night out. I know it is last minute, but I thought I'd ask."

"Of course, of course, that is fine. More than fine, it's perfect. We were due for a night with them."

"Thanks so much, I really do appreciate it."

"Have a great time, we will have them in bed by the time you get back."

"See you tonight, we won't be too late." Ethan hung up the phone. He marched upstairs ready for a hot shower, although he felt quite refreshed already.

MISUNDERSTOOD

People assume you aren't sick unless they see the sickness on your skin like scars forming a map of all the ways you're hurting.
—Emm Roy, author of *The First Step*

*R*obert Samuels could not remember the last time he had slept peacefully. The interruptions kept coming and coming endlessly. Sometimes at 1:00 a.m., other nights at 3:00 a.m. His entire being felt drained. He knew it affected him every waking moment of his life. The toughest times were during work hours. There, any little event could set him off. It didn't take much. Perhaps a late arrival or a missed sales call by one of his staff. Such petty circumstances could send him into a rage.

The medical world referred to it as a "delusional disorder." His mother, one of the strongest women he had ever known, had changed almost instantaneously. One day, two years prior, out of the blue, she began hiding all her jewellery and personal belongings. She claimed thieves were planning an attack on their home, and she must protect her castle. She often roamed the house in the middle of the night, staring at the street, as if some crazed stranger would show up and try to break in. Every time Robert heard the creaking in her room followed by her footsteps, it immediately woke him up. One time, he found her in the basement trying to install firewood on the windows to lock out the imaginary bad guys.

He constantly debated what he should do. Was it time for her to receive professional care? Could he actually live with himself if he had her sent to a home of some type? Did he have the time or patience to continue taking care of her? He knew something had to give. His own mental health was suffering to the point of exhaustion. And as he thought it through, he glanced over as the clock blinked 4:00 a.m. *I can't do this anymore…*

He slowly got himself out of bed, not wanting to wake her. Entering the kitchen, he opened the highest cabinet and pulled out a bottle of vodka. Pouring a quarter glass, he walked into the den. Through his bay window overlooking the Lake of Two Mountains, he stared as the leaves rustled without care.

His mind went back again, as it often did, to the decisions he had made and the subsequent consequences he now had to live with. He had dedicated incredible energy and time to his career at Premier Marketing, and it really showed financially. Now a senior-level manager making more money than he needed, the seventy-hour workweeks had paid dividends. But what had he sacrificed? He couldn't hold a relationship during those years. His friends all had wives and children. They no longer bothered inviting him to their get-togethers. Not that he would attend given his single lifestyle. And he knew deep down that the company had sucked out a more precious, indescribable element from his life. Was it positivity? Compassion? Empathy? All of the above? He wasn't always so difficult and stubborn.

The situation with his mother took fatigue to a new level, but his attitude at the office bordered on neurotic and had for some time. He fully grasped the negative effect it had on his colleagues and direct reports. Yet he felt helpless to overcome it, and the top brass encouraged his behaviour. His reputation as a bullheaded, relentlessly unforgiving authoritative figure seemed to be admired by upper management. As he continued growing in importance and status, so too did his aggressive managerial style. The vicious circle continued to expand and ensnare those around him. He would never admit it openly to anyone, but he dreaded going to work every day.

His health had become a depressing hurdle in his life. When working such excessive hours, he lost track of keeping his body in any type of respectable condition. Late hours equalled frequent junk food binges. Wine and beer were always available and accessible, even at the office! He never stood a chance, or at least he used that as his excuse. The scale stayed in the closet by choice.

He downed the vodka and went to the kitchen for a refill. As he entered, he caught a glimpse of his mother peering through the front door window. *I didn't hear her come downstairs.*

"Mom, is everything alright?" he asked.

She did not answer.

He walked over and grabbed her shoulders. She spun around and sent his glass flying against the wall, shattering into hundreds of little pieces. Her hand was bleeding.

"They're coming, I see them!" she screamed.

"There is no one there, Mom."

"You blind fool, you have no idea!" She wrestled away from him, slapping him in the face in the process and ran upstairs, slamming the bedroom door.

Robert stood in place for several minutes, staring at the mess. He grabbed the broom and started cleaning. He tried fighting back the tears with all his will but did not succeed.

ALL YOU NEED IS LOVE

Maybe that's why I wanted to get lost somewhere,
because I wanted to be found.
—Corey M. P., author of *HIGH*

S everal people were speaking at once. Verbal jabs were being thrown between territory managers, fighting for their piece of the pie. It could have been mistaken as a political debate between two fiercely opposed candidates.

"Don't deny it, Martin, the Home Hardware account started in Toronto. I brought that business to the table. It is completely centralized, so you're angle about the franchises is nothing but hogwash!" screamed Paul.

"I'm getting the calls," answered Martin, "so maybe you should realize we are a team here. I'm taking care of your work."

"What! All you are doing is taking my commissions!"

The bickering continued on and on. Normally, Ethan would have jumped in, trying to validate every point while mediating the entire argument. Today, he was positively distracted. He kept thinking of Ravi's simple steps and how it could help his situation. He thought about Eva. He could not wait to take her out. It would be the first time in months, hence the reason these petty discussions flew over his head. His daydreaming caught up to him.

"What are we going to do, Ethan?"

Ethan had no clue who had asked the question and what it pertained to. "Excuse me?" he muttered.

Paul looked at him furiously. "About the territory. About the Home Hardware account? How will we handle the commission split and the lead with the marketing manager over there?"

Ethan stared at him thoughtfully. "You and Martin are both senior sales managers. I expect you can work this out on your own."

With that, he got up from his seat and marched out of the conference room. He did not look back. Entering his office, he closed the lights and grabbed his jacket on the way out. As he closed his door, he came face to face with his boss. He did not hesitate. "Hello, Robert."

Robert scowled. "Off already, Ethan? Seems a tad early, given it is four thirty in the afternoon. Do you have a sales call?"

"Not at all."

"Perhaps another important commitment then?" questioned Robert.

"Actually, that is exactly right," said Ethan, but he did not elaborate.

Robert tilted his head ever so slightly to one side, staring intensely at Ethan, as if this strategy would give him all the answers he was seeking. Surprisingly, Ethan did not flinch in the least.

Robert persisted. "Care to elaborate, Stone?" He knew Ethan hated it when he used his last name. But again, no reaction came from Ethan.

"Honestly, Robert, I have an important family situation, or rather opportunity, that I should have attended to for some time now. I would prefer not to give more details, but let me say it matters deeply to me. I hope you can understand where I am coming from."

Robert Samuels was not accustomed to this type of discussion with Ethan. Something seemed different about him today.

"Don't you think I am entitled to know where you are going?" asked Robert with less conviction this time.

Ethan took a second, then another, to formulate his response. He realized this conversation could head in several negative directions. He thought about Ravi's advice. *Listen, and do not judge.* He realized only he could make this relationship better. Perhaps it would be a pointless journey, but he decided then and there it was time to do his part in making this a moment of fair, honest communication. "I understand, Robert. You deserve an answer. I am leaving early so I can take my wife, Eva, out to dinner and truly listen to her for the first time in months, or maybe even years. I have ignored her needs, and we have grown apart. I feel it is important for us to connect again and make things right."

Robert stared dumbfounded. "Oh, okay, um, yeah, I get it, Ethan. Do what you need to do. Just make sure you are available tomorrow morning so we can review some numbers."

"Absolutely, I'll be here bright and early, Robert!" Ethan patted his boss on the shoulder and made his way out of the office.

Robert watched him leave, scratched his temple, and went back to his office for another long night of work.

***

Eva was rushing. She had a million things to take care of and no time for anything. She needed to get moving if she wanted to pick up the kids on schedule. Guilt always overwhelmed her when she missed the pickup and her sweethearts ended up at the after school babysitting service. Purely an internal emotional conflict, as both Luca and Kayla seemed ecstatic playing with their friends whenever she arrived late.

The phone startled her. "Hello".

"Hi, Eva," said Ethan.

"Hi."

"What are you up to?"

Eva had been caught off guard. Ethan never called at this time of day. "Rushing as always so I can pick up the kids on time."

"No need today."

"What do you mean?" asked Eva.

"Your parents will be taking care of that."

"Why?"

"I am taking you out to dinner. Actually, we are going to Le Filet."

Eva looked at her phone, surprised by the news. "But it's Tuesday night, Ethan."

"A fine night as any I have seen for us to spend enjoying a great meal together."

Eva could detect something distinctly different in the way Ethan sounded. He seemed different somehow, more energetic. She liked the sound of it, although she would not admit as much. "You sure my parents are cool with this? I know the children can be quite a handful, and Mom and Dad aren't spring chickens anymore."

Ethan laughed. "Are you kidding me? Your parents have more energy than most twenty-years-olds I know. Nothing to worry about. I spoke to your mom, and everything is settled. I will be home in one hour to pick you up. Does that work for you?"

"Uh, sure, okay," she muttered.

"Perfect, see you then. I love you," said Ethan.

"See you soon." She hung up knowing she could have been sweeter, but this whole situation felt suspicious. *He must be feeling guilty about something.*

***

They arrived at the trendy, inconspicuous restaurant just after six. Le Filet had become a true hangout for foodies from all over North America. Mostly fresh, local ingredients were used, and getting a reservation was never easy. Luckily, Ethan had done some marketing work for the restaurant and knew Chef Claude Pelletier personally. They were able to sneak in at the last minute.

As they were taken to their seats, Ethan offered Eva a seat overlooking the stylish décor. In the car ride over, they had talked about the kids' school activities and upcoming birthday parties—mostly lighthearted stuff. And through it all, Eva could sense a positive energy radiating from Ethan's demeanour that she had rarely seen in the past months. She held herself in check, not yet fully grasping this shift in attitude.

"I'm really happy to be here with you," said Ethan.

"It is definitely unexpected," she answered.

"We need to do this more often!"

Eva nodded her head, smiling ever so lightly.

"You know, I did want to talk to you about a few things. No hidden agenda or anything like that, just sharing some thoughts."

Here we go. He does have a reason for bringing me here. Too good to be true. I should have guessed.

Ethan could tell Eva had her guard up. He couldn't blame her, given the shakiness of their relationship over the past few months.

"This may sound funny, but I must do some of the talking first. I will try to get to the point quickly, because ultimately we are here for you."

Eva stared, unmoved.

"This morning, I went for a run with a potential customer," said Ethan. "An incredible man—Ravi Channa."

"Wasn't that strange?" asked Eva. "You have never run with a customer before."

"First time for everything! And yes, I did find it bizarre that a customer I visited for one meeting invited me to his house for a run on the Lakeshore waterfront. But I do care about my customers and felt compelled to accept."

"You do care about your customers."

Ethan continued, "What a riveting experience it was, Eva! We talked about a great deal of different things, from our careers to our families. We shared ideas, and mostly, Ravi explained his philosophy on life that has taken him to the highest level of success and happiness."

"This sounds somewhat cultish, Ethan."

"I know, I know. Just bear with me for a few minutes. We discussed so much, but I don't want to bore you with too many details. Essentially, he made me realize how short life really is. And how I have been wasting valuable moments every day. He strongly encouraged me to speak with you tonight about some small but important changes I will be making."

Eva was unsure if she should be happy or annoyed. She could see genuine enthusiasm from her husband and did want to hear more. Before he could continue, a smart-looking waiter arrived. They ordered a bottle of Sauvignon Blanc. He took the order and left them to their conversation.

"Continue where you left off," said Eva. Ethan smiled, seeing Eva using the listening skills Ravi had mentioned and picking up their conversation from before the interruption.

"I should give you some background. Ravi is different from anyone I have ever met. He is quite a handsome man whose level of fitness could put most twenty-year-olds to shame. His business is called the Elevation Leadership Institute, a place so warm and inviting you can almost feel the positive vibe envelop your whole being as soon as you walk in. And most importantly of all, from the time I spent with him this morning, I learned his life philosophy is incredibly focused on happiness and pursuing a greater good."

Eva looked surprised. "He made quite an impact on you over one run."

"He did. And we only grazed the surface. We talked in depth about certain specific actions he takes every day that allow him to be a better person. I have to admit, Eva, it made me realize I need to change for you and the kids."

This last statement came out so naturally, Eva couldn't believe her ears. She had been telling Ethan for months that he needed to make different choices. Now, after a morning jog with a complete stranger, he decided it was time! She repressed her frustration and decided tonight was no time for a fight. *I want this for my family too.* "Go on, Ethan."

Before he could continue, the white wine arrived. "Here you are," said the waiter. "Do you have any questions about the menu?"

They both shook their heads.

"What can I offer you?" he asked, directing his attention to Eva first.

"I am torn, but I have decided to go with the Lobster Gnocchi."

"Excellent choice. And for you?"

Ethan smiled. "The Scampi Risotto sounds too tempting to resist."

The waiter seemed pleased with Ethan's selection. "I will get these orders in. Can I offer you anything else right now?"

Again, they both politely shook their heads.

He smiled and made his way to the back.

"Nice guy," said Ethan with a dashing grin.

Eva nodded, bewildered. *He is being very friendly.*

"I know I'm taking up all of the spotlight right now, but I promise in a few short minutes the floor will be all yours."

Eva acknowledged his statement with a simple nod.

"Ravi encouraged me to talk to you about it. He explained how important it is for you to understand what I am trying to accomplish, because it has a major impact on our life together. The first part, which is all we discussed this morning during our run, involves three specific components, or steps if you will."

Eva felt a tinge of nervousness. She hoped none of these steps involved Ethan leaving for a six-month cleanse in the Himalayan mountains to become a monk. The conversation seemed headed that way.

"Here it is," he said excitedly. "Meditate a few minutes morning and night, listen intently without judging, and be super nice to every person I meet."

Ethan looked at Eva with genuine happiness and satisfaction. He awaited her response.

Eva stared back, unsure what to say. She processed the information. "What does *meditate* mean exactly?" She had heard about the concept, but never really took the time to understand it.

"I looked it up at the office today. Basically, the first thing to do is sit in a comfortable position, in a quiet place, and breathe. Well, more than just breathe. Concentrate on breathing with as much focus as possible. Understandably, the mind tends to wander and get caught up in the many daily stresses we live. But when that happens, we are supposed to ground ourselves again and return to our breathing. By doing so, the mind totally calms, and we are meant to feel rejuvenated." Ethan just happened to give that entire explanation without taking a breath.

"I can see how that would work," said Eva.

"I am excited to try tonight! Maybe we can do it together?"

Eva quickly shook her head. "I will let you try first. We can see how it goes for you."

"Fair enough."

"And moving on, you are going to listen intently without judging. That will be a challenge, given your recent track record," said Eva.

Ethan accepted the jab, knowing full well it was deserved. "I will make every effort to listen to you and all those around me with true concentration. And without simply tuning out when I don't agree."

"Does this apply to the kids also?"

That one hurt a little more, like a punch to the gut, but again, he knew the result of Eva's sarcasm came from months of frustrating behaviour on his behalf. "Absolutely."

"I look forward to seeing this listening technique in action," said Eva. "For the last part, I must say, you are a nice-enough person. What will change?"

"Ravi made it clear that I must take it to a whole new level. It comes with understanding my surroundings, making a more conscious effort in certain situations."

"Such as tonight with the waiter?"

"Exactly. He is giving us great service, and I want to show my appreciation."

It all seemed positive in theory, but Eva had seen far too many negative situations in recent times to accept this as the new reality. She expressed her doubts. "I see you wanting to make a real effort here, Ethan. But I will be honest. I will believe it when I see a significant change."

Normally, such a comment would have completely dampened Ethan's spirits. But he got where Eva was coming from, and he agreed. He nodded seriously.

"I know it's harsh," she continued, "but I want us to be open with each other."

"I couldn't agree more," said Ethan. "I plan on putting these ideas into practice right away. Let's leave it at that and see the results. I have talked enough tonight. Now I want us to talk about you."

Eva looked around, unsure if she wanted to delve deeper into their conversation, considering the proximity of the other guests in the restaurant. "Maybe later, Ethan," she whispered.

"You don't feel comfortable here?"

"There are a lot of people."

They were sitting at the window seat. As if by more than just coincidence, the couple next to them finished their coffee and strode out of sight. Ethan and Eva looked at each other and burst out laughing.

"Well, if that isn't meant to be, I don't know what is," said Ethan.

"I have to agree," said Eva.

"I haven't been around much lately," continued Ethan, "and it seems you have a lot on your mind. Is that a fair statement?"

She nodded.

"Do you want to tell me about it? I promise to listen without judging."

"To put it frankly, I have been dwelling on the past."

"In what sense?"

"I am going to say a few things that are for our ears only, Ethan."

"Of course."

"I love our children more than anything on this earth. They are my reason for living. Only, I sacrificed so much when I got pregnant. I'm not sure if society's sexist expectations influenced our decisions, but

I find myself wondering why I left my entire career and my dreams behind."

"And I continued with mine."

"I'm not questioning that part," said Eva defensively. "But we could have done things differently. I had such passion for cooking, such ambitions to start a real project and make a dent out there."

"You still can! Nothing is stopping you," blurted Ethan.

"Let's be realistic, Ethan. I have been out of touch for almost eight years now. The market has changed, culinary techniques have evolved. I wouldn't know where to start."

Ethan just nodded, choosing not to throw out more suggestions. Listening to her, truly hearing her speak for the first time in months made Ethan understand the complexity of her thought process.

"I am at a crossroads, Ethan. And you haven't been there for us. I have felt so alone."

The last statement caught him off guard.

"It's rough to hear, I know, but it needs to be said. It is great to see you want to change and improve your view of the world. I can say that I also need a new direction to follow, and I need your help with that."

"How can I help?" he asked. "I mean on top of the changes I want to make personally to be a better person."

"I don't have that answer, Ethan. I don't have any answers right now." Eva looked down at her hands. She stayed in that position for several seconds. Ethan wanted to comfort her, or better yet, jump across the table and hug her, but he felt she needed space right now.

The waiter arrived at that precise moment with their meals. This helped lift the mood, if only slightly. They gave each other a look, neither negative nor positive, but rather of acknowledgement.

Eventually, the conversation shifted back to the kids and the crazy things they did. A more positive vibe returned, well encouraged by the lively crowd in the small restaurant. For the first time in forever, Ethan and Eva shared a meal without arguing once. The only exception came when they could not agree on the chocolate pot de crème, as desired by Ethan, or the famous key lime pie, Eva's favorite. In the end, both desserts found a way to their table, to be shared.

The night had been a smashing success. They both hoped it was a sign their relationship had turned a corner.

THE TURN

Be the change that you wish to see in the world.
—Mahatma Gandhi, political ethicist

ᔐ

Sylvia removed her glasses, gently laid them on her desk, and rubbed her watery eyes. Thick documents were scattered in every direction, in stark contrast to her typically organized desk. She leaned back into the leather chair, tension weighing down her shoulders. She glanced at her computer screen. Her inbox showed 164 unread emails. She slowly closed her laptop with a sigh.

Walking over to the window, she stared at the Montreal skyline. Sylvia could not appreciate the view, not with a Sales and Marketing meeting looming. She didn't have the energy to deal with incompetent employees. Premier was bleeding cash, and her mission was to save every penny she could. Perhaps that meant cutting a few corners or overbilling a large client here and there. *What choice do I have? Who else is going to make the tough decisions?* She knew some people questioned her ethics, but they had no idea how much stress she carried for them. They were simply pawns in a game they could never comprehend.

Her father, the current president, skipped these meetings and most everything else these days. She couldn't remember when they had last spoken. He was too busy traveling the world and enjoying the fruits of her labor. The VP of Sales, Robert Samuels, would be in attendance. As would the infamous Ethan Stone whom she still resented after their heated exchange weeks earlier. She had played coy and put on a stoic face, but every encounter with him left her fuming.

Grabbing her bulging briefcase, Sylvia left her office and made her way down to the conference room.

***

Ethan sat four seats to Sylvia's left, in a state of wonder. He had been practicing meditation for the last six consecutive days—small fifteen-minute increments morning and night—and could sense a whole new way of thinking taking over his life. It was as if a cloud had been lifted from his mind. Everything seemed less hazy now.

The first few times had been very difficult. He found a quiet spot in the corner of his bedroom and sat there for several minutes trying to concentrate on only his breath, but his brain just kept wandering. From his sales reports to thinking about breakfast, he could not hold his attention in place for more than a few seconds. But Ravi had explained as much to him. He needed to practice and stick with it. By day four, he experienced an indescribable moment of clarity. He was able to concentrate on breathing in and out repeatedly for several minutes. Nothing else penetrated his thoughts. His mind quieted, and he entered a state of complete freedom he had never experienced before. A pang of pure happiness entered his body for a few brief moments. He felt free, as if his body and soul were now in a new place of complete serenity. He knew it sounded corny and very hippy, but he had become a believer in the past days.

Sitting in the boardroom, observing Sylvia kick off the meeting with such open disdain, he shifted his past frustrations to an attitude of positivity and open-mindedness. He had no idea what could be done to change the course of their relationship or the incomprehensible direction of the overall company, but he would try his best to stay calm and look for solutions.

***

Robert Samuels sat two seats down to Sylvia's right. His mind was elsewhere. The previous week had taken its toll. It had gotten worse on the home front, if that was even possible. His mother got lost the previous day for several hours before being found by the police wandering aimlessly at the mall in her pajamas. He knew the time had come to have her placed in a specialized institution where professional care could take over. Yet he couldn't get himself to do it at the moment. Guilt overtook his rational mind every time he tried to research the subject.

As for work, he always took time before the monthly Sales and Marketing meeting to prepare the numbers and, more importantly, determine the issues that must be dealt with. Not today. He came without a shred of information. He hoped Sylvia could carry the load, and he could stay under the radar just this once. Not one person at Premier knew his family situation, which meant no one could understand his fatigue and frustration. Furthering his anxiety was the fact he had ignored several customer calls in the past few days. A lack of energy and motivation. Not ideal when starting a meeting with a ferocious, power-hungry executive completely incapable of empathy.

He glanced around the room and observed the frowning faces and worn-out expressions. The tension could be cut with a knife. For many years, he had enjoyed the competitive nature of the company. It had always been tough, but fun at the same time. The latter no longer applied. Now every individual cared only about two things—survival and making an extra dollar.

He stopped when his eyes arrived at Ethan. They had not spoken since the awkward moment in the hallway two days earlier when Ethan left early, stating the need to see his wife as the reason. He looked different. Robert couldn't figure out exactly what had changed, but there seemed to be a new confidence and fresh energy about him. Robert sipped his coffee while indulging in a double chocolate muffin. He watched as Sylvia launched her dreaded meeting.

***

"Welcome everyone," said Sylvia, without the slightest hint of warmth or sincerity. "Unfortunately, we have to start this meeting on a negative note once again. Sales have been down for the fourth month in a row. This continuing trend is unacceptable. I am tired of hearing senseless plans that have no true direction. I want real solutions!" She turned directly to Ethan. "Your numbers are plummeting! I am trying hard to see some positive, but I'm at a loss. We've lost ground with existing accounts, haven't opened any new ones in a long time, and now Thomas Lumber is threatening to leave!"

The first comments slid off Ethan's back like water, as he had become familiar with this line of attack. The last comment should have caused serious anger to boil to the surface. Sylvia blaming him for her lack of ethics was unthinkable. Normally, he would have launched into a furious counterattack, defending his position with a number of over-used clichés. The old Ethan would definitely have thrown the Thomas Lumber overbilling fiasco back in her face. After all, Sylvia had made that incredibly devious decision. And on top of that, Robert never took any slack. He was running sales for the entire company. The meeting would have continued in awkward embarrassment for all present and ended with even less resolution. That pattern repeated itself quite often.

But Ethan had clarity on his side today. He knew it made little sense after only a few days, but he believed the meditation practice had changed his entire perspective. It allowed him to think and take a moment before reacting.

"I understand your frustration, Sylvia. The entire sales team is out there day after day trying to gain new business. The economy is tough, but that's no excuse. We must bring in new customers, I agree." Ethan kept calm.

Sylvia showed genuine astonishment for a split second, having expected a confrontational answer. She ploughed ahead, thinking she sensed weakness, "Trying and talking are very different from bringing in actual revenue. And your answer does not address any sort of specific game plan. What are your people going to do to make an impact?"

Out of nowhere, Robert Samuels intervened in such an unusual way it caught Ethan by complete surprise. "Sylvia, you continue to direct your questions at Ethan, but I am the VP of Sales and should be taking full responsibility for our current failures."

The entire room shifted their attention to Robert. In this bizarre meeting, Robert had actually succeeded in taking the strangeness to a new level. His ever-consistent behaviour of agreeing with Sylvia's every comment had taken a sharp turn. And she did not appear impressed in the least.

"Robert, you are not the one at fault here. Mr. Stone needs to reassess his team's priorities and achieve some sales targets in a hurry."

"To be completely fair, I will repeat that the entire sales force is under my umbrella, and you should be addressing your concerns directly to me," insisted Robert.

Ethan looked at this bull of a man who had just made a very critical decision that may cost him dearly in the long run. Defying a person like Sylvia Massa meant trouble. To do so in front of this crowd could be viewed by some as career suicide.

"I appreciate your support," said Ethan, looking at Robert, "but I take full responsibility for our current situation. Thankfully, it isn't a lack of effort but rather a need to refocus the team's time and energy."

Robert looked dead tired. He seemed in danger of either falling asleep on the spot or leaving the room. He did neither. "Sylvia, I will work closely with Ethan and our team to get the numbers back on track. Why don't we see where we stand next month?"

She immediately opened her mouth, then stopped. It happened twice more and caused the others to laugh quietly under their breath.

"Fine, Robert, have it your way. But let me say you have decided to share your faith with a man needing to prove his worth in a hurry."

"I've always liked a challenge," responded Robert, somewhat defiantly.

If looks could kill, Robert would have been in trouble. A few moments of silence hung in the air as they stared at each other.

Visibly agitated, she changed the subject and reviewed other issues from accounting problems to HR disasters. Most in attendance tuned her out. Robert still looked abnormally distracted and dazed from Ethan's point of view. As the meeting ended, and people began shuffling out, Ethan walked in stride with Robert.

"Hey, Robert, is everything good?" he asked.

Robert hadn't even noticed he had company. "Oh, um, yes, fine, fine."

"You sure? I don't mean to pry, but you look preoccupied." Ethan had never imagined approaching Robert in this manner, but things had changed in the past few days.

"A few issues at home," said Robert, "but I am dealing with it." His tone did not indicate any real confidence in his situation. Ethan wanted to help, to talk more about it, but didn't want to probe. He decided instead to practice another of Ravi's philosophies.

"I want to thank you, Robert. I appreciate what you did in the meeting. Standing up for the sales team and encouraging teamwork is definitely the right direction to go. We will be better for it."

"Sylvia exaggerated. And I know about the Thomas Lumber fiasco. I may be a jerk sometimes, Ethan, but I am no thief."

Ethan stared dumbfounded.

Robert suddenly walked away without another word. He entered his office, closed the door, and shut the wood shutters. Ethan went his own way, not unhappy with the unexpected turn of events.

FINDING THY SELF

Yesterday I was clever, so I wanted to change the world. Today I am wise, so I am changing myself.
—Rumi, Persian poet and mystic

He no longer needed an alarm. At 5:30 a.m. sharp, his eyes opened, as did his mind. Slowly exiting his bed without making the slightest sound, Ethan moved to his recently discovered favourite space in their bedroom—the Persian rug. He sat down on his meditation pillow and let all his muscles relax.

Ethan absorbed himself in his practice. Every few seconds, his thoughts drifted off to random places—his work or his tasks for the day—but he didn't follow them. He had learned to acknowledge his thoughts, work through the distractions, and regain focus very quickly. Tension melted from his shoulders. He could feel his body adapting to his breathing, following the smooth rhythm. He entered a state of calm, finding a peaceful place for his mind.

Entrenched, he did not notice his daughter Kayla standing there watching him. She touched his arm, and he opened his eyes, seeing his precious princess staring in confusion. "What are you doing, Daddy?"

"Oh, sweetie, this is called meditation."

"Is it like the Yogi Mommy does sometimes?"

"Yoga, yes, honey," replied Ethan with a smile.

"Can I try?" she asked.

"Of course!"

He knew a moment like this would stay ingrained in his memory forever. Kayla sat down next to him. "Now, you have to breathe through your nose only."

She followed his instructions with exaggeration, sending her nostrils into a wild flaring motion.

"A little softer, sweetie," he said, laughing. "What you want to do now is think only of your breathing."

"How do we do that?"

Ethan knew his explanation would not make any sense to a five-year-old. He decided to take a different approach. "Think of someone you love."

"I love my cousin Juliette."

"Perfect. Now think about sending her your love."

"Can we send her a card in the mail?"

"Of course, we can." Ethan chuckled. "I have one more idea. Think about a food you enjoy."

"Grapes!" she exclaimed.

"Good! Now imagine you are eating grapes. Take the grape and taste the delicious flavours. Think of the juice and the best way to eat it."

Kayla shot up in a flash. "I'm hungry, Daddy!"

Ethan appreciated the moment, knowing it would be cherished. He scooped up his daughter, and they made their way to the kitchen. They found quite a surprise. Luca's hands were covered in a healthy mixture of butter, chocolate, and flour. The kitchen counter could not be seen. Most cupboard doors were open. The stove had been turned on, which made Ethan very nervous.

Two weeks earlier, Ethan knew this exact scene would have played out very differently. Seeing the disaster and danger, he would have screamed at the top of his lungs and would have sent Luca to his room, causing panic around the house. But he sensed such good intentions from his son. He still felt his anger growing, but a newfound patience allowed for a level of self-control he rarely experienced in his life.

Placing Kayla gently on the floor, he turned the stove off. "Luca, I see you wanted to make us pancakes. That is such a sweet gesture. But you know the stove is only for adults. It is very dangerous and cannot be used by children, ever. Do you understand?"

Luca's lip quivered ever so slightly. "I'm sorry, Daddy." He jumped into Ethan's arms and buried his head into his father's shoulder.

Eva watched the entire scene from the corner of the hallway, mesmerized. She hadn't witnessed compassion from her husband in years. His level of stress seemed to have almost disappeared. He actually took the time to talk, not scream, at his children. She could feel the tears coming, which also took her by surprise.

She entered the kitchen and embraced the Ethan-Luca bundle while simultaneously pulling Kayla into their family hug. After a few seconds, all of them started giggling uncontrollably. It was a step. A small step. But a step nonetheless.

GO LONG

A kite can't soar without some kind of force against it.
—Dakota Kirk, actor

⌒〜

*R*eaching as far as possible, he placed his palms flat on the floor, followed by his feet, feeling the deep stretch in both hamstrings. Sleepy muscles expanded forcefully, eventually yielding to the exercise. Nothing felt better than a yoga session first thing in the morning. Sharing this moment with his wonderful wife and best friend, Daniella, made the entire experience that much better. They shared a knowing glance every few minutes, never lingering too long, wanting to give each other space and respect.

Completing the one-hour session, Ravi headed for the kitchen to make them both a light and healthy breakfast: a grapefruit, whole-wheat toast with all-natural peanut butter, and tea with milk. They talked about politics, travel, books, food, never seeing time pass them by. As exquisite a morning as any Ravi could have asked for. Suddenly, his cell phone rang. "Hello?"

"Hi, Ravi, it's Ethan…Stone."

"No need to specify, Ethan. I recognize your voice," Ravi answered in his smooth accent. "It's been a few weeks. It is wonderful to hear from you! How are things?"

"Very well. Things have certainly been different since our last meeting. Or *run* I should say."

"Different how?"

"Without wanting to sound overly confident, I have made some serious strides with your three principles."

"I like confidence. I'd love some details."

"Well, I must say I have put the meditation techniques into practice. I did a bit more research to ensure I knew the proper way to start. I have begun to truly listen to those around me without judging—most specifically at home with Eva and the kids. At work also. And I am trying hard to be genuinely nice with every person I meet. I make an extra effort to consciously treat others with a higher level of respect, including strangers. I am feeling the circular reciprocation!"

"That is fantastic!" exclaimed Ravi.

"I can see the positive changes. I still have a lot of work to do. I have a ton to make up for with certain people in my life. Which leads to the second reason for my call."

"What's that?"

"I know you run several times a week, and I was hoping I could join you again sometime."

"How about tomorrow morning?"

"That would be perfect. Where do you suggest?"

"Do you know where Centennial Park is?"

"Of course."

"It is an amazing place to run," said Ravi. "A small lake, a mountain to run up, trees with no cars in sight. Who could ask for more?"

"I agree!" Ethan paused for a few seconds. "Ravi, I have to ask you something."

"Sure, anything."

"I learned so much during our last run together. Now I am asking to pick your brain again. I have seen such benefits in the past weeks that I know I am following the right direction, one that is very necessary in my life. Through your Elevation Leadership Institute, you do this for a living. And from our meeting there, I also understand you work with various people all over the world on improving their personal and business lives." Ethan felt uncomfortable, but he soldiered on. "I guess what I am saying is, I am not looking for a free pass. We should probably sign some paperwork, maybe a contract? I mean, I want to work with you to improve my life. I want you to be my coach. But it feels like I am taking advantage of you."

Ravi burst out into laughter, which immediately broke the awkward tension caused by Ethan's request. "Ethan, first of all, that is not a great negotiating tactic to get a better deal! But I am at fault here if I misled you in thinking our time together has a hidden agenda of any sort."

"Absolutely not!" exclaimed Ethan. "I want to be clear with you. I am not the type of person to take things, or people, for granted. Or I should say I will no longer be that kind of human being. You are helping me, which is what you do, so I assume it deserves compensation. I want to be able to call you and meet with you if need be. But I respect your time, and I know how busy you are."

Now Ravi took a few seconds before answering. "I will be direct and honest with you now, Ethan. There are two very specific reasons why we are spending time together. At this time, I will not be telling you either of these reasons."

Ethan stared at his phone, dumbfounded. "I don't follow, Ravi."

"You can call me anytime. We can meet whenever you feel the need. This is not a contract or a business dealing. You will not receive an invoice from me at any point."

"Ravi, you are killing me here! I am completely confused."

"Let me say one thing, and then we will hang up and meet for our run tomorrow morning at seven o'clock sharp." Ravi paused for dramatic effect. "From the words of the respected Sakyong Mipham, 'Like gravity, Karma is so basic we don't even notice it.'" The phone clicked, ending their conversation.

Ethan stood in his room, astonished. *Like gravity, Karma is so basic we don't even notice it.* He paced around the house, trying to understand how the cryptic words affected his relationship with Ravi. He eventually gave up and went to work, wishing he could find the answer.

***

Ethan had learned from their previous experience and did not want to arrive ill-equipped. He entered Centennial Park in full running gear, from new Nike runners to a dry-fit long-sleeve jacket. Of course, Ravi had made it before him, looking ten times more impressive and stretching in unfathomable positions. This could easily be explained by Ravi's level of general fitness being ten times superior to Ethan's. But at least he was here and ready to go.

After a quick greeting and a few more stretches, they started running. A warm breeze welcomed them with open arms. Ethan felt much better this morning. He expected to lose his breath soon, but for the moment, the pace suited him nicely. They followed the gravel path, heading toward the lake. Trees surrounded them on every side, the sun glistening through the leaves. In the water, a family of small ducklings followed their mother. The scene reminded Ethan of his own children, making him smile.

They hadn't spoken a word up to this point, yet Ethan felt completely at ease. He knew this resulted from Ravi's affable nature. Ravi projected a friendliness, a certain universal acceptance of the world which transcended petty issues. Ethan did not feel the need to fill the void of silence. It seemed appropriate. After a few more minutes, with Ethan just starting to feel a burning sensation in his legs, Ravi broke the ice.

"Tell me more about the changes. Start from the meditation."

"Eye-opening," said Ethan. "The first few attempts were impossible, and I almost gave up. But I remembered our talk and researched it further. I kept thinking about random issues at home, or work dilemmas, or irrelevant topics like sports highlights. Frustrating to say the least. I now understand these thoughts that keep popping up into our heads are referred to as 'chatter.' My first instinct was repression, but fighting only made matters worse. By the fourth session, I managed to acknowledge the thoughts and move on quickly enough, as per the suggested solutions. Now, after the first two or three minutes, these thoughts don't bother me."

"Excellent," confirmed Ravi. "You made it further than I expected in a short time."

"It has made a world of difference. I have found a patience I never knew existed within me. I dealt with a tough work situation in a calm manner, which has never happened before. By breathing before reacting, I worked through normally explosive emotions with my son when he almost set fire to the house. And I sense I still have so much room to grow to another level."

"By pursuing the practice, and even trying different forms of the art of meditation, you will eventually attain complete self-composure. Not many people in our hectic world can claim to have a full grasp of their mental state of mind. But it takes time—years, I would say—to achieve the highest form of understanding."

"I am determined to pursue it," confirmed Ethan.

"Tell me about the second step we discussed, the art of listening intently without judging."

"This also took much more effort than I expected," said Ethan. "It made me realize how little I have been listening to those around me. Even when I did listen, it was definitely with some form of judgement."

"It is normal. All of us have opinions. But when we consciously take the time to think before talking, and truly hear the other person, we come to realize there is no reason to force an assessment."

"Exactly!" exclaimed Ethan. "I took Eva out to dinner, and we talked for the first time in months. I finally listened. She had so much to say. In fact, it may sound strange, but she expressed some serious negativity, which I see as positive."

"The fact she is confiding in you?"

"Yes. I mean, isn't it better I know how she feels inside? I see that as a step in the right direction."

"I completely agree."

"I also realized during our conversation certain things need to change in a hurry. She is really down right now, and I can clearly see how my attitude and selfishness contributed to her state of mind."

"I understand. I sense you are motivated to improve the overall situation." Ravi quickly changed directions and headed straight for the daunting mountain in the park. "Don't worry, we'll only go up seven or eight times," said Ravi with a smile. "Tell me about the third step we discussed last time, circular reciprocation. Being incredibly nice to every single person you encounter."

"I had a few opportunities to put this into practice with strangers, but this change in attitude positively altered one of my most frightful relationships."

"Which one?"

"I have experienced pure frustration when dealing with my boss, Robert Samuels. The man has been impossible, or so I thought. Two weeks ago, I took the time to speak with him honestly and act friendly, as opposed to my usual instinct of running away. It worked wonders. In a staff meeting the following week, he defended me while the company's controller unfairly attacked my division. I couldn't believe it."

"That is an interesting story, Ethan."

"It is, but in the process, I came to realize Robert has an issue plaguing him. Now that I have removed the shutters, I can see the man is unhappy about something personal. And I think it is serious."

"In time, you may be able to help him in some way," said Ravi.

"I sure hope so." Ethan wanted to add a few words, but being in full flight up the mountainside made this unthinkable. The lack of air in his lungs left no room for debate.

To Ethan's surprise, they actually conquered the large hill seven more times. Ravi pushed him further than he expected, making good on his earlier comment. Talking remained at a strict minimum, although Ravi continually encouraged him. His legs felt heavier than cement, and he could be close to passing out at any moment, yet Ethan respected the process. He had been the one to call Ravi and request this morning run after all.

Finally, they trotted down the mountain, and Ravi announced the end of the gruelling workout. Ravi pointed Ethan toward the drinking fountain and allowed him to gulp down several greedy swigs before giving up his spot. Ravi gracefully dabbed a touch of water on his face and took one small sip. "How do you feel, my good man?" asked Ravi.

Ethan struggled to answer. "I will survive. Maybe. You may have to drive me home."

"Don't worry, in a few minutes, all will be back to normal. Unless you faint. Then things may get complicated. I suppose I could drop you off at Lakeshore's Emergency Room. They will take good care of you."

"Very funny, Ravi."

"As you try to regain some sense of composure, I must say I am blown away by the amount you have accomplished in the past few weeks. It should have taken much longer. Your determination has been exemplary."

Ethan sat up, embarrassed by the compliment. "I knew I needed a change—or to change, I should say."

"Still, talk is cheap. You backed it up from what I can tell."

"Thanks, I do appreciate your kind words. They mean a lot to me."

Ravi nodded and smiled. They continued stretching in silence for a few more minutes, enjoying the warm spring air. A few more people were making it to the park now. Some were walking, others jogging with their dogs. The day could not have started in a more positive way. He felt physically tired, yet mentally refreshed. Sitting in the park, taking in the view, he sensed a new way of viewing his world. He worried about Eva and his children, wishing he could turn back time. Having gained some insight on patience and understanding in the past weeks, it made him realize how badly his attitude had affected his family. "You know, I have made some pretty ridiculous mistakes in the past while," he said suddenly.

Ravi looked at him thoughtfully. "All of us make mistakes. Some worse than others, but the past can only be looked upon as a great tool for learning where we need to go now. The present and the future are the keys to happiness. Not dwelling on the past, but learning from it. I have a question for you. What was the mistake you made on February 10 of last year?"

Ethan stared in confusion. "What do you mean?"

"Very simply, what mistake did you make? What stressed you that day? What happened that ruined your chance at happiness?"

"I have no idea," answered Ethan. "That was nine months ago."

"Fair enough," continued Ravi. "What about April 17? What unforgivable comment did you make?"

Ethan took another second. "Well, I am stumped again."

"I could throw out another date, Ethan, but my point is this: the past is just that—the past. It is what I call the *time-anger gap*. We move on, and our days and lives thankfully continue. We can always start over. Life is very short, very limited. The number of minutes we have is precious and not to be wasted. We only get 86,400 seconds per day. We can't waste them on frustration, unhappiness, or regret. Move on and make it right. Spend your time investing in those you care most about. Any time a tough situation arises from now on, please remember that it will pass. You won't even remember it happened. Find the solution, be overly positive if necessary, and it will work out."

Ethan continued nodding, even as Ravi finished. He agreed with him. It made sense, and time did come at a premium in this hectic world. "Thanks, Ravi, your words always leave me feeling capable of more."

Ravi smiled. "Actually, I am very happy you said that, Ethan."

"Why?"

"Because your recent change in attitude combined with your determination to be a better 'you' have led to us discussing the second part of the philosophy. You are well into the initial self-awareness process you decided to implement a few weeks ago. Time for a new challenge, although I fully expect you to continue harnessing your remarkable progress with the meditation, nonjudgement, and thoughtfulness."

"A new challenge?" asked Ethan, surprised. "You don't let up!"

"That much is true," confirmed Ravi. "When we discussed calming the mind and various techniques to improve patience and understanding, the goal consisted primarily of starting fresh. It is only when we release ourselves from everyday predisposed beliefs that we can attain a measure of true self-acceptance. Once this process is undertaken, many positive opportunities suddenly appear before us. Would you agree?"

"Definitely."

"Perfect. Now that your mind has been put on the right path, it is time for us to discuss the physical aspect of the journey."

"That sounds both interesting and bizarre at the same time."

"That did sound funny, didn't it?" Ravi shook his head, smiling. "Take a few seconds to reflect on the improvement in your running over our past two sessions."

Ethan took the time and agreed he felt better than he had in months, if not years. But he had just begun. "I see what you are saying, Ravi, although I am still new to the game. Or coming out of retirement if we consider my younger track days!"

"Yes, Ethan, that should be considered. In fact, it will serve as the basis of our discussion."

"I am not sure where this is going, Ravi."

"I have come to realize that our bodies are incredibly strong, impressive specimens. Much more powerful than our minds will allow us to believe. In the right circumstances, we can achieve unthinkable feats when we open up to the possibilities."

"All right," said Ethan. "I am starting to get your flow, but not quite."

"Stay with me. Once you have created that renewed state of mind, the body can follow. Staying active and in shape is great. And yet determining a lofty goal and working to attain that goal will provide such confidence and belief, it will make a world of difference in your life. I call this *barrier breaking*. The idea is to break through self-imposed limitations," Ravi spoke with certainty and passion.

"What are you suggesting?" asked Ethan, curiously yet cautiously. He had made strides, but Ravi clearly had a plan, and it could very well stretch beyond his capacities.

"Stop me if I am wrong. You ran short track at a younger age. You have been losing levels of fitness continuously over the past few years. Eating habits have gone down the drain. You have been stressed at work and at home. You wish for a way to improve your overall health tenfold. Does all of this sound right to you?"

"Unfortunately, yes," said Ethan, nodding his head.

"There lies the answer."

Ethan tried acting as if he had some clue what any of this meant. But he couldn't figure it out. "Sorry, but I am still unsure what we are talking about."

Ravi's face beamed with excitement as he said the next five simple words. "You will run a marathon."

Ethan gaped at him for a few seconds before breaking into uncontrollable laughter. "You had me, Ravi. You really had me there." He shook his head with a smile, pointing his finger at Ravi in a mocking fashion. Seeing Ravi's facial expression filled with both enthusiasm and seriousness, the reality of his words began to sink in. Ethan's grin disappeared.

"I will ask you to refrain from saying another word," said Ravi with a smile. "Go home, take a hot shower, breathe, and think about our conversation. We will speak in a couple of days."

Ethan nodded. He got to his feet and began walking out of the park in a daze. He turned, but Ravi had not moved. Seeing Ravi planted in the same spot, he gestured toward the parking area questioningly. Ravi shook his head. "I am going to take on the hill a few more times." Ethan looked at him, shook his head, and gave the thumbs-up sign. And then he left to think on his own.

DEEP DIVE

Good judgment comes from experience, and experience comes from bad judgment.
—Rita Mae Brown, author and activist

*D*espite the very late hour, several patrons crowded the bar area. The aggressive sounds of video poker machines filled the air. Clouds of smoke circulated, cutting off access to even the slightest amount of fresh oxygen. Establishments in Montreal were no longer permitted to allow smoking, but this location did not follow the same rules.

Robert sat at a table in the farthest corner of the room. Although his stillness could be mistaken for composure, that could not be farther from the truth. He had been sitting there for over six hours, consuming close to a complete bottle of Jack Daniels by himself. He stared blankly at the other customers as they yelled over the hard rock music. He teetered on the line between unconsciousness and utter confusion. Strangely, despite his current condition, he appeared fairly normal to those around him. He did not look incapacitated.

Suddenly, the lights became brighter, and Elton John's "Tiny Dancer" played softly throughout the bar. This none-too-subtle sign served as notice that three in the morning had arrived. Time to leave. Some customers would go home. Others would hit up a pizza joint to satisfy their light night-binging routine.

The place emptied quickly. Robert, however, hadn't moved an inch. The head bartender, a burly man in his early fifties, made his way over. "Hey, pal, time for us to close shop. You gotta leave."

Robert didn't move a muscle.

"I'm serious," he repeated. "Are you listening to me? Time is up. Drinking is over. Clear the premises, please."

After a few seconds, Robert slowly turned his head toward the man, registering the fact that someone was speaking to him. "I understand," he managed to blurt out.

"You need a ride or something. Want me to call a cab?"

Robert did not look at him this time. He rose sluggishly, somehow managing to keep his balance intact. It took him another few seconds before he moved toward the door. Exiting, he pushed past a group of rambunctious college kids and walked toward his car.

He fumbled for a few minutes, searching for his keys. First checking his jacket pockets, then his pants, with no success. It took another few minutes for him to discover they were already in his hands. He accidentally triggered the car alarm and could not get the highly annoying sound to stop. It took the gracious help of a young woman to accomplish the insurmountable task. She could see Robert's condition and immediately questioned his ability to drive. "Don't worry, I'm just trying to get in the car to sleep," he stammered. She looked at him unimpressed and shrugged, walking away.

Once in the front seat, he attempted to start the car. *If I could only get the key to enter the small hole of this damn ignition.* He eventually succeeded and sped out of the parking spot, clipping the side mirror of another car and damaging his own in the process. He didn't notice.

He drove down Sherbrooke Street, zigging and zagging his way around the various cars on the two-lane boulevard. Horns honked endlessly as he attempted passes most race car drivers would avoid. On three separate occasions, he narrowly missed crashing into other vehicles, two of which were stationary.

Robert felt tired despite his adrenaline-pumping antics. Exhausted and confused, he eventually found himself on the highway heading toward his home. Finally, following more dangerous encounters, he turned on Church Road, one street away from his final destination. The weight of his eyes could no longer be controlled. They slid closed, and he had to slap the back of his neck to open them again. This happened once more, with his head lowering to his chest this time. He had no idea how long this lasted.

A powerful sound startled him awake, and all he could see were two bright lights piercing his vision. He violently yanked the steering wheel to his right, avoiding the oncoming car. But the jerking manoeuvre sent his Audi straight into the sidewalk, then the bicycle path, and finally into the luscious trees on the roadside. Somehow, his sporty car did not flip.

Robert tasted the blood before seeing it. He realized his hands were glued to the steering wheel and had not moved throughout the entire tailspin. He touched his nose and winced from the pain. His fingers were covered in blood.

The car was still running. He put the shaft into reverse and attempted to back out. The sound of tires spinning filled the air, but no movement occurred. He tried and tried for several minutes but had to admit defeat. Stumbling from the car, he pushed away the various branches impeding his exit. A few of them scratched his bruised face even further. He stood, but the spinning in his head forced him to grab his car for balance.

After a few seconds, he walked around and noticed the passenger side front wheel had completely burst during the fiasco, leaving the tire rim exposed. This would require a tow truck. Finally gaining some semblance of composure, he realized his state of mind, or lack thereof, and knew he could not get caught at this moment. A police patrol would question him and discover his drunken condition very quickly. He could feel the panic rising. His brow sweat profusely.

Robert pulled out his phone and looked through his contacts. No true friend he could call. He would not call either of his sisters. That would lead to disaster. He placed his head on the car hood and tried his hardest not to break down or put his fist through the window. *This is pathetic. I am pathetic.* He let his body fall to the ground, sitting against the wheel.

He looked through his phone again. One name stuck out. *Can I call him? Should I call him?* He was running out of options, fast. There was a possibility the other car had called the cops on him. He needed to decide. He slammed his hand against the car, leaving him in more unnecessary pain. He grabbed his phone. More hesitation. Finally, he decided he had no other choice.

THE DEAL

The purpose of life is not to be happy. It is to be useful, to be honorable, to be compassionate, to have it make some difference that you have lived and lived well.
—Ralph Waldo Emerson, philosopher and poet

*T*he savory smell of Italian Sausage and fresh vegetables floated out from the barbecue. Ethan cooked away, excited about spending an evening with his wife and children. Luca and Kayla were both playing and arguing at the same time, the way only kids can understand. No intervention needed. Eva was preparing a salad in the kitchen.

He was having a hard time containing his excitement from his morning run with Ravi. *A marathon. Can I really do it?* Thinking of this new challenge brought butterflies to his stomach. He had taken a few minutes in the afternoon to look up the subject. Most explained the necessary training plans. Others focused on nutrition, hydration, and resting the body as to not cause overload to the system. After his research, he believed it could be accomplished with the right amount of focus and dedication. He also understood the importance of including Eva in this discussion.

The last few weeks at home had been very positive. His efforts to listen and be calm were having the desired effect on the overall mood of the household. The kids seemed happier, and Eva was coming around, albeit slowly. He couldn't remember the last time they had spent a night together as a family. They were both sipping at their wine, sharing a few knowing glances while the kids played. He truly looked forward to sitting down to dinner with them.

They set the kids up first, as both Luca and Kayla only took about five minutes to eat. Once they finished up dessert, Ethan put on *Beauty and the Beast* and gave each a healthy portion of popcorn. Ethan and Eva decided to eat in the dining room, where they could dim the lights and relax. Ethan put on the Smooth Jazz channel and poured them both more wine.

"How was your run with Ravi this morning?" asked Eva.

Ethan smiled. "Funny you should ask me that."

"Why?"

"Because we discussed some very interesting things."

"It seems you always have the most intriguing conversations with your new friend."

"I can't disagree! The man is bright and insanely fit too."

"Having a hard time keeping up, are we?"

"We should not even be mentioned in the same sentence."

Eva took a long sip. "The last time you met with him resulted in some major changes. It's only been a few weeks, but I appreciate the efforts you have been making."

Ethan couldn't describe the warm feeling this simple sentence brought to his heart. He could not recall the last time his wife had complimented him. He did not know how to respond. "I simply followed basic instructions."

"Easier said than done," said Eva. "Although I have tried convincing you in the past with little success. I guess I should be insulted Ravi convinced you so easily!"

Ethan didn't quite know if she was serious or playing. He did not want to take any chances. She was making a very valid point.

"Fair statement. I can't explain it, to be honest. I think when a complete stranger communicates something that really hits home, it takes us out of our comfort zone. Ravi made me realize how my attitude only led to frustration for everyone, including myself. Had I been listening to you from the beginning, much of the heartache could have been avoided."

Eva nodded, keeping her face unreadable. She took another sip of wine, even slower than the last one. She looked down into her glass, moving it in a circular motion, causing the red liquid to dance in various directions. After a few seconds, she spoke, "I would rather focus on the future. Tell me about today."

Ethan realized he was holding his breath. He relaxed. "It started smoothly, with us running around the forest path in Centennial Park. Slightly less amusing when we started the hill repetitions."

"He made you run the Centennial Park hill. That's not too bad."

"Seven times."

"What! You must be joking."

"I am not."

"And you survived!"

"Want to know the craziest part?"

"Tell me."

"Ravi continued. As I left, he got back up and just kept running. I have no idea what he did, but I suspect he probably ran it a dozen more times."

Eva shook her head with a mixture of astonishment and awe. Ethan nodded with the same expression.

"And that leads to the content of our discussion."

"Go on," said Eva, her interest piqued.

"Without wanting to bore you with every detail, Ravi explained how the next step in his life philosophy involves the body. How we need to challenge ourselves to reach farther and higher than ever before—that we need to take on a goal that seems almost impossible. He calls this *barrier breaking*."

"A physical challenge?"

"Exactly. One that forces us to reach beyond our self-imposed limits."

"What did he suggest?"

Ethan took a sip from his glass, letting the sumptuous red wine linger a few seconds on his tongue. "You will be surprised."

"Tell me!" she exclaimed.

"Ravi wants me to run a marathon."

Eva looked confused. "A marathon. You mean a six-mile run or something of that distance?"

"No, the full marathon. He wants me to run twenty-six miles!"

Eva's eyes bulged open. "He can't be serious. You can't be serious."

"I am, but I wanted to discuss it with you first. You see, it will require quite the commitment of time. And I know I have been missing in action over the past months. But I believe Ravi when he says this challenge will teach me many things about perseverance, discipline, and willpower." Ethan waited for Eva to respond.

Eva looked down, seemingly in deep thought. She did not react, leaving Ethan bewildered. He began panicking internally, nervous she would get upset at his new time-consuming project. As seconds ticked by, he could feel the butterflies in his stomach. He began to sweat ever so slightly.

Eva then spoke a few simple words he could never have imagined would come from her mouth. "I will do it with you. I will run the marathon by your side."

Now Ethan's eyes opened wide. A massive smile appeared, taking over his entire face. He leapt from the chair and kissed Eva, hugging her warmly. "That is an amazing idea! It will be great! We can make a plan together, improve our nutrition, and get in tip-top shape!" He could not contain his excitement.

Eva pushed his face back a few inches with both of her hands. "One condition, Ethan. If we do this, we do this right. No excuses, no missed runs, and absolutely no giving up. We commit to each other, here and now. Can you make that promise?"

Holding back his natural instinct to shout "yes" at the top of his lungs, he instead made eye contact with her. "I promise."

They hugged for several more seconds before proceeding to put the children to sleep.

***

Floating. He was watching his own body rise into the air. He soared across the city, able to fly for the first time. He finally understood how birds felt. The sheer freedom brought by the sky overwhelmed his senses. Speeding past trees and buildings, he came upon a field filled with bright, glittering shapes he could not identify. He glided lower until he reached the mysterious place. Landing on his feet, he began to understand what these objects were. Large diamonds, bigger than soccer balls, in a variety of incredible colors. He reached for the first one. Before his fingers made contact, a ringing distracted him. Then a shaking sensation. Then Eva's voice. "Ethan, get up, wake up…"

Startled, Ethan lifted his head, only to realize Eva had his cell phone. "Someone is calling you."

"What time is it?" Ethan answered, still unsure of his whereabouts.

"Just past four o'clock."

"What?" He looked at his phone in confusion. "Hello."

"Ethan, I'm sorry to bother you at this late hour." The voice sounded groggy.

"Who is this?"

"It's Robert. Robert Samuels."

Eva looked at Ethan questioningly. He had no idea how to react. He shrugged and shook his head. "Yes, Robert, is everything alright?"

"I have a problem."

"What is it?"

"It's a long story. Bottom line is that my car is stuck in a very strange place. I can't really call the authorities for help, if you catch my drift. I'm sorry, I had no idea who to call."

Ethan sat up in complete surprise. *Is this happening? Is my boss calling me in the middle of the night?* He could see the man needed help. The image of Ravi popped up in his mind, reminding him of his new way of treating those around him. "Where are you?"

Robert hesitated. "Well, I am a mile from my home. I am just off Church Road. You will see me. You may or may not notice my car. It's kind of deep in the trees. I can't walk, my head is turning. I mean shaking. Or spinning. Whatever."

"Oh," answered Ethan. "I see. Well, I am on my way"

"Thank you, Ethan. Thank you."

Ethan quickly got out of bed. "Eva, weirdest story ever. I have no clue what happened, but Robert Samuels is stuck and seems in desperate need of help."

"Why did he call you? I mean, you know each other, him being your boss and all. But you've never had that type of relationship? In fact, you haven't said many positive things about the man."

"Something has been wrong with Robert in the past few weeks. I didn't mention it because I assumed it was just a phase. It must be more serious than I thought." Ethan finished putting on his track pants and hoodie. "Go back to sleep, my love. I'll be back soon." With that, he grabbed his keys and made for the car.

The distance between Ethan's home and Church Road could be covered by a long run. Ethan couldn't make out Robert's sports car at first. Only upon closer review did he finally notice the tire tracks leading into the forest and the damaged back tires. Then he noticed Robert. He could see something on Robert's face. As he made his way from his car, Ethan gasped at the sight. Blood dripped from his forehead, down his left cheek, and onto his shirt. He resembled a beaten boxer who had just gone twelve rounds with Ali. Robert did not seem in the least bit concerned with the blood, although he wore an expressionless look on his face, the same look from the office a week earlier. Ethan didn't like that look.

"Robert, are you okay? We need to take care of that blood."

Robert glanced up at Ethan, noticing him for the first time, staring with empty eyes. He said nothing. After a few seconds, he turned his head back down to the ground.

Ethan stood confused. He decided to go back to the car and grab some tissues to help with the blood. He brought them to Robert but got no reaction. It felt strange, but he decided to play caregiver and dabbed at Robert's cut. It helped reduce the blood flow. For his part, Robert did not make the slightest movement. *Is he sleeping?* In answer, a groaning sound came from Robert's mouth. "Take me home, Ethan. Please just get me out of here." Barely audible, Ethan knew enough to react without needing further explanation.

He grabbed Robert by the arm and dragged him to his feet. Putting Robert's arm around his shoulder, Ethan carried him the best one can carry a 230-pound man. Opening the passenger side door, he attempted to ease him into the car, banging his boss's head on the door frame accidentally. Again, no reaction.

They drove in silence for the six minutes it took to arrive at Robert's house. Ethan remembered the place. He had been asked, or rather ordered, by Robert to drop off copies of an important presentation late one evening a few months earlier. No appreciation was shown at that time. He remembered the frustration of being treated like an assistant and not the actual Director of Sales he was. A common occurrence at Premier.

Ethan pulled into the driveway. Robert had kept his head slumped the entire time, his breathing coming out in short, laboured bursts. Thankfully, the blood had stopped, although a dry streak still remained on his cheek. He tried shaking him awake. "Hey, Robert, wake up. We're home." Robert stirred but did not move. "C'mon, buddy, can you hear me? We need to get you inside." Ethan attempted another more aggressive push. This time, it worked.

"Where, uh, what, my car..." Robert could not have been more disoriented.

Ethan got out and made his way over to the passenger side. He opened the door and helped Robert from the car. As they climbed the last step to the house, a woman in a bright pink nightgown and red curlers appeared in the doorway with some form of a cooking spatula in her hands. She held it as a weapon. "Get the hell away from my house!" she yelled frantically. It startled Ethan, and he had to use near superhuman power to keep Robert from tumbling backward off the stoop. The screaming woke Robert immediately, and likely woke the majority of their neighbours in the process.

"Get back inside," groaned Robert, coldly. "And put that thing away."

"Bobby? My Bobby? What happened to your face? Why did this man hurt you? Oh my God. Police! Police! Someone help!" she screeched at the top of her lungs.

Ethan looked on in horror, genuinely nervous. He no longer needed to support Robert's weight because his boss had suddenly become incredibly sober. He moved to the front screen and pushed it open, forcefully ushering the woman inside. He also ripped the spatula from her hands. "Wait at your car," said Robert.

It took a good ten minutes before Robert reappeared in the doorway. Ethan had just begun creeping toward his car door, wanting to get away from the whole scene. His boss descended the steps and made his way down the driveway, his collar and upper shirt soaked. He had washed away the blood.

"Ethan, I want to thank you for helping me tonight. I hit rock bottom and had nowhere to turn. I will tell you the God-awful truth. I was drunk and completely incapacitated. I am still not fully sober. In my emotionally unstable frame of mind, I decided to drive home and narrowly missed a head-on collision. My car being stuck in the middle of some trees is very minor to the alternative course my life could have taken tonight."

Ethan had no clue how to respond so he kept quiet. Robert continued, "I am under tremendous stress right now. You may have identified

Premier Marketing as the culprit, but that is the farthest thing from the truth. That woman you saw a few minutes ago is my mother. She used to be strong, caring, and full of life. The doctors call it a delusional disorder. She believes dangerous kidnappers want to take her and everything in our house. She spends her evenings roaming the floors, staring out of windows, and even sneaking away on occasion. She refuses to accept her medication, often tricking me when I try to assist her in taking the necessary pills. None of my siblings are providing even the smallest amount of help or support, so I am on my own. She should be in a specialized home, a place where her condition can be addressed. But they say her case is not severe enough. I have no answers or solutions. The system has failed us. I no longer sleep properly as this massive issue clouds my judgement every waking minute of my life."

Ethan stared at the bull of a man he had feared for so many years. A person with such direct aggression coupled with a complete lack of sympathy, you could only squirm away from his towering threats. Yet today, Robert stood at his most vulnerable, confiding secrets normally reserved for one's most precious friends or family members. The openness gave Ethan the necessary confidence to lend a genuinely understanding ear. "That must be incredibly difficult to deal with. I can only imagine how truly draining it must be for you, given the fact you are alone to face the issue."

"It is, and I don't see what the next step is."

"Well, I'm not sure I can help, but I have a cousin who works as a nurse at the Victoria Square Medical Center. She always finds ways to help me out. I think the first step may be finding the right doctor. I remember when a friend of mine had a burnout, which I know has nothing to do with your current situation. But he had the wrong diagnosis from his doctor, and it caused months and months of incorrect medications, which, in turn, affected every aspect of his life. My cousin sent him to a more specialized and experienced psychiatrist, and everything got back on track. Perhaps we could find that same solution for your mother? But I may be stepping over some boundaries here, it is just a suggestion."

Robert stared and said nothing for a few seconds. His eyes seemed to water slightly, the creases in his forehead gaining in size. Suddenly, he grabbed Ethan by the shoulders and spoke in a soft yet determined voice, "Yes, that would mean a great deal to me. Truly, it could make a real difference." He slowly let Ethan go.

Ethan knew their relationship had changed. The events of the bizarre night, or very early morning rather, had created a bond of some sort. He sensed in Robert a man who needed friendship, who could use a person to talk to. Under the hard, confrontational shell hid a man with the same wants as others. Robert had been living the most difficult of personal challenges and had decided to react in his own way. Who knew how long the deterioration of his mother's health had been affecting him? Perhaps Ethan had only known his boss in the worst of circumstances. With all these thoughts running through his head, he thought of his own father, realizing how much baggage he himself had been carrying around—until Ravi had opened his eyes.

"Things will get better. Tough times make us stronger. We will figure this out." Ethan reached out and hugged Robert, holding him for several seconds. And with that final gesture, Ethan entered his car as the sun began to wake the world up for another unpredictable day.

WATER PLEASE

*We will go far away, to nowhere, to conquer, to fertilize until we
become tired. Then we will stop and there will be our home.*
—Dejan Stojanovic, Serbian poet

than never considered a knee to one's stomach as the most desirable way to wake up on a Saturday morning. There were exceptions to this rule, he realized.

Kayla and Luca jumped on the bed with an enthusiasm only children can express. Throughout the rambunctious bouncing, Ethan received a few bumps and knocks, as he tried to pry open his eyes. Considering he had arrived only a few hours earlier from the fiasco turned confession with Robert, his body still needed sleep. That would not happen this morning. It didn't matter.

He grabbed both of his kids in a bear hug, finding their ticklish spots in the process. They were laughing uncontrollably as Eva entered the room. "Let Daddy wake up, munchkins. He got home very late."

"But we're having too much fun!" exclaimed Luca.

"Yeah, it's true, Mommy!" screamed Kayla.

"No worries, Eva, I'll catch up on my sleep tonight," said Ethan. He stretched his arms and made his way out of bed. The kids giggled their way downstairs. He threw on his trusted slippers and made his way downstairs with Eva by his side.

"So, what happened last night?" asked Eva.

"It's one heck of a story, nothing I could possibly have expected. I'll tell you about it for sure, but I don't think Luca or Kayla should hear the details."

"I get it. Do you remember I asked my parents to hang out with the kids this morning so we could go for a run? I figure we will have plenty of time to catch up then. Plus, we need to start getting in shape for the marathon. I know it is five months away, but considering I never

123

ran a mile in my life, I assume we should get started sooner than later. Although I am questioning your energy levels for today, no offense."

"None taken. Ravi suggested a few sites where we could put together a complete training program. I spent some time reading up on marathons and most experts confirm the training plans should be followed carefully to ensure a successful experience and to avoid injuries. They also mention sixteen to eighteen weeks of training, so you are right on the money. I think a small run won't hurt me. It may even give me some jump!"

Eva decided to prepare a special breakfast. She put together a toasted bagel sandwich, with tomatoes and eggs cooked to perfection with yoke covering the sides, melting in with a touch of pesto. Ethan made cappuccinos, adding chocolate on top of the creamy foam. They ate the sumptuous meal, chatting about running and stretching. Suddenly, Kayla and Luca started arguing.

"I want to play with it!" cried Kayla furiously.

"It's mine, get away from me!" responded Luca.

Eva and Ethan watched the interaction, not wanting to jump in too quickly. But the escalation happened fast. Kayla ripped the toy car from Luca's hands. Before either of the adults could intervene, Luca pushed his sister hard to the floor, causing her to bump her head. She screamed out bloody murder, sobbing uncontrollably.

Ethan was mad. He shot up from the table, ready to punish both kids and send them to their rooms. But he knew his own fatigue had the better of him at this moment. As if on cue, Eva softly touched his arm before he made a move. The look she gave her husband stopped him dead in his tracks. No anger or frustration. Simply patience. He knew his old self would have overreacted in this situation and ruined the morning for his family. Instead, with the newfound communication he shared with Eva over the past weeks, combined with his meditation practice, he approached the kids, holding down his anger.

"Kayla, are you alright?" She nodded, throwing herself into his arms for dramatic effect. "You know, sweetie, Luca was playing with that car. What do we do if we want to share a toy?"

Kayla answered through her subsiding whimpers. "We ask nicely."

"Exactly." He turned his attention to Luca. "Buddy, we never push others. There is never a reason to be aggressive. Do you understand?"

Luca nodded. "I'm sorry, Kayla. I got upset when you pulled my car away." He went over and hugged his sister.

Eva watched the entire scene unfold, dumbfounded. *Ethan has never shown this type of patience.* It made her feel ecstatic. She hadn't imagined it possible. She had read many articles about sibling rivalry and fighting. She had spoken to Ethan about the best ways to handle cases just like this. He never seemed to be listening before, but his actions today showed the necessary amount of directness and compassion to immediately diffuse the problem while leaving the children feeling good about themselves. She also knew his meditation had played an important role. All of it suggested the new Ethan could be permanent. And she wanted to believe—she had to believe.

The doorbell rang, causing more excitement. Luca and Kayla sprinted to the sound, unlocked the front door, and smothered their grandparents with hugs and kisses. They hadn't even crossed the threshold but were already being coaxed into treasure hunts and pirate costumes. Thankfully, they did not look or act their age and succeeded in keeping up with their beloved balls of energy.

Managing to take their jackets off despite the small beings strapped around their legs, they entered the home. "Something smells rather enticing," said Eva's father, poking his head around to locate the source.

"I cooked a quick breakfast. Are you hungry?" asked Eva.

"Although your food is always an exceptional experience, I will pass as my stomach is highly unimpressed with my eating habits over the past few days. Besides, don't you have some running to do?"

"It is time for less talk and more doing," confirmed Ethan. "Thanks for coming this morning. It means a great deal to us."

"Eva mentioned running," said her mother, "but she did not specify any details."

Eva finished up in the kitchen and walked over to her parents. "I have some interesting news. We've decided to run a marathon. Together."

They looked at her with a confused smile, not grasping the enormity of the task. "How long is a marathon?" asked her mother.

"Well, according to Ethan and most other reliable sources, we're talking twenty-six miles."

Her father gasped. "That is some serious running. When I drive that long, I get tired. And you guys will do it on foot? Incredible!" He shook his head in disbelief.

"We have a long and exciting road ahead of us," said Eva. "Ethan put together a full training plan for the next twenty weeks. We would love your help and support during that time. It will be time-consuming but well worth it, we hope."

Robin knew her daughter needed this. They had spent so much time together in the past months discussing difficulties on the home front. Something told her this could be a great turning point for her daughter's marriage. She wanted to be part of that solution. "Eva, you have our full support. We are here for both of you, and we know you will achieve this remarkable goal. Right, honey?" She stared at her husband, who agreed enthusiastically even though the decision had already been made for him.

"Thanks, Mom, it is very important to me." They hugged. Ethan and his father-in-law stood by, smiling, not quite willing to take their relationship to that level. They were satisfied with a firm handshake.

Ethan and Eva kissed the kids and made their way into the sunlit street, ready for this new challenge. They were running three miles today. Not a long distance considering the marathon challenge, but a great start nonetheless.

***

Today's run took them toward Baie D'Urfe, a picturesque town adjacent to their own. This route was a haven for runners and bikers alike in the summer. Beautiful, towering oak trees shadowed the perfectly smooth pavement. At this time of year, in the late fall, the roads were much quieter, and they had their own space to enjoy.

They hardly spoke at first, choosing to concentrate on the task at hand. As beginners, they often ran out of breath and needed some walking time. They happily shared the silence, understanding that energy conservation took precedence.

Slowing the pace down, Eva decided to try speaking and running at the same time. "I know you may have wanted to take on this experience on your own. Thanks for including me."

"Of course! It is so much better being out here with you. And I am happy you wanted to try it."

"The idea struck a chord with me right from the start," confirmed Eva. "It feels…right."

They continued jogging several more paces, taking in the refreshing breeze.

"Eva, can I ask you something?"

"What is it?"

"It's kind of deep."

Eva kept her eyes glued straight ahead. She wondered where this was going and if she could let herself speak freely and openly. "All right, what is it?"

"Are you happy?" asked Ethan.

Her throat suddenly felt dry. How could she possibly answer this question? It was intense, filled with underlying meaning and baggage. Yet the time had come to set things straight. She decided not to hold back.

"Ethan, I want to be completely honest with you. It has been really tough. You have gone on with your career, trying to achieve your goals. I know this has been important for you. On my side, I have stayed with the children for several years now. I love them. I would do absolutely anything to ensure their complete happiness. By doing so, I have refused to give my own ideas any attention. They have been put aside, discarded, seemingly never to be looked upon again. It hurts to think I can't pursue my dreams, that I can't follow my passion." Instead of slowing down throughout her speech, she found herself running faster and harder, trying to outpace the frustration.

Ethan kept up. Within a few seconds, they returned to a more sustainable pace, one that wouldn't force them to call an ambulance. "I truly want to know, what is your dream? I mean, if you could do anything at all, what would it be?"

Eva pondered the question, wanting to express herself the right way. She could feel the emotions creeping up, tears welling up. She knew if one single drop broke the plane, the floodgates would open. She used massive willpower to move forward, to keep her emotions under control. "To create wonderful food others can enjoy."

Baking sent her into a timeless flow of happiness. Hours flew by in what seemed like minutes. All outside pressures and stresses magically disappeared when she could concentrate on crafting delectable chocolate soufflés or vanilla truffles. It just seemed right when she had her cooking tools in her grasp.

"I get it, and I hear you," said Ethan. He knew this already, even though he needed to hear it again. And the conviction in his wife's voice made him realize she must find a way back to her roots. Or perhaps he must help her get back to doing what she so loved. "I'm not sure how, but considering the key to your happiness lies in the food industry, we must work as a team in getting you back to your passion. I promise we'll figure it out." He made every effort for Eva to understand his conviction.

They continued running in silence. They did not compete with each other. But they did push one another.

They descended the main boulevard, preparing to turn east toward their home. Only half a mile separated them from unlimited water and rest. Neither stopped to walk even though it would have been the easiest solution. Eva decided once again to push the envelope and see what her body could do. She picked up the pace, forcing Ethan to reach new levels of stamina he wasn't sure he had.

They passed the final stop sign, now only three hundred yards away. Eva began sprinting. Her legs pumped furiously. Ethan switched from short strides to long, impressive leaps. He could sense a serious cramp forming at the back of his left calf. He struggled on, ignoring the pain. They entered the last hundred yards side by side, and despite the gigantic effort, both were smiling.

As they arrived into the driveway, Eva threw herself onto the grass, exhausted. Ethan walked around the block, trying to regain his composure. Eventually, Eva got up and did the same to avoid any sort of muscle tension. They stretched slowly, knowing it would help to get their heart rates back to normal.

After several minutes, they ended their training session by entering their house and gulping down a boatload of water. No words were spoken, nor were they needed. Sharing this moment with a simple yet meaningful look meant the world to them. They could feel a deep connection returning and decided to accept it with open arms and sore feet.

THINKING OF
ANOTHER

No one has ever become poor by giving.
—Anne Frank, author of *The Diary of a Young Girl*

*I*t made complete sense. The idea played in his mind the way a film image projects on a theatre screen. *She wants to follow her passion.* Ethan had spent the past day thinking of his meaningful conversation with Eva during their run. He had come to certain realizations. He had completely ignored her need to start a career ever since the kids were born. Eva had dedicated herself to raising their children. Once they started daycare and then school, she gave clear signs of wanting to pursue new opportunities. He had avoided those discussions, perhaps knowingly, if not selfishly, protecting his role as the family provider. His growing unhappiness at Premier Marketing made him forget the coveted bliss of waking up full of excitement to take on the new challenges that lay ahead. By falling into the vicious circle of accepting boredom and duty, he had lost complete sight of his dreams. Daily monotony had become the norm.

These thoughts engulfed his mind and made his morning meditation session difficult. He couldn't find clarity, his attention constantly returning to Eva. But it didn't matter because he had an idea. Not a plan, but a small step in the right direction.

He dialed Ravi's number. It was early, but he knew Ravi started his days at the first sign of dawn. "Hello, Ethan."

"Ravi, how are you?"

"Could not be better! I am currently sitting in my den, sipping my morning tea with Daniella by my side and reading Simon Sinek's excellent book *Start with Why*. Quite a remarkable piece on the importance of discovering the heart and soul of any business."

"I've heard of it, but can't say I have had the privilege yet." Ethan made a mental note to get a copy. "I'm actually calling for some advice again. But I don't want to disturb you."

"Of course not, but you have the wrong person," said Ravi. "I don't offer advice, only experience sharing and suggestions."

Ethan laughed. "That's right, you mentioned that before. Fair enough, I will be careful not to probe you for advice. Eva and I had our first official run yesterday."

"Where did you run?"

"We followed the water from our house toward Baie D'Urfe. We covered a few miles."

"That is wonderful!

"It is the first time we went in that direction. Very beautiful with all the old trees. Not to mention the gorgeous properties."

"I agree."

"While we were out there, we shared a very significant moment. I asked Eva about her dreams and her passion. Remember how I told you about her culinary past?"

"I remember quite clearly."

"It has never left. I see she loves baking and creating all sorts of amazing dishes. Unfortunately, I have continuously ignored her need to follow her heart and pursue her passion."

"I see. Can I presume you want to help change this?"

"Yes! During that enlightening visit to your Elevation Leadership Institute, you spoke to me about the concept of dream facilitation. I want to know more about it."

"I do like where this is going," said Ravi. "Do you have time to meet for lunch tomorrow?"

"Sure. I have a few appointments at the office in the morning, but I will be done by noon."

"Perfect. There is someone you should meet. We'll have lunch at a restaurant called Vertigo. It is in the Nelligan Hotel. Near your office. Do you know the place?"

"I have never been, but I've heard of it."

"Sumptuous food, truly. See you there at twelve fifteen."

"Sounds like a plan." Ethan hung up the phone and marvelled once again at the great fortune of having encountered such a wonderful and genuine person. Ravi had managed to change the way he thought, listened, and lived. And it seemed there was still much more for him to learn. How he could ever repay Ravi for his kindness remained a mystery to Ethan. Take and take is all he had done. *One day I will find a way to give back.*

***

The morning at the office passed uneventfully. He spent some time with a long-standing customer looking to change the packaging concepts for his specialty lighting fixtures. Sasha had done most of the talking, being a masterful expert in that domain.

Later, he had a brief conversation with Robert in the cafeteria. Being a very public place, they avoided any mention of the fiasco from the previous week. But Robert looked slightly better, and Ethan promised he would spend some time with him outside of Premier to talk. When he had told Eva the story, her maternal instincts had immediately taken over. She wanted to help Robert, find a way to support him with his mother. Although Ethan agreed, he felt his boss needed some time after the accident to regroup. He also didn't see how Eva could jump into the situation at this point. She had only met Robert Samuels a few times and had heard nothing but negative comments from Ethan. He had changed his perspective recently, realizing the truly difficult familial predicament Robert was in. Another lesson Ethan learned about the fundamental need not to judge others, as taught by Ravi. Deep in thought, he realized it was time to leave for his lunch meeting.

Arriving at his destination, Ethan took in the chic lobby of the Nelligan Hotel. The frosted glass doors, held open by a smartly dressed doorman, led to a large space filled with welcoming dark furniture. To the left, several patrons surrounded high bar tables, sharing drinks and laughs. He noticed the restaurant seating area just beyond the crowd of people and walked in that direction.

There sat Ravi in a corner booth, talking animatedly, waving his hands left and right. Ethan approached and noticed a lunch companion by Ravi's side he had not yet met.

"Ethan, so very happy to see you! Sit, please, sit!" said Ravi, getting up to greet him. "Let me introduce you to a close friend of mine. This is Amber Voss."

No more than thirty-five years of age, the woman sat with heavily curled brown locks surrounding a radiant freckled face. A very familiar face. In fact, too familiar to be a simple coincidence. *Do all of Ravi's friends beam with joy?* Amber took his hand confidently. "I've heard a lot about you, Ethan."

This surprised him. "Really? Can I ask what he has said, because you shouldn't believe him."

"Well, I wouldn't divulge such confidential information," said Amber jokingly.

Ethan found himself immediately impressed by Amber's friendliness and sense of humour. Of course, if she spent time with Ravi, this should not be shocking.

"Ethan, I invited you here today for a specific reason. She is that reason." He nodded toward Amber. "You can learn a tremendous amount of information by simply sitting with her and listening."

"That is an exaggeration if I ever heard one," said Amber, shaking her head mockingly.

"I can only agree with Ravi," said Ethan. "His judgement has been impeccable since we met."

"Oh, that will change, just give it time," said Amber with a wink. Ravi shook his head, amused.

"All right, enough joking, young ones, let's focus." The irony that despite the ten years of age difference, Ravi looked younger and healthier than he did was not lost on Ethan.

"When you called me this past weekend, Ethan, it got me thinking. Your wife Eva has a passion. Most of us do, but often we don't allow ourselves to figure it out or truly believe in it. In your case, from what you have explained, Eva had grand plans that somehow did not materialize. Those details are not important right now. I happen to have a wonderful contact, a person who understands an industry not too different from the one Eva wishes to pursue. And perhaps naively, I felt the need to bring you both here to talk."

Ethan sat in stunned silence. Once again, this man running a multimillion-dollar business with a hundred other places he could be chose to help a man he had only known for weeks. "I don't know what to say to either of you. Your willingness to help in any way is deeply appreciated."

"Amber is the one you must thank. I'm here for the food," said Ravi. "And the free lunch."

"I suggest you hold back the praise until you can honestly determine if you're left with the right information," said Amber with a coy smile on her face.

"I have absolutely no doubt."

"Amber, why don't you give us the story of your career path?" asked Ravi. "Such inspiration is hard to come by these days."

"That is the last time you get to compliment me today," said Amber, threatening Ravi with her fist. "You've set the bar high enough for one day."

Throngs of people filled every corner of the restaurant. The crowd was diverse, with as many bankers as there were locals. Tourists in the city completed the picture. Waiters and waitresses worked hard to keep up with the bustle of the place. Despite the many possible distractions, Ethan focused on listening to Amber's intriguing story. He wanted to know more about this young entrepreneur.

She turned her attention to Ethan. "I want you to know I don't make a habit of talking about myself. But if it can help you in any way, it's my pleasure."

"It means a lot," said Ethan.

"Of course," answered Amber. "When Ravi and I talked, he mentioned Eva and her culinary education. That is when I realized I knew her. Not too well, but from the Montreal Culinary Academy. She came in the year after I started. You can't really miss someone like Eva, given her exceptional talent. She made quite an impact during her time. Very impressive, given the competitive nature of the school."

Ethan felt a pang of pride, which he did not hide very well considering Amber's grin. "I have noticed recently how small the world is. Or at least how small Montreal is."

"Indeed. When I graduated from the Academy, I worked at a few well-respected restaurants where I learned to put my newfound skills into practice. There were many nights grinding out long, arduous hours, but I loved it. Time flew unnoticed."

"Can I ask where you worked?"

"Europea and Toqué."

Ethan's mouth almost dropped to the floor. "Wow, you've learnt from the best!"

"I have, but luck played a huge role," said Amber. "One of my professors happened to be a very well-known chef with many contacts in the industry. Once he got me going at Europea as an apprentice, it became easier to continue in the high-end restaurant category. And keep in mind I didn't get paid a single penny during that first apprenticeship!"

"Someone once told me you make your luck," said Ethan.

"I knew from my first day that I had found my passion. Surrounded by the hustle and bustle, creating exquisite dishes, I couldn't have been happier, except for one small detail—I wanted my own place. And I could not ignore this burning desire, as much as I tried. Those wonderful establishments taught me how to work with the customer in mind and showed me the importance of always using the highest-quality ingredients. And above all else, how to hire and empower the best people in our industry. Learning all this during my first five years, I knew I could do it. I saved every dollar I made. I created a detailed cash-flow budget with my father, the family accountant. I asked my best friend—a marketing guru with an MBA—to prepare a thorough market analysis. I begged and borrowed, and finally after six attempts, I miraculously convinced a bank to offer me a line of credit. All the persistence was well worth it in the end. I was able to open my first restaurant." Amber's face glowed with childlike delight.

"Which restaurant?"

"This one," said Amber happily.

"You own Vertigo! That is incredible." Ethan did not exaggerate his enthusiasm. Here sat a woman who had taken her dream and made it a reality. Very inspiring. "How did you make it happen?"

"A combination of things really. Timing played a role, and I received a ton of support from my loved ones. And we cannot forget about Lady Luck."

"Luck? I'm sure that only played a very small role."

"You hear so many people talk about making luck," answered Amber, "but I can say with complete honesty that sometimes life just works out in a way you would never have expected. At that time, the economy was not at its peak. Tourism in Montreal hit rock bottom, and the food industry suffered greatly. As a young chef in training, I felt terribly nervous about the future. Even Toqué, an establishment with a flawless reputation, pursued every avenue to bring in new clientele. But through tough times, many opportunities arise. In my case, it all happened when the previous owner, Mr. Karakis, wanted to retire. He couldn't stand the constant worry. He had made plenty of money being a very frugal man. Even seeing a few dollars dwindle away with the quiet nights frustrated him to no end. When Ravi informed me about the situation, I immediately sought a meeting with this legendary man."

"Wait a second. How is Ravi getting into this story? You cannot tell me he knew Mr. Karakis," questioned Ethan.

"He's a friend," said Ravi innocently. "We worked together on a few projects. Long story for another day."

Ethan should not have been surprised at this point. Ravi's influence reached far. The man seemed connected to everyone. "Sorry for interrupting you, Amber, please continue."

"I will never forget the day we met in his office on the second floor. He brought me in, and we sat for over four hours talking about the business and our experiences. He told me about his career, his early beginnings as a hard-working immigrant in Montreal. He truly started from scratch. I went on to tell him all about myself, and we just sat there getting to know each other. At the end of it all, he looked at me and told me his time had come, and he wanted me to own the restaurant. We put together the most reasonable of payment plans—another stroke of luck—and here we are. He still remains a great mentor and friend. He comes for lunch once a month, and we discuss the state of the business." Amber looked incredibly happy. She spoke with confidence and poise.

Ethan sensed a person filled with passion and dedication. "I am thoroughly impressed with your perseverance and creative spirit during a recession. Not many people could have pulled it off."

"Thanks for your kind words, but I had so much help." Amber looked over at Ravi. "Most notably, Mr. Channa over here. What an example of selflessness."

Ravi waved away her comment. "I simply suggested two entrepreneurs get together and review a mutually beneficial proposition."

"I think we both know there is more to it," said Amber. She leaned over and grabbed his forearm. "I owe you dearly. You gave me the opportunity to shine."

Ethan didn't know if it was his memory returning or something in the way Amber had spoken, but it finally hit him like a rocky wave. "You are on the Food Network! I've seen you. It just came to me. *Amber's Night Out.*"

Amber blushed. Clearly, she hadn't become accustomed to the attention yet. "Yeah, that's me. It's very new. It fell into my lap."

"Sorry, but I will respectfully disagree with that statement," said Ravi. "You earned every bit of that opportunity, and now they have a star in the making!"

Amber smiled, clearly wanting to change the subject. "Enough about that subject, you're embarrassing me. The show just started a few months ago, so who knows where it is going!"

"Now that we are on the matter of your embarrassing success, I would like Ethan to hear more about your subsequent path. In all seriousness, it will be great for him to understand your thought process."

Amber continued her story: "The restaurant had many great qualities. The staff loyalty could not have been stronger. In terms of location, we can all agree it is second to none. But I felt we needed a fresh start, a unique flavour. We decided to revamp the décor and completely change the style of food we offered. We went with a 'market fresh' concept, where we brought in the freshest ingredients from around North America and changed the menu daily. From swordfish to tuna tataki, P.E.I mussels to braised short ribs, we designed every dish to excite our regulars and attract many new customers. We were able to grow quickly and expand into the empty location next door. We added over thirty tables. Most lunches and dinners are served at full capacity, and the crowd is wonderfully diverse. We couldn't be more grateful."

"I must be one of the best customers!" exclaimed Ravi. "I eat here several times a month."

"You are here very often," confirmed Amber. "But you're not a great help. You constantly exclaim how exquisite every meal is. A touch of objectivity would help. I'm sure we can improve."

"Fortunately, I have never had the opportunity or need to bring any concerns to the owner."

Ethan knew enough about Ravi to understand he would never criticize Amber's restaurant. That being said, being a sound business mind, he did believe Ravi would provide feedback if something didn't seem right. From the look of things and the number of customers, Vertigo's concept didn't need too much tweaking. "Have you thought about other projects?" asked Ethan. "Between the Food Network and this place, you must be very busy. But I wonder if you have other ideas?"

Ravi's face lit up with glee. "This story contains another plot or two." He looked over at Amber.

"Last disclaimer, as there have been a few, but I want you to know Ethan, I don't spend my days talking about myself and my business. But Ravi asked me to tell you this story, and I dare not refuse a request from this demanding, unforgiving man." She tried keeping a straight face but failed miserably. "When Vertigo achieved financial autonomy, I decided to explore the Montreal food industry and learn what worked and what didn't. I also had the desire to try different ideas. To make a long story short, I discovered three areas somewhat lacking in options: high-end breakfast restaurants, Spanish tapas, and Indian fusion. One by one, I found willing partners to start these new ventures. Although there were many major challenges from cash flow to leasing concerns, I can happily say today each location is working well."

"I think we both know 'well' is an understatement," said Ravi.

Ethan did not quite grasp what this meant. "I'm sorry, are you saying you opened a restaurant in each of these food categories?"

"Yes," answered Amber, still visibly uncomfortable to be speaking about herself.

"I can tell you with absolute confidence that each of these establishments is doing fantastic," said Ravi. "I spend plenty of time at each as do many of my friends. One only has to visit Trip Advisor for a few minutes to see all of Amber's restaurants rank in the top fifty in Montreal. Bisou is the breakfast place. Cantana is the Tapas restaurant. And Rajan is the Indian fusion. Honestly, you really need to try each one."

Ethan was utterly blown away by this woman's creative entrepreneurship. She had managed to pursue her dreams in the most difficult of times. And then she found a way to build on that success. Ethan felt in awe.

They continued talking over lunch about many things, mostly food related. Amber shared her experiences in greater detail, and Ravi threw in interesting stories. Ethan listened. It could possibly have been the most productive two hours in his life, certainly from a learning perspective. Eventually, Ethan realized he needed to get back to the office. He tried taking the bill when it arrived, but Amber brushed him away quickly.

"Amber, thank you so much for this lunch. I don't know what to say. Hearing you speak with such enthusiasm and getting insight into your many accomplishments is extremely inspiring."

"It was my pleasure, Ethan. In the end, good luck and hard work came together for me. A bit of fortunate timing too! I will leave you with a thought. If Eva has any cool ideas and wants to discuss them, I am always available. We never know what can come from some brainstorming."

"Absolutely. She may take you up on that!"

Ravi hugged Amber in a fatherly embrace. Ethan shook her hand.

"I will walk you back to Premier," said Ravi.

"Are you nervous I will try to skip out on work?" asked Ethan.

"Not your style."

They made their way onto the cobblestoned streets of the Old Port. As they passed the main square, it became difficult to walk. The sunny weather had brought out the masses, even in late October. The atmosphere was electric, and Ethan felt at home. Having become a man of the suburbs, he missed the downtown core where he had once lived with Eva for a few years. Their apartment, a small loft at the corner of Queen Street and William Avenue, had been a steal. The same location now rented for triple what they paid years earlier.

"Interesting person, isn't she?" asked Ravi, rhetorically.

"Very. It seems almost surreal. What she has accomplished in so little time."

"I thought she would inspire you. That was the goal. It has to do with step three."

"In your philosophy?"

"Indeed. You are well on your way with step one, Self-awareness. I can clearly see how you have adapted. Taking a quick look at your energy level, I know step two, barrier breaking, is in the works. The time has come. Do you remember my office setup with the funky rooms?"

"Of course!"

"That is where we conduct dream facilitation. The idea is to help someone around you accomplish their deepest desires. You serve as the catalyst in making that person believe they can do anything they put their mind to."

"I remember."

"You spoke to me about Eva and her culinary background. I simply put two and two together and thought meeting Amber could have some type of positive effect. I am leaving the rest to you."

They arrived at Premier just as Ethan's mind began to reel. "Wait, you can't leave me hanging like this, Ravi. I need more information."

"In fact, you don't. Giving advice serves no purpose. Take the knowledge gained and think about the possibilities." Ravi shook Ethan's hand and smiled. "Take care, my friend. Keep running, listening, and caring. Good things will happen." With that, he walked away with his uniquely debonair manner.

Ethan stood there, feeling the energy of his thoughts engulf him. *Yes, I understand. I know what to do.* He went inside and walked the eighteen floors up to Premier Marketing, ignoring the elevator.

THE TURN OF TIDES

In chaos, there is fertility.
—Anais Nin, novelist and diarist

ᴛension smothered the air of the Premier offices. Interns and VPs alike struggled to stay focused on the task at hand. The company's biggest customer, TSS Solutions, had planned a last-minute visit with their top brass. This could only mean one of two things: either they wanted to pursue new opportunities, or they were coming to announce a change of partners.

The Massa family had gathered the entire staff in the cafeteria two days earlier to explain their plan of action. To the dismay of all, this meant cramming approximately four weeks of work into forty-eight hours. They wanted a full market analysis, new branding strategies, ideas for a new marketing campaign, and, last but not least, a complete review of the previous three years of work.

Ethan knew TSS, like most accounts at Premier Marketing, had not been given enough attention in the past months. It so happened that Robert, Sasha, and Ethan had partnered up on the last project for TSS—ideas for their new web strategy—but due to the constant lack of resources and manpower, they had only managed to present a few generic solutions. They had all worked very hard but knew the final result barely met expectations. Now, in full panic mode, the entire company was dedicating every asset to retaining its most important customer.

As Ethan finished up a report showing a small increase in sales for the technology goliath stemming from an Ad Words campaign earlier in the year, a knocking on his door interrupted his thoughts.

"Can I come in?" asked Robert.

"Of course, come in!" answered Ethan cheerfully. He looked at his boss carefully, trying to gauge his state of mind. Unreadable.

Robert closed the door quietly and sat down on the retro-style cushioned brown chair. "How are the reports coming along?"

"Okay. Trying to make the numbers look better than they are."

"I'm sure you will do your best. You have always done good work with TSS," said Robert. "With all customers really."

He rose slowly from the chair and walked over to the window, standing there, gazing for several seconds without moving.

The silence became uncomfortable, but Ethan didn't want to speak merely for the sake of it. He had learned through his own meditation practice that patience often brings answers.

"I need your help with my mother. Can you put me in touch with your cousin, the nurse? The one you mentioned the other day?

"Yes, of course." Ethan was surprised he remembered their conversation.

"As you are aware, my mother is no longer able to care for herself. I don't know what to do. I feel lost in the medical system, and I am basically hoping you can assist me. The problem is psychological, which makes it very difficult to deal with."

Never had Ethan seen his boss show this kind of vulnerability. In fact, Robert had never projected even the slightest sign of weakness. In the past three weeks, between the accident and his behaviour at Premier, Robert clearly needed a helping hand. "I've heard Maria talk about the type of care they provide, and I think she is the right person to speak with. Let me call her, and I will get you in contact with each other."

Robert nodded, and his shoulders slackened. A weight had been lifted, but another still remained. He stood fixed in place at the window, gazing into the distance, his face hidden from view. "I have noticed a significant change in you recently," he said after several moments. "You have become more patient, calm, and determined. Little things no longer affect you, and your level of general happiness is definitely on the rise. I would like to know what exactly has happened."

In the past, any inquiry from Robert came with an aggressive undertone or a hidden agenda. Most questions were rhetorical, making Ethan feel small and unimportant. But today, Ethan understood the impact of his personal change in attitude. And he wanted to share his learning experiences with this man who was desperately searching for answers.

"I met a man, Ravi Channa, who made me realize how very short our lives are. He lives by a simple yet deeply meaningful life philosophy, which focuses on self-awareness, change, and selflessness. He runs the Elevation Leadership Institute, a place I highly recommend you visit. Spending time with him will definitely improve your outlook."

"Can I please have his contact information also? Maybe he can help me?" Robert turned and Ethan could see hope in his eyes.

"Of course," answered Ethan.

Robert walked over to Ethan and leaned in close. "I haven't treated you with much respect over the past years. A part of it came from this poisonous environment, but mostly my negative attitude was caused by the frustration with my mother's illness. In the end, it doesn't excuse my behaviour. You have been performing very well under strenuous circumstances. Never once did you overreact or try to undercut me. I want to thank you." He held Ethan's shoulder for a few seconds and left without saying another word.

Ethan sat in place, stunned by this short meeting, or rather confession. He wondered why the past three months had brought such a whirlwind of change to his world. *Ever since my first encounter with Ravi.* He could try to analyze the situation for hours, but instead, he chose to accept the current circumstances for what they were. He had work to do with little time to waste.

Two days later, despite the last-ditch efforts and endless hours, Premier Marketing lost TSS Solutions—their most important, profitable, and prestigious account. And all hell broke loose.

PART III

BELIEF

LEAP OF FAITH

When we give cheerfully and accept gratefully, everyone is blessed.
—Maya Angelou, author and civil rights activist

⟨⟩

*J*t felt strange for both of them. After training anywhere between forty and fifty miles per week, this taper-down period two weeks before the marathon consisting of shorter distances defied all instincts. But they knew this was the way it had to be. All the books and training plans confirmed this, and who were they to question experienced running gurus?

Ethan could not be happier. Out in the serene landscape, jogging next to his amazing wife, he appreciated every second of it. Today had an even greater sense of importance for him. After the meeting with Amber and Ravi, Ethan had made a dramatic decision. He wanted to pursue the idea of dream facilitation to its deepest level. This meant throwing caution to the wind with Eva.

They turned the corner around Luca's school, located right in front of the shimmering lake. He wondered how long it would be before his son could appreciate the beauty of this place. *Probably a few years still.* So close to home, the winding path had proven to be the perfect spot for their training.

They reached the area where they would walk the rest of the way to cool down. He looked over and noticed the lack of sweat on Eva's face. "You look ready."

"I don't know about that," she answered. "It's not so bad when we're running a few miles. The real test is coming. I'm pretty nervous."

"You'll do great, I know it."

They walked a few more minutes, taking in the invigorating cool morning air. Ethan made a note to offer his in-laws a nice bottle of wine after the marathon. Their commitment to spending day after day with the children made a world of difference in allowing Eva and Ethan to get out and train.

He decided to jump right into the subject he so desperately wanted to bring up. "I had a surprising lunch a few days ago."

"Let me guess—with your new man crush Ravi," she said affectionately.

"In fact, yes," laughed Ethan. "But also with a remarkable woman," he teased. Ethan sensed the slightest sign of jealousy from Eva, something he hadn't seen in a long while.

"And pray tell me who you are referring to."

"You went to culinary school with her. Amber Voss."

"You had lunch with Amber Voss and Ravi! You do realize she is big-time now. She has her own restaurants and TV show on the Food Network. I can't believe you didn't tell me!"

"Yes, but embarrassingly enough, I didn't realize that when I met with her and Ravi. I'm no connoisseur. She is a very ambitious person."

"And wildly successful."

"Her restaurant Vertigo was completely full. Seems very trendy. Anyway, the point is that we discussed many things that are relevant to you."

"How do you mean?"

"First, she remembered you. She greatly complimented your culinary skills."

Eva blushed. "You are being ridiculous, Ethan."

"Sorry, I know how it makes you feel, but that is the simple truth. We continued talking in greater detail about her career path and the industry, which you are familiar with. She explained she is always looking for new and exciting opportunities."

"That's an interesting topic. I would have loved to attend."

Ethan realized the unfairness of having kept this from Eva for a few days. He soldiered on to avoid any further frustration. "Over the years, you've spoken to me of several great ideas. We put everything on hold for the children. Except that hold has become a permanent reality. I realize now how incredibly frustrating that must be for you. My career has continued forward, untouched by family responsibilities. I know it has been difficult for you. With the talent you have, it makes little sense."

Eva had no understanding of where this discussion was headed. They had talked briefly in the past about the decisions they had made, but with little consequence. She gave Ethan a quick glance without uttering a word.

"When I sat with Amber, I realized she had taken her passions and turned them into the most spectacular of opportunities. Then I began to imagine. I thought about your abilities and your drive. I took the time to remember your talent. You always dreamed of starting your own business. You told me as much the very first day we met. Sure, we can't always predict the way things will turn out. But I have come to understand that the only thing, or rather person, holding you back is me."

A flood of emotions bubbled up inside of her. She did not blame Ethan in any way. Circumstances and events happened. Life happened, and she had two incredible children to prove it. They had lived through tough times as a couple; there was no denying it. Ethan's attitude had not helped. The old Ethan, she reminded herself. But throughout these issues, never once had Eva believed her husband responsible for her own inability to pursue her goals. He hadn't always listened. But she never pushed the envelope. Perhaps there was even a level of comfort for her, knowing Ethan's job provided for their family. After all, they couldn't complain. They lived well enough, had great neighbours and everything else they needed. Not to mention highly supportive grand-parents. It was no secret she wanted more from life and felt capable of accomplishing what she put her mind to. Something did hold her back, but it wasn't Ethan.

"No, it wasn't you," she said, barely holding back the tears.

As they turned into the final street near their home, they stopped to stretch. "I could have done more for you," said Ethan.

"I had ambitions, but I didn't take the time to formulate them. Then we had a surprise with Luca, which still means more than the world to me. But you are certainly not the reason I didn't follow my heart."

"I'm not sure I agree," said Ethan. "What if now is the time to follow your passion?"

"What are you saying?"

"You should chase your dreams. Put pen to paper, decide what you want to do, and we will find a way to make it happen. Together."

The conviction in her husband's voice left no room for debate, yet she did not understand the plan. "I appreciate your support, Ethan, but this makes no sense. Where would we start?"

"At the beginning," answered Ethan, smiling. "Amber left the door wide open for you to contact her. She basically told me she is looking for new ideas and loves partnerships. She has been successful in launching new ventures. She respects your skill and ability. Why not put a concept together and see where it goes?"

Eva's mind raced faster than ever before. Butterflies took over her entire being. She felt the rush of potential. Could she actually pursue her heart's desires? Her entire adult life had been spent thinking of the moment she could run her own business. But so many questions remained. Her mind shifted back to those limitations.

"What about money? And the children? I've never run a business. How will I start? What is the first step?" She rambled all these concerns without taking a breath. Her eyes were wide as she sensed the opportunity slipping away. And then she looked at Ethan's calm demeanour and understood things had changed.

"We will work through these questions one at a time. I have some business experience in the field of sales and marketing, wouldn't you agree? Amber brings vast restaurant knowledge to the table. Sure, it will be a major challenge. But that's the point! I know how badly you want this. Concerning money, we have savings put aside, and the mortgage is well on its way. With the right strategy, we have the leverage for financing. Leave that side to me. You can concentrate on the most important part—making your dream a reality."

A tear escaped her eye. Eva suddenly flung herself into his arms, bowling him over onto the grass. "I do want this," she whispered, grabbing his face tightly with both hands. "More than I can put in words!"

He sat up and held her close. "I know. And we'll make it happen together." They walked to their front door, arm in arm, seeing endless possibilities ahead of them.

SAIL AWAY

For there to be betrayal, there would have to have been trust first.
—Suzanne Collins, author of *The Hunger Games*

⌒⟩

*H*e hadn't arrived late in years. Nor was he late today, although the time was later than usual to be arriving at Premier. He had informed Robert he would take a few hours of personal time that would be made up later in the week. Ethan had driven both Luca and Kayla to school that morning, after taking them for their favourite breakfast treat at the corner bakery. His shift in mindset and attitude had brought upon the realization he needed to spend more time with his children. *I am not going to miss them growing up.* It felt truly refreshing closing his cell phone and focusing on his family. It had been a spectacular start to the day.

Whistling the tune to his favourite Beetle's song, "Eight Days a Week," he waltzed into the Premier lobby, feeling energized. His positive mood came directly into conflict with the litany of long faces. He knew there would be consequences to losing TSS. From his recent analysis, Premier was losing money by the boatload. They had tried to manipulate and overcharge so many customers over the past years. Some had taken their business elsewhere. But the bigger customers took the necessary time to assess the damage to their margins. Some were on the edge, as made evident by their demands for contract renegotiations. Others accepted the status quo by virtue of bureaucratic ignorance, but they would catch on soon enough. TSS had figured things out way earlier than expected. It actually gave Ethan an eerie sense of satisfaction. His Premier Marketing salary provided for his family, but he didn't know how much longer he could stand the blatant disrespect and lack of integrity toward their valued customers.

Passing Diana's desk, he noticed the empty boxes. She was crouched low, filling them up with her personal belongings. He could hear her sniffling. She looked up at him, teary-eyed. No words were spoken.

The meaning was clear. He shook his head, frustrated. He hugged her as she tried to hold back the tears. This would be her last day.

As he entered his office, he found a handwritten note from Robert Samuels. It explained his desire to move on from Premier, wanting first and foremost to take care of his mother. Nothing negative in the tone. Only facts about his decision and the greater roads ahead, including a section thanking Ethan for opening his eyes and being there in tough times. He didn't know how to react. Reading it gave Ethan a genuine feeling of happiness for the man, or rather friend, Robert had become. Yet it was absolutely shocking. He never imagined Robert leaving Premier. Ever. Now two people who had both significantly affected him were gone in the span of an hour.

As he gathered his thoughts and emotions, the door burst open. Sasha entered at full steam, fuming. "Sylvia just fired me!"

Ethan had learned a great deal about Sasha's mental and emotional strength over the past year. A few months back, as the lead on a highly important pitch to a multinational conglomerate prospect, she somehow managed to forget her laptop bag in a taxi. With no time to react and no other person with the most recent presentation on hand, she winged the entire meeting and closed the account by virtue of her charm, composure, and business savvy. This story went through the ranks at Premier and made her a legend.

Now she stood in front of Ethan, trembling. He could not tell if she would cry or smash her fist through the window. She sat down slowly, staring at her hands. "I've given everything to this company. Four years of loyalty and dedication. So many times, I could have moved on to bigger and better things. I've always tried to do the best for Premier. Never complaining or asking for more. I can't believe they would do this to me." And then she cried, letting her protective walls crumble.

Ethan handed her some tissues. "I'm at a loss, Sasha. You are such an amazing person. Honestly, you have impressed me so many times I have lost count. No company in their right mind would make a decision like this. It's inexplicable. Unforgivable." Ethan meant every word.

"Probably for the best," said Sasha, dabbing her cheek. "I haven't been happy in months. Part of me wanted to look for another job, but we've been busier than ever. I never thought this day would come.

I have never been fired from anything!" Ethan could sense her pain turning to anger.

The intercom in his office rang. He stared at the phone, unsure whether to answer. Sasha nodded. He picked up the receiver. "Uh, hello?"

"Ethan, it's Sylvia. I need you to come up to my office."

"All right." He put down the phone, shaking his head. "She wants to see me."

Sasha quickly set aside her own frustrations, her concern now solely on her colleague and friend. "They can't. They need you."

"You are twice the business mind I am. They are letting me go."

She looked at him but didn't throw encouraging words his way. Premier's brass had shown how ruthless they could be.

He walked around his desk and hugged Sasha, holding her for several seconds. Their friendship meant the world to him. "I will call you later."

He made his way to the elevator and thought about his predicament. He felt strangely calm and almost serene. Perhaps the time had come for him to move on. With the crop of talent that had been let go or had chosen to leave in one day, it didn't matter if they fired him. They had decimated a key division and lost three of the most remarkable people with whom Ethan had worked.

Arriving on the executive floor, he found a surprising scene in Sylvia's office. Her father, Massimo Massa, sat cross-legged in a chic white leather chair. The man embodied old-school Italian style with flair. His silver-grey hair had been slicked back in the tightest way possible. Ethan didn't know much about fashion, but he could tell the man's brown suit must have come directly from the highest-end tailor in the city, given the impeccable cut and fit. The wing-tipped, brightly polished shoes completed the look. He looked a cross between the Godfather and Gianni Versace. His face left no room for compassion. Stern, rugged, and ready to tear you apart at the slightest imperfection. "Come and sit, young man." He had a hoarse voice filled with malevolence. Or perhaps a regular voice Ethan had transformed into pure evil in his own mind, given the circumstances.

Ethan sat down uncomfortably. Sylvia didn't make eye contact with him. *There it is, the surest sign of my demise. Game over, adios, sayonara, sucker, you don't have a job.* He began to imagine the packing process in his office. What would he tell Eva and the kids? A moment of panic gripped him. He realized how difficult it would be for Eva to pursue her dreams if he lost their main source of income. Suddenly, the meeting took on critical importance. He straightened himself and tried to look confident.

"You may have noticed a certain panic downstairs," said Massimo. "We have made some important changes. It's no secret the loss of TSS has forced our hand. We cannot afford to carry around dead weight anymore."

Ethan couldn't believe he had to hear this nonsense. Did they actually believe Diana and Sasha were unworthy of Premier? They were clueless.

"Essentially, we have decided to restructure the entire sales and marketing force," he continued. "We have let go of fourteen people today."

That number took Ethan off guard. *Who else had they fired?* People were dropping like flies.

"Which brings us to your situation," said Massimo. "You have been with us for some time now. Always loyal and dedicated, doing your work without complaining."

How did this man know anything about Ethan's performance? Ethan had only met him in person twice and had seen him speak to the entire company one other time. Sylvia kept her head low. *She knows I am being let go.*

"It's not easy for our organization right now. We have lost major ground in the market. Our reputation is taking a beating. Many key staff members have underperformed. The carelessness has been poisoning even the best of us." Massimo Massa used both his hands to slick back his already perfectly positioned hair. He did not do it with any purpose in mind. Simply a gesture of habit. "If we want to survive, many difficult decisions must be made. Starting right now."

He had expected stronger, negative emotions at a time like this. As with Sasha, Diana, and Robert, he too had dedicated sleepless nights to the cause. He had even missed Kayla's third birthday party to finish a presentation. All for naught. None of it had brought him happiness or a sense of satisfaction. Perhaps the time had come for something new.

"We have decided to change the way we function. Better communication, focused attention on details, and specifically doing more with our resources. It is with this in mind that we are promoting you to the position of Vice President of Business Development. You will report directly to me and will manage a team of seven dedicated sales and marketing staff. This will be effective next Monday. We will increase your salary by fifteen percent and a more aggressive bonus structure will be implemented." Massimo did not smile, frown, or flinch. His face remained stoic, expressionless. Sylvia fidgeted with a loose string on her skirt. Clearly, she had no input with this decision, nor was she thrilled.

Ethan had no clue what was happening. They had fired those he worked closest with. Over the past months, he had challenged Premier's executive management team quite thoroughly. His division had suffered significant losses in accounts, and by natural consequence in revenue. Yet one of the Massa family's ruthless leaders had given him a fancy title, more money, and bigger management responsibilities. It made no sense. But as he thought about it, as he realized their true motives, clarity found him. *They have no one left. This has happened before.* Ethan recalled when the major shift had occurred at Premier following the death of its founder, Vincent Massa. Many of the company's great minds had left then. Now, in a similar situation (although somewhat self-imposed), they were stranded. They cut where they could, leaving only a few desperate souls to fend for the survival of the business. With Robert taking leave and Sasha being grossly undervalued and underestimated, they wanted Ethan to right the sinking ship.

Before he could react, Massimo Massa continued, "You will be given more information in the coming days regarding staff and the new org chart." He got up and ushered Ethan to the door. "We know you will turn things around for us." Massimo patted him on the back and ushered him away. Sylvia stayed put.

As he entered the elevator to go back down to the dark unknown, Ethan had never felt so sick in his life.

26.2 MILES

What seems hard now will one day be your warm-up.
—Anonymous

⟅‿⟆

The atmosphere was electric. Strangers smiled at each other warmly, sharing words of encouragement. Runners stretched their muscles. The sun glistened, shining on the Jacques-Cartier Bridge. You couldn't see past the thick crowd of brave souls ready to embark on this daunting journey. And there stood Ethan and Eva.

Months of endless training had brought them to a place far beyond their wildest dreams. They had supported each other through thick and thin. If one felt tired during their training, the other stepped up and carried the emotional and physical load. Sharing their deepest thoughts became a tradition during long runs, to the point where Ethan joked about doing an Ultra-Marathon with Eva to ensure they stayed inseparable.

Coincidentally, the date of this race fell on his mother's birthday. Had she still been alive, Nora Stone would be turning seventy-eight years old. He hadn't realized as Eva had registered them months before, but it hit home now. Already feeling immensely emotional, it further heightened his senses. He was running for his family. He was running for his mother. She had died much too young. He desperately wanted to make her proud. He missed her dearly.

The time had come to line up with the masses. They had chosen to follow the four-hour bunny—a highly experienced runner who would guide them to the finish line at the perfect pace if they could keep up. Neither expected to accomplish or surpass this ambitious goal. Simply crossing the line would be a huge success.

A powerful voice bellowed out the countdown for everyone to hear on a loudspeaker. "Ten, nine, eight, seven, six, five, four, three, two, one!" A horn sounded loudly, sending a cheer of excitement throughout the crowd. Everything moved at a snail's pace. The number of runners did not allow for a fast start. But considering the excessive distance, no one dared complain. Two minutes and twenty-one seconds later (according to the large screen at the marathon start line), Ethan and Eva crossed the starting block and heard the critical beep signaling their chip was activated. And with that began a day of trials and tribulations they would never forget.

They jogged comfortably side by side around Saint-Helene's Island, soaking in the surroundings. There were many runners around them, affording little space to change speeds. This early in the adventure, they were feeling fantastic. The masses of people were connected, the excitement contagious. Ethan talked to the racing bunny. He asked about her race history, how she got to this point in her life. She had participated in fifteen marathons, seven triathlons, and, most impressive of all, one Iron Woman in Hawaii. Her lean figure gracefully covered ground with ease. After a few minutes, Ethan decided he better stop talking and get back to concentrating on his running pace.

They arrived on the Concord Bridge, and the view of the city left them both speechless. On the downslope, gravity pulled the athletes relentlessly. Some runners sprinted, using the downhill section to their advantage. Ethan knew his best bet was to keep his pace steady. Passing a refreshment station, Eva grabbed two cups of water. The first to drink, the second to pour onto her head, splashing down her back. Volunteers were screaming positive clichés to motivate the runners. Everyone returned high fives and fist pumps. Eva made a mental note to take on that role at next year's race. Their personal commitment impressed her. Turning left onto the first street after the bridge, she spotted Kayla and Luca with her parents. The energy boost felt Hulk-like. Running right to them, she hugged all of them, not worrying about losing a few seconds. Ethan did the same. The kids were beyond excited, flapping around noisemakers and hooting like crazy. Her parents carried a look of pride. She waved once more, desperately hoping she would see them again later in the race.

They crossed one of the Old Port's most-storied areas. Ethan felt a weight in his legs. *Fatigue?* He had been here before. He knew his body had been trained to handle much more distance given the number of long runs in their training program. Runners were more dispersed at this point. There was room to breathe. He carefully concentrated on the road ahead, his focus on his breathing. A glance over at Eva told him she was feeling very strong. It gave him the strength to push forward.

They arrived at the steps of City Hall when Eva felt a deep pang in her side. It was a disheartening pain, one that drudged up negative thoughts of failure. The very same thing had happened during a training run four weeks earlier. She had walked for about five minutes, and thankfully her body responded to the rest, allowing her to get back on track quickly. She grabbed Ethan's arm, and immediately he understood. No words were shared, nor were they needed. Without worrying about matching their bunny's pace, they took a few minutes to gather their strength with a brisk walk. In no time, Eva felt her energy return. Nodding at her marathon partner and closest friend, she slowly got back to a light jog, breathing in the fresh air. The episode was past her now, although she suspected the sheer unspeakable distance would bring more drama before the day was over.

Running a few more miles, Ethan couldn't believe his eyes. *Putting a steep hill in the middle of the race. Are you kidding me?* He started the climb, the incline causing his legs to burn furiously. He took solace in the life-saving power drink station to his right on Berri Street. He attacked the refreshments and barely had enough energy to smile at the selfless volunteers but still made the effort. It mattered to him, showing his appreciation. He had seen the impact of opening the door for a stranger or offering his place in line at the grocery store. Good Karma paid forward. The simple effort of returning a wave offered him a spark of energy. He decided he would find and thank the course planner for showing him the meaning of challenging oneself. The hill would not defeat him.

They passed the thirteen-mile marker, meaning they had run half the race. Eva was feeling better. Her momentary lapse in composure had passed. She knew there was much ground to cover, but running a half marathon was no simple feat for a beginner. She soaked up the atmosphere, appreciating the opportunity. They were passing the Lafontaine Park. As a child, she remembered her parents taking her there to enjoy the rare greenery within the city. You could always find an eclectic crowd, from flourishing artists to wannabe politicians. On this race day, a little-known band was blasting rock music to encourage the runners. It put a smile on her face. All the small, positive distractions helped alleviate the enormity of the task at hand. Most people refused to believe the articles they read or the comments from other brave finishers. There was a point where the body no longer followed the mind, no matter how hard you tried. They called it "the wall." Eva had sensed being very close a few times during the long runs, but they always stopped before the severe pain or panic kicked in. There could be no avoiding it today. The question was how she planned on handling it when it arrived.

They were covering the longest stretch of straight, flat ground near Villeray. The crowd was thick as they passed the innumerable apartment buildings and townhouses. Supporters were donning funky clothes and colourful wigs and waving flags to show their encouragement. To many, running such a distance didn't make sense. They saw it as a form of torture. Punishing the body in such a way forced the participants to dig deeper and farther to find a way across the finish line. That was the point. To test the limits of the will. Ethan knew this and kept his focus on the remaining miles. He could not let doubt creep in.

The joy of seeing her family again lifted Eva to new heights. Turning the corner, she saw them, full of happiness. Eva immediately noticed their excitement upon seeing her and Ethan. Nothing else mattered at that moment. She sprinted around two other runners and hugged both her children, not wanting to let go. Ethan enveloped the three people who meant the most to him in the world. He knew this moment would be engraved into memory for life. They took a few more seconds and knew it was time to keep moving. Eva smiled as she got back on track, looking over her shoulder several more times. Ethan stared at his partner, knowing what this day meant for them.

As they approached the twenty-mile marker, Eva felt a shift in her legs. She assumed hitting the wall meant a sudden shock to the nervous system or a scathing pain throughout her body. She imagined keeling over and rolling on the pavement, screaming for help. Instead, her body stopped. It was impossible to keep going. Every part of her physical being told her to pack up and go home, steering her toward a premature ending. That little voice told her she had done enough. Her mind was playing games. She looked over and saw that Ethan was still trudging forward. She whimpered. Ethan finally noticed her condition. He was alert, supporting her, willing her forward. He knew this moment would come for both of them. Ethan thought back to the articles he had read. He knew they could not completely stop under any circumstance. Muscles would give in—they would actually take over the mind and add physical limitations. He put his arm around Eva and started taking baby steps. She followed, using his strength. They covered a few inches, then a few steps. Eventually, Eva could feel the blood circulating through her legs again. She used every ounce of mental toughness left in the tank to regain her composure. Lifting her head higher, it became manageable. The dull ache of every single body part got buried under the incredible desire to finish the race.

They could see the Olympic Stadium from this point on the course. Flowers from the Botanical Gardens lent a freshness to the air. All around them, runners had become walkers. This late in the event, many of the undertrained and some of the overtrained hit their own physical limits. A few were limping along. One older man, most certainly in his seventies, looked distraught, dragging his left leg ever so slowly. A course volunteer stepped onto the paved road to provide assistance. The man waved her away, determined to keep going on his own. This entire scene impressed Ethan. How a man of that age was able to battle through the pain was miraculous. He was running on a personal reserve of "Don't tell me I'm too old for this." Another runner, this time a woman, jogged by Ethan with ease. She gave him a friendly pat on the back and told him to push on. Despite excessive fatigue and dehydration, the atmosphere was wonderful to experience. There was a communal vibe, as if everyone involved wanted those around them to finish the race. No feelings of competition—just a bunch of runners with the same goal in mind. They were all running to their own beat. Only trying to surpass their own limits.

Seeing thousands of screaming supporters sent shivers down her spine. Eva never realized how difficult this would be. Fans of all ages wanted to see how the runners would handle the final part of the course. Loud clapping, whistles, bells, and horns filled the air. Everyone was shouting, cheering them on. Eva fed on the crowd's energy to keep going. Tears welled up in her eyes. She couldn't help it. Ethan saw her face and gave her a look of concern. She returned a thumbs-up sign. He smiled at her, not wanting to show his own pain. He was hanging on by a thread. Both of his calves were on the verge of cramping. The only important thing right now was to cross that finish line. Together. He would not stop.

They turned the final corner and saw the massive poster that read "Montreal Marathon Finish Line." It seemed impossible to finally be at this place. Months of training, talking, sharing, and rebuilding had brought them together, perhaps closer than ever before. Eva had changed. Ethan was becoming a new man. The marathon made them both realize there was more to life—and to do it as a team inspired him. There was still a physical struggle, but nothing could hold them back now. A weight had been lifted. The pressure of failing, of stopping along the way, had disappeared. Their goal would be accomplished today. The throngs of spectators were jumping around wildly, encouraging every single runner to cross the finish line. They used this energy as their own motivation to finish strong. It was no longer about the body. It went much deeper, much further into the depths of the soul. Ethan felt the tears coming, shocking him. Eva was already weeping quietly, happily. This journey, a cleansing in reality, was reshaping their relationship. They felt it, understood the power of committing to the challenge, but more importantly to each other. It represented a bond stronger than any words could describe. This was a new beginning.

They crossed the finish line into the majestic Lafontaine Park holding hands, arms raised, beaming with joy. They had done it! Their first marathon—together. Hugging tightly, they shared a kiss. Being ushered along, they received their medals and went in search of their family. Ethan could no longer stand and hit the ground, exhausted. Almost immediately, he was surrounded by his children, who appeared out of thin air. Eva was hugging them and her parents at once. She was shaking with excitement, clearly in much better shape than Ethan. She lifted Kayla high into the air and spun her around. Her daughter shrieked with joy. Luca jumped on his father.

Ethan had learned many important things on this journey—faith, courage, and determination. Above all, however, belief topped the list. Belief he never imagined possible. He had accomplished barrier breaking, and it felt spectacular.

He accepted some water Luca had brought him. Sipping gingerly, he looked at the three people he loved most. Something in him had changed on this crazy day. Despite his physical agony, his mental fatigue, and his inability to speak, he had just attained the unattainable in his life.

THE CURSE

When ill luck begins, it does not come in sprinkles, but in showers.
—Mark Twain, writer and humorist

a sharp pain surging up his left hamstring woke him abruptly. A merciless cramp with a death grip on one of his many aching muscles. It took Ethan several desperate seconds to find the right stretch as a remedy. His entire body shook, and sweat had broken the plane of his skin. He limped around the room, happier than ever despite his agony.

This natural post-race consequence mattered very little. He had accomplished his goal. Eva had crossed the finish line by his side. Their emotional roller coaster led to a beautiful ending, one they would both cherish forever. He looked forward to celebrating with his family.

His cell phone rang. Grabbing it from the nightstand in a slow and methodical fashion to avoid any further damage to his already overextended muscles, he was surprised by the name on the caller ID. "Robert, how are you?"

"I'm doing very well, Ethan, thanks for asking. I hope I am not waking you?"

"Of course not. I slept in later than usual, but I've been up for about five minutes. Your timing is perfect. But I am embarrassed as I should have called you in the past few days."

"No worries," answered Robert. "I heard about the craziness over at Premier that went down the day I decided to move on. Seems like all hell is breaking loose."

"It's out of control! They are firing key people left and right. Soon there won't be any team left at all!"

"It's not right. But congrats on your promotion. I heard it through the grapevine."

"I'm barely surviving, Robert. The past few weeks have been frustrating, to say the least. I'm not sure I have what it takes to keep going in that environment."

"Sometimes it takes a difficult situation and a helping hand to see what matters most."

Ethan grasped the deeper meaning at play.

"I also saw on Facebook you and Eva posted impressively identical times of four hours and six minutes for the Montreal Marathon yesterday. I am speechless and didn't know you had it in you. I mean Eva, sure. But you?"

Ethan liked this new Robert, full of jokes and friendly sarcasm. "Since when did you become so connected?"

"I decided I needed to join the masses, a few years late, I'll admit."

"We're definitely happy," answered Ethan. "The relief I felt crossing the finish line was like no other. My biggest fear was to fall short of the distance. And to finish with Eva was something special."

"I'm impressed. Not many people run that kind of distance in a month, let alone a day." Robert paused, and Ethan sensed he had something else to say. "Ethan, there is another reason for my call today. It will sound strange." Another hesitation. "I met your father yesterday."

Ethan dropped his cell phone, accidentally or perhaps subconsciously. That last statement sounded so ludicrous to him he couldn't grasp its meaning. He quickly picked up his device. "I think I misheard you, Robert. Could you repeat what you said?"

"I met your father," Robert confirmed uncomfortably. "I took my mother to the Westmount Square Clinic for her checkup. Thanks again, by the way. We were sitting in the waiting area when the doctor stepped out of his office with a patient. He called him Mr. Stone and said he would see him again next week. I know Stone is a very common name, but something about him reminded me of you. I decided to ask him if he knew you. He then told me he is your father."

Ethan's hand quivered. He had worked so hard to suppress the emotional turmoil his father had left him with. Years of repressing deep anger and frustration. He knew this played a role in the detrimental way he had treated his own children in the past. Ravi's paternal story, combined with his own renewed philosophy, led him to the conclusion he should seek out his father and reconcile one day. But doubt lingered, and the pain of that awful betrayal still stung. He was not ready.

"What, um…and then what happened?"

Robert had difficulty getting the story out. Every word stuck in his throat. "I don't mean to sound negative, but he looked rather fragile. He had a cane and a severe limp. I asked him if everything was okay. He wouldn't say, but he asked for you to call him if it felt right. He mentioned a story he must tell you, and that time had its unforeseen limits. But he couldn't call you out of respect for your wishes nine years ago. He left me with his number to pass on."

"Did he say anything else?" asked Ethan, hesitantly.

Robert paused before continuing. "He said he couldn't possibly have more regret, and he wished he could make things right. But he would settle for sharing a lesson that he learned much too late in life."

Ethan found himself fighting back tears. He could never have expected this. It seemed surreal. He had buried so many emotions into the deepest recesses of his heart. The decision to sever ties with his father now seemed harsh and regrettable. Francis Stone had made many mistakes. But he was still Ethan's father. Perhaps it was time to make amends.

"Thank you, Robert. I know the entire situation must have been very awkward for you. I appreciate your call." Ethan took the phone number and hung up.

He paced around his bedroom. Then he sat, breathing deeply. He meditated for twenty minutes before making any decisions. Opening his eyes, he knew what he must do.

***

Ethan arrived at the coffee shop early. He needed time to settle in and get ready for a meeting he hadn't anticipated ever having. His father's voice had surprised him. Francis Stone used to speak in a deep, monotone voice. Now it came out hoarse and barely audible. Their conversation had been brief. Neither wanted to use a phone call as their first method of communication after so many years. They quickly agreed upon a spot near Sherbrooke Street in NDG, where his father now lived. He couldn't travel much farther apparently.

Several headphones-wearing students crowded the tables, typing papers on their laptops or texting their friends. After making small talk about the weather with the cashier, Ethan took his mint tea to a private table that had somehow escaped occupation. He sat down slowly, peeking out of the window. *Will I even recognize him?* It had been almost a decade. It seemed absurd. At one point, it had just become the norm. He didn't want to linger on regrets, but it made no sense in hindsight. This was still his father after all. Ethan knew he was justified in his anger. But he had carried the weight of their broken relationship for years. He wanted to move on.

A young woman held the door of the coffee shop open for someone as she left. An older man, wearing a tweed hat and with silver hair covering his ears, limped in with a cane. He thanked the woman and stood, seemingly regaining his breath. Ethan looked at him carefully. Embarrassingly, he wasn't sure if it was his father. This man looked thin, small, and significantly older than Francis Stone should look at sixty-three. Upon further observation, the Irish traits came through. Most specifically his eyes—a bright green that still showed life. Ethan suddenly felt a deep sadness. He had to fight very hard to hold back tears. Had his father been alone all this time? Where did he live? Who helped him get groceries or go to the bank? Not the questions he thought he would be asking himself seconds before their first meeting in many years. Nothing felt normal.

Ethan stood carefully, afraid he might lose his footing. Francis saw him, smiled, and slowly made his way over. Although he needed his cane to support him, there still remained a stable quality about his movement. He looked more solid than Ethan felt at that moment.

They stood two feet apart, staring at each other. The chatter around them disappeared. Nothing else existed, as if they were standing in their own little universe. Ethan expected to feel so much frustration and anger, but being in the presence of the man who had brought him into this world only carried sadness and regret. His emotions were running high. He extended his hand, not sure how else to proceed. Instead of taking it, Francis Stone took Ethan's arms and brought his son close, holding him for several seconds. Ethan did not know how to react. This was the first time his father had ever held him. Ever. Francis eventually let go, and they sat down.

"How have you been?" asked Ethan.

"I'm doing fine, son."

Already more affection in this simple statement than Ethan had received his entire childhood. "Where exactly are you living in this neighborhood?"

"Just around the corner in a quaint little condo."

"Alone?"

Francis hesitated. "You could say that. Some medical attention is always around to help." His Irish accent seemed to have deepened.

"When did you get the cane?"

"Oh, not too long ago." He did not seem interested in pursuing the subject. "What about you, Ethan? Is everything good? Are you happy?"

If his father only knew how much time he had been spending on his pursuit of happiness. That story alone would take Ethan hours to tell. "I'm doing great, Dad. I'm sure you remember Eva. She is working on some projects right now." He paused, realizing his father had no idea he was a granddad. "You…have grandchildren." He took out his cell and showed a few pictures. "This is Luca, and that's Kayla. My reasons for being."

He had not meant the comment to be spiteful. Francis looked away, his face halfway between a smile and a frown. His father did not dwell for long and quickly returned his gaze to Ethan, regaining his composure.

"I've been wanting and waiting to see you for a long time. Ever since the day we stopped speaking, truth be told. In the past months, the urge has been almost unbearable. But I wanted to give you space. I consider it a blessing to have run into your friend Robert at the hospital. A true gentleman. Please thank him for me."

Ethan nodded.

Francis continued, "We can speak about regret for a long time. I know it has been on my mind every single day. I owe you the deepest apology. What I did to this family is unforgivable. I treated you and your mother with such disrespect and threw away our precious bond. For that, I am so very sorry. More than words could ever express."

Ethan did not know how to react. But he understood the pain his father must have been feeling for years. His mistakes had cost him his family.

"If you will indulge me, I have a story to tell you. Would that be okay?"

"Sure, Dad."

Francis sighed, relieved. "Following our rupture, I continued living a miserable and selfish life for years. I went into a tailspin, drinking all night, partying, and, worst of all, jumping from one sad relationship to another. I missed your mother's funeral, as you know all too well. No one could find me, not that I was worth looking for. Life had lost all meaning for me. I treated every stranger with arrogant disregard."

He spoke with such passion; Ethan did not recognize this man. A father who had refused to even acknowledge his own child's feelings.

"I had no plans, so a few months ago, I decided to visit Dublin. I wanted to see my family and drink with my cousins. I was at the lowest point in my life." He paused, shaking his head, eyes lowered. "One evening, a simple-looking man was sitting at the pub, minding his own business. Being out of sorts as usual, I bumped into him and sent my drink all over his clothes. Instead of making amends, I berated this innocent patron and accused him of being a clumsy fool. He tried to ignore me. He didn't want a confrontation. But I couldn't help myself. All my anger, my frustrations, were coming out in their nastiest forms. I insisted, provoked him with relentless insults. I could see him beginning to boil. I wanted him to explode. That was my only goal at that moment." Francis's voice quivered. "I pushed him, and again he tried to ignore me. But once I punched him in the back of the head, he finally lost patience. This hulk of a man rose from his chair, grabbed me by the collar, and dragged me into the street. He only needed one hand to put me to the ground."

Ethan could feel sweat on his brow. Hearing his father tell this story made him feel a terrible sadness. His legs felt weak.

"That wasn't the problem. I didn't mind being physically punished. I deserved it. But what happened next has forever changed my life."

Ethan sat mesmerized, wanting to hear more.

"That mysterious man started walking away from me. I could barely get up, but I managed to follow him. I needed him to acknowledge me, to hurt me. I wanted to feel *something*. I continued shouting obscenities, but he did not turn around. He walked straight into the dark woods in the park, and I followed as best as I could, given my drunken state. After a few minutes, I could no longer see him or much of anything. The only light came from the moon. I eventually tried turning around but couldn't find my way. Suddenly, I could hear a voice. More of a wailing really. I followed the sound and came upon the most beautiful woman I had ever seen. She was as pale as snow, with red hair flowing down her back. She was wearing a grey cloak, and she seemed to be glowing in the darkness. I couldn't believe my eyes. I knew with absolute certainty I had come upon a banshee."

Ethan stared in disbelief. As a child, his grandmother had told him stories of the banshee. She was a female spirit from mythical Irish stories whose high-pitched wailing warned of imminent death. But that was just folklore. Nothing real. Ghost stories.

Francis could read his son's expression. "I know how this sounds. Let me finish the story before you make any judgments. I was completely mesmerized by this apparition. She looked so real. I had nowhere to turn, so I decided this must be my fate. I approached her carefully, and she looked right into my eyes. She was holding a mirror. She handed it to me as she continued wailing, although it became much softer, more like a hum. At first, I could only see my reflection in the mirror. As I stared, images began forming. It was my life. As if a movie had been made. I saw you. I saw your mother working at the hospital. Our home. Memories from our time as a family. But I quickly realized everything was negative. I was seeing my contemptuous attitude. I was being shown how little I cared for those around me. I had to relive the moment I broke your mother's heart. Scene after scene of me being selfish, arrogant, and shameless. I started crying, realizing I had spent most of my life hurting my loved ones. I fell to the ground, shattering the glass mirror, and held my face, unable to move.

"That is when the banshee moved closer to me. I looked upon her, thinking this was the day I would die. And I believed I deserved it. She then spoke to me. Her lips did not move, but I could hear her as if we were having a conversation. She told me I had one year to make things right. I could still salvage what was left of my time to bring good to this world. She said I had one year to find the path of righteousness and save myself. If I didn't, it was over for me. She told me to return to this very same place one year later to prove I had changed. She said she would be wearing either the black shroud of death or the white gown of love. That would be the answer to my fate. And just before disappearing, she said my health would deteriorate every day until we met again as a reminder of the little time I had left for redemption. And then she disappeared."

Holding his breath for a moment, Francis continued, "I stayed there, in shock, and eventually passed out. When I woke the next morning, I thought it was only a terrible nightmare caused by excessive drinking. I was back in my tiny apartment, having no idea how I made it back. There next to me lay the broken mirror. And I knew it had happened."

Ethan hadn't moved a muscle during the entire story. "What did you do?"

Francis Stone shook his head. "I was very afraid and confused. I spoke to only one person, my cousin Aiden. He knows everything about Irish folklore, being a history teacher. He also loves wild stories. I knew he wouldn't judge me, whether he believed me or not. He comforted me, telling me to take it easy for a few days before doing anything."

"Then the next morning, my urine turned red. I felt nausea, unable to breathe. They took me to the hospital. Days I stayed there, losing blood, unable to function properly. Doctors began running tests, trying to figure out the problem. They tried every avenue to no avail. Blood specialists, cancer experts, none could find an answer. I continued losing weight. After several weeks, my mind drifted back to that strange night. I began wondering about the cryptic words the banshee had spoken. I am not overly superstitious, as you know, Ethan, but the coincidence of my ill health struck me as near impossible. I had no other solution, so I told Aiden I needed help. He suggested we go see a very special person he knew of—a seer."

Ethan's eyes popped open.

"I know it is hard to believe. Trust me, I feel foolish even telling you. But I was lost. We travelled over six hours down to Cork and found the seer in an isolated home by the Celtic Sea. Her home was simple enough. There were butterflies floating around the house. Beautiful flowers decorated the garden and gave it a very welcoming feel. I was comforted. I had pictured a dark and terrifying place littered with animal bones and war relics. I still felt ridiculous, but at least the scenery resembled something out of a romantic comedy as opposed to a horror film. And I was desperate for an answer. We made our way to the front door, and as I attempted to ring the bell, to our surprise, a young child of no more than five years of age opened it and smiled at us. A precious thing with dark skin, bright blue eyes, and an impressive lock of curly brown hair. Without asking us a question, he walked back into the home, motioning us to follow him. We obliged and made our way through a weave of beads. It smelled of burning incense and honey. As we crossed the threshold, there sat a woman whose age seemed impossible to determine. Her smooth, chocolate-coloured skin complemented the calmest of expressions. She sat cross-legged on a large white futon, sipping from a steaming cup. Her face showed no change of emotion when she saw us. She pointed toward two large cushions on the floor and invited us to sit down. She welcomed us to her home and thanked us for making such a long journey, given the pain I was in."

"She knew why you were coming?" asked Ethan.

"I never told her anything, nor did Aiden. The information I received was to simply make the trip and show up. But I didn't look too good by any means, so her assumption that I was sick made sense. What followed next was the strangest part. She didn't waste time jumping into the story of my life. She started the dialogue by speaking about friendship, spirituality, and kindness. In the most serene tone, she explained the circle of life and the need for the world to change. After a few minutes, she spoke of my time in Ireland. She went into my excessive drinking problem. She pointed to my carelessness, not in a judgmental way, but rather factually. And then..." Francis Stone paused, shaking ever so slightly. Ethan stared, unsure if he should say something. His father went on after a few seconds, "She explained in frightening detail the events of that awful night. This seer knew the story. She described the appearance of the banshee. She retold how my lifetime of selfishness had brought this situation to me. And she explained how the banshee was the spirit of death, but that it did not necessarily mean my physical death. I was given an ultimatum to fix what I had broken. Either I would die or my mirror image, who had caused so much pain, would perish. I had to make the right choices."

The fantastical nature of this revelation threw Ethan into a defensive state of mind. *My father has lost it.* He hated having that type of thought during such an important moment, but he couldn't deny his feelings of disbelief and frustration. Nothing made sense, and he didn't think himself capable of listening to some imaginary tale from his father. Francis Stone instantly read his son's thoughts, anticipating them.

"Son, please hear me out. I recognize the lunacy of my words. I promise you I have not gone senile just yet. Maybe one day soon, but not right now. Remember that I myself never had time for such nonsense. I have never been superstitious or believed in mythical stories. That day, when I heard this from the seer, I made my way toward the door, and only by virtue of Aiden's insistence did I stay."

Ethan nodded, making every effort not to seem incredulous. He decided to put his opinions aside for now. "What happened next?"

"The seer pointed out how my provocations led to the events of that night. From my painful physical state, and given the fact the doctors couldn't find the source of my pain, it became obvious to her that the banshee had indeed inflicted this upon me. She went on to describe my weight loss. She knew about the migraines I was beginning to suffer. She described my sleepless, tormented nights. Ethan, she knew everything of the past weeks and was recounting such facts that I had to accept this seer's supernatural vision. I asked her for advice. I felt closer and closer to death, afraid my days were numbered. No one had answers, and I needed to believe I could continue living. I had only regrets, nothing to show but a wasted life." A single tear streamed down his face as he looked down at his hands.

Ethan reached out and held his father's wrist. He no longer knew this man. Nine years went by fast, but it also gave people time to change. The sincerity and sheer openness of their discussion gave Ethan hope. He still did not know what to make of the story, but he no longer saw his father in the same, negative light. "Please go on."

Encouraged by his son's willingness to listen, Francis Stone continued, "First, the seer gave me a few cures to help ease my suffering—special herbs and natural concoctions. She also told me to stop eating meat, eggs, and all dairy products as these would hinder my soul's healing process. And I must stop drinking immediately. She then explained how she believed I could find redemption. It was simple in concept but very hard to do. I must dedicate the coming months to making amends. I must apologize to those I hurt and find ways to help those in need. Essentially, I needed to be the exact opposite person I had been for so many years. Replace the terrible mirror image I was shown that night by someone much better. Become a person who loved, not abandoned, his family and friends. And then the seer explained how I must return exactly one year later to that same spot in the woods and find the banshee to prove I had changed."

"What did you do next?" asked Ethan.

"Aiden and I left the seer, greatly thanking her for everything she had done. In truth, I was petrified by her knowledge and foresight. Upon returning to Dublin, I immediately changed my diet and used the concoctions she had given me. It worked to the point where I did stabilize, although I did not regain my complete health. I then took several days to write down my goals, identifying the people I had hurt so badly and how I would make amends. I visited many of them, expressing my deep regret for my behavior. I wrote letters to others. A few had passed on, and I visited their families. I gave most of my money to local charities and volunteered at the local food bank. I did what I could. I know I had the banshee on my mind, but I genuinely wanted to make amends for my wasted life. In fact, the only person I did not contact was you. I didn't feel ready and didn't want to hurt you again."

"How long ago did all of this happen?"

"Seven months, one week, and four days."

They sat there quietly for a few minutes, lost in thought. Ethan could feel the strain on his emotions. He knew his father believed the story had happened word for word. Francis Stone had spoken with such candour and conviction that his belief in the events could not be questioned. For Ethan, such far-fetched voodoo hearsay seemed highly improbable. But how to explain all the details? How could the seer have such privileged information? And the fact his father's sickness had not been diagnosed medically raised questions.

"What are your plans now?" asked Ethan.

His father looked him straight in the eye. "To make things right."

LOST AND FOUND

Yes: I am a dreamer. For a dreamer is one who can only find his way by moonlight, and his punishment is that he sees the dawn before the rest of the world.
—Oscar Wilde, author of *The Critic as Artist*

That night, Ethan struggled to find sleep. His mind kept coming back to the strange day he had experienced. Never in his wildest thoughts could he have expected to sit with his father and listen to such a story. It defied logic. Trying to make sense of it was a futile task.

When he finally did manage to close his eyes, his mother came to him. He found himself alone in a forest—completely lost. He had been wandering for hours, searching for a way out. Every time he would come to a passage, darkness would engulf him and throw him back into a confused sprawl of trees. Strange sounds made him jump. He couldn't escape. It felt real to him, as if he were lucid but could not wake himself from this dream prison.

Then, when all hope was lost, he saw his mother. Her face was different, but her voice could not be mistaken. She called to him. As he approached her, ready to embrace the person he missed the most in this world, she disappeared into thin air.

He woke sweating profusely. He felt empty, drained of all energy. Dawn had arrived, but Ethan needed to stay in bed. He thought of his mother, a beautiful woman who did her best to protect her son. Nora Stone had cared deeply. Ethan always felt safe around her. As many people do, he regretted not finding a way to spend more time with her. Only when sickness overcame her being did he drop everything to be by her side. Years later, he wished he could speak with her, express his sorrow. He had never confronted the loss, and he knew deep down the pain simmered, waiting to explode.

The quality he appreciated the most about his mother was the one he struggled to cultivate: patience. He could not remember one time when she had lost her cool. Despite the many challenges with Francis, and Ethan being no cake walk either, she remained composed, always ready to help. She was a rock. She kept the family together, even when she was treated unfairly.

In recent months, Ethan had taken much time for introspection during his meditation sessions. He came to realize he carried a melting pot of character traits, evenly split between his parents. He wished he had more of his mother's temperament. She always put others first, never taking care of herself. For Nora, helping a family member or friend took precedence every time. There were times as a teenager when Ethan judged her, wishing she could stand up to Francis and live her life the way she wanted to. But with time, he understood the sacrifices she made for her family. She could never have enjoyed any independence because she felt a duty to maintain their family unit at all costs. And it did cost her dearly in the end.

Reaching into the drawer next to his bed, Ethan pulled out his journal. This morning, he thanked his mother for all she had been. He honored her memory, writing all her amazing qualities one by one: *caring, loving, protective, selfless, empathetic, sincere, honest, genuine, kind, compassionate, forgiving*. And then he detailed the ways he would try to emulate her. It would be his goal. He knew if he could be half the person his mother had been, he would be that much better off.

His last written sentence touched a sensitive topic that had made its way back into his life: forgiveness. Ethan had decisions to make regarding his father. He truly wondered if he had the courage to let Francis back into his world. He wished his mother could help him answer that daunting question. But he was alone and had to face his new reality. He couldn't wait for a miracle. Time was of the essence, and only he could move forward and do the right thing.

IS THIS REAL?

*H*er mind, always overflowing with exceptional ideas, seemed empty tonight. Whenever she thought about her dream concepts in the food industry, she could talk anyone's ear off. But her inspiration was clearly lacking. She shut her laptop and walked over to the kitchen. Pouring a glass of Taylor's Port, then tasting a bite of dark chocolate, she went to sit in the den.

Eva knew this was simply a case of nerves. Ravi had called her a few days earlier and given her Amber Voss's number. He confirmed what she had already discussed with Ethan regarding a new and exciting opportunity. Without wasting a moment, she had contacted Amber and set a meeting date. She promised to bring a creative flair and contagious energy. And some brilliant ideas. The last point wasn't going so well.

She wanted this. Badly. Since her conversation with Ethan, it was on her mind every day. She needed to be taken seriously, and the path for this to happen was through her abilities. Her bookshelf filled with several cookbooks and culinary guides attracted her attention. It always felt good to read about mouthwatering dishes or Michelin Star–rated restaurants. She decided to rummage through the dessert recipes.

As she leafed through page after page, her attention returned to the port she was drinking. Her friend Ines had brought back two cases from Portugal months earlier and had given Eva a bottle. Only after carefully researching more about Taylor's Port had she realized the privilege her taste buds were enjoying by drinking a Select Reserve Port that had been aged for over four years in oak vats.

She had called Ines after the first sip, and her friend had passionately described the traditional fermentation process. Surprisingly, most of the port houses in Portugal were situated in the city of Gaia, not Porto, contrary to popular belief. Ines explained the various intricacies of Taylor's way of producing their port, most importantly the fact they were one of the very rare places still employing actual human beings to crush the grapes with their bare feet. Machines had taken over most of this labour across the world's vineyards, but the owners at Taylor's refused to accept the tiny decrease in quality caused by robotic foot copycats. They claimed only human feet could ever produce the perfectly squished grapes. Eva couldn't argue. It tasted full-bodied and wonderfully fruity without overtaking the taste of the dark chocolate she was indulging in.

She took another bite, then another sip. Pausing, Eva closed her eyes and let the taste wash over her senses. She had quite the sweet tooth. Yet this combination managed to perfectly unify the bitterness of 70-percent dark chocolate with the sweetness of port wine, providing the perfect dessert for any person. She sat up. Her "Aha!" moment had arrived.

She had been searching for this idea for hours. She knew exactly what she wanted to do. It would take time and hard work, but the uniqueness of this concept would make all the difference. She threw herself back into dream mode, using her newly found inspiration as motivation to create the perfect plan. Excitement flowed through her veins.

***

The revitalizing warmth of the April spring air washed over her. It was weather that let you easily walk around in a long-sleeve shirt and avoid a jacket altogether. This filled the streets with walkers, shoppers, and students.

Amber suggested meeting at Milos, Montreal's most famous Greek restaurant. The chic hotspot would cost you dearly for dinner, yet remained affordable for lunch.

They arrived at the exact same time, almost bumping into each other at the front entrance. Eva recognized her former classmate immediately. It was hard not to, given her recent success in the industry.

They exchanged the customary two kisses on each cheek and made their way to a window table for two.

Eva was nervous. Just a few years ago, she had studied at the same academy as Amber. But things had changed quite drastically since then. Their lives had taken very different paths. She felt the need to prove herself but didn't want to come across as desperate. Thankfully, she had prepared her plan rather meticulously, not wanting to waste this opportunity.

"Thank you for meeting me, Amber."

"Of course. Why wouldn't I have lunch with a former classmate? Not to mention a friend of a friend."

"I do have to say that recently, the circle of my life has often come back to Ravi."

Amber laughed. "Somehow he finds a way to be the humblest human being I know while constantly connecting people from every walk of life. I am still trying to figure him out."

"I haven't spent much time with him, but Ethan is thoroughly impressed."

"How could he not be! His vision and willingness to help has led to this meeting."

"It means a great deal to me. I know your time is valuable, and I haven't been too involved in the industry for the past few years."

"You brought up your children, from what Ethan told me. I haven't reached that point in my life yet, but I can assure you I will do everything in my power to follow your lead."

Eva was surprised and flattered. She had never expected this career-minded woman to think that way.

"I can see how those words can be hard to believe," said Amber, "but my mother brought me up until I went to school, and it changed my entire perspective. I want to be able to do the same one day."

Eva nodded. "It has been very rewarding. At the same time, I feel I am now ready to try something new." She paused. "Not just new, but to follow my dreams. Oh God, that must sound so cheesy."

Amber smiled. "We all want to follow our dreams, but heaven forbid we say it in those words! Trust me, I know exactly what you mean."

Just a few minutes of conversation and Eva felt completely at ease. It felt good speaking with a strong, successful woman. It gave her the confidence to move forward. "How were you able to accomplish so much in such little time?"

Blushing, Amber answered awkwardly, "You make it sound too grand, Eva. I am blessed to be a partner in a few interesting restaurants, that is true. I had some luck along the way. But the secret is simple—surround yourself with exceptional people. The rest will come together. That has been my experience."

"How do you find these key people?"

"Our hiring practices are based very specifically on two essential components—culture fit and reference checks. We put in place core values that represent our core beliefs. These include respect, teamwork, passion, and optimism. If a candidate can demonstrate how they fit with our values, that is a great first step. By the way, I'm not talking about simple buzz words. We ask real-life questions, bring in actual scenarios where potential employees have no choice but to answer from the heart. Next, we carefully contact every reference they give. We ask for these references during the phone screening interview. If a person doesn't have the respect of their former supervisor, how will our team be able to trust them? That is our process in a nutshell. Very powerful stuff when implemented correctly."

"Your team must be very reliable."

Amber paused, reflecting on the comment. "Truth be told, I had to learn the hard way."

"What do you mean?"

"All three restaurants are doing well right now. I don't take that for granted because I have seen many talented chefs head in the right direction for months only to see their businesses suffer through difficult times. I hit rock-bottom within a year of opening my first restaurant, Crimson. Ever hear of it?"

Eva shook her head politely.

"Not many people have. The launch went spectacularly well. Rave reviews from the critics with customers in abundance. We could hardly keep up during those first months. But it was a mirage. I had so many problems, but I ignored them completely and tried to use hours and then more hours to fix them. I thought I could do it alone. I didn't realize how untrained my staff members were. Our service and quality steadily decreased. My marketing strategy went nowhere. And the worst possible thing happened: I found out my sous-chef had been stealing for months, leaving my bank account dry."

Eva couldn't believe her ears. "That is awful!"

"My own fault," said Amber. "I never paid any attention to my finances in those days. Sounds silly, I know. But when business is rolling, and you can hardly keep up with the daily hustle, cutting corners seems natural. It is, in fact, the worst possible decision. I had to learn through experience."

"What did you do next?"

"The only thing I could do. Closed up shop, took some time to regroup, and started from scratch. A tough lesson, but one that has made me the person I am today."

"How about your employee? Did you sue or try to get some form of compensation?"

"That was part of my learning curve. I had built an impressive bank of frustration and animosity. For weeks, all I thought about was revenge. Lawyers and accountants sucked up my time and energy. I lost my joy, the positive vibe we all need to move forward and accomplish great things. My father could see it draining me. That is when he suggested I sit down with Ravi."

"I can see where this is going," said Eva, smiling.

"Indeed. It is a question of perspective. He made me realize how time was ticking away, being wasted on negativity. My own precious time. One philosophy he shared completely changed my way of seeing things. You see, I would constantly get weighed down and stressed out by minor inconveniences. It didn't matter what it was. If it got in my way, it could ruin my day. Ravi asked me a simple question that I could not answer."

"I am intrigued."

"He told me to carefully think about something specifically annoying or stressful that happened twenty-eight days earlier. When I couldn't answer, he repeated the question but changed the date to twenty-three days before. As he continued to inquire with new dates, I began to understand his point.

"In his philosophy, he calls this the *time-anger gap*, and he explains how stress is always floating around, but we get to choose how to handle it. We deal with potentially difficult situations every day. But it comes to pass, and we move on. Ravi believes the key to happiness is our ability to accept life for what it is and realize that we will very quickly forget that rude waiter or an angry customer. We decide how we react in every circumstance. We choose if we will let our frustration get the better of us, or if we will embrace the idea that every negative moment will quickly enough come to pass. Acceptance, positivity, and foresight. Knowing it will pass and we won't even remember."

Eva soaked in this information. She hadn't thought about life in those terms. Until recently, she had spent most of her time regretting certain choices or flabbergasted by the daily grind of life. The marathon training had given her focus. Throwing herself into business ideas had helped also. But those two projects had kept her busy. Taking a different outlook on life in general, one where she could have been more positive would have done a world of good.

A young waiter arrived at their table and greeted them warmly. He meticulously described the lunch specials and had both women's complete attention. The choices were delectable and impossible to refuse, but they couldn't eat every dish. Amber chose the Greek Salad followed by the Salmon Tartare. Eva craved the Organic Heirloom Beets and decided to try the American Sea Bream. They laughed at the quantity of food they were preparing to eat during a working lunch.

"I am even more impressed with your success after hearing that story," said Eva. "Many people would have given up or gone back to working for someone else. You persisted in following your dream."

"It worked out. But my goal in relating that experience has more to do with our ability to change perspectives. We can start from a new vantage point and eliminate the preestablished misconceptions we hold on to. I have become much more open-minded, and I avoid letting a bad hour turn into a worse day, which could eventually become a ruined week. I try to make the most of every moment. Ravi played an enormous role in this process. Hearing myself talk, I should probably apply to his marketing department at the Elevation Leadership Institute!"

Eva was enjoying herself. She felt completely at ease with Amber. Her calm yet joyful attitude brought an infectious energy to their meeting.

"I have talked too much!" exclaimed Amber suddenly. "You've asked me great questions, and I could go on for days with this subject, but we came here to discuss your business ideas. Where do you want to start?"

The starters arrived before Eva could utter a word. They looked spectacular. "Looks like I will be talking with my mouth full!" said Eva.

"And I will be skipping dinner tonight," answered Amber.

Eva took her time savoring the first few bites before focusing her attention back on her presentation. She felt her nerves tingling.

"I thought about many different ideas throughout the brainstorming process. My biggest question always came back to the value of launching an entirely unique concept versus the pursuit of a proven idea. In the end, originality won the day."

"I like the sound of this already."

"As you may know from our conversations, my passion lies primarily in the dangerous delights—pastries, cupcakes, cheesecakes, tarts, and of course, cheese. Traditionally, these are served in coffee shops, bakeries, and restaurants. We have seen more recently the small emergence of wine bars that offer certain finger foods to accompany the alcohol. While these do satisfy many customers, lacking is a place where a person could enjoy digestives paired with delectable desserts in a stylish setting. I am proposing a new take on all these existing venues. I want to bring a port house to Montreal." Eva hoped she didn't sound too rehearsed.

"A port house," said Amber thoughtfully. "That is different. It definitely strikes a chord. Give me more details."

Eva felt a hidden confidence emerging, and her heartbeat sped up. "First, I have been scoping out various locations. I don't feel Crescent Street or the St-Laurent area cater to the type of crowd we are looking for. After walking around town for the past days, I came up with two key areas: Outremont or the Plateau. Each has its charms and advantages, and I know the crowd is perfect in both areas. It's more a matter of finding prime real estate at an affordable cost."

"Both great spots, I agree," said Amber. "There will be plenty of negotiating to get a fair deal on rent. But that will come later. Please go on."

Eva nodded. "Next, I visited various restaurants and cafes to get a feel for décor. My friend Rosa is a wonderful interior designer. She gave me the info on the latest trends and styles. She gave recommendations and places I could find inspiration. She graciously assisted me in putting together these very temporary renders of a potential port house." She handed the 3D drawings to Amber.

They could not have looked more realistic. The attention to detail was superb. Frosted glass doors tinted in a blue hue made up the front design. The name *Gaia* had been chosen and placed on every window in a silkscreen style. "I picked that name for a reason," said Eva. "I read quite extensively about the Porto region in Portugal. Ironically, most people don't know that port wine actually comes from a city called Gaia across the river. I certainly didn't. I thought we could use that as a fun story for our customers. Explain the history to them, give them information about the various port houses, and how they came to be. In Greek mythology, the word *Gaia* means 'mother of the heavenly gods,' which seemed fitting."

"Love it," said Amber with conviction. She then moved on to the next render, which looked much more like a photograph than a computerized drawing. The entrance, with a beautifully sculpted dark walnut reception desk, took up most of the space. In the background, a shiny metallic pyramid filled with port wine bottles reached the ceiling. Its appearance made the foyer one of the more attractive places Amber had seen.

"This image is breathtaking and very realistic. It looks nothing like a render!" exclaimed Amber. "I don't know what this will cost, but so far, I'm feeling very excited about this place. Did you come up with all these ideas?"

Eva took the opportunity to move the next image forward as she answered. "I imagined a concept, but the credit must go to Rosa. She is a true visionary. Anything she touches turns out wonderfully. Sometimes we get lucky, and I am certainly blessed to have such a friend. I gave her a few cues, which she then transformed into a true work of art."

Amber worked hard at becoming a good listener. A talent taught by Ravi. But already having the next picture in front of her made it almost impossible to focus. She was staring at the main lounge area.

A combination of white avant-garde chairs and tables mixed with relaxed, unassuming chocolate sofas created the perfect contrast. It immediately made sense how the patrons could choose to sit in groups or have more intimate conversations. At the back of the room stood a long, narrow bar. The glass shelves on the main wall were stocked with various liqueurs and glowed with various hues of red, blue, and purple. "I have a friend in lighting," said Eva. "They offer this very cool LED tape lighting that can change colors with a remote. We could actually control the mood in the bar area at any time and even adapt to different occasions."

Amber was speechless. These images went so far beyond her expectations. She had come here for a nice lunch and an informal chat. She was being presented with a very attractive venture. It had nothing to do with money or success. It never did for her. It came down to passion and belief. Eva had both, and Amber wanted to hear more.

"One last thing," mentioned Eva. She pointed to an area in the back corner of the room. There was a small, triangular space with a frosted glass panel on the façade that went hip high. The words "Artist at Work" made up the top part of the glass in embossed lettering. "This will be the DJ booth. Music invigorates me, and I believe it will bring that extra special vibe to have a live DJ on most nights. Nothing too loud or crazy, but mostly to complete the mood. A little funk, jazz, chill vibes, and we could even throw in some international flavor."

Before Amber could ask another question, their main courses arrived. She hadn't thought about eating. She didn't care right now, given her current interest in Eva's Port House idea, but the smell immediately intoxicated her senses. She had chosen Milos for a reason. They put aside the paperwork and dove into the attractive dishes. After a few long seconds of bliss and enjoyment, Amber turned her attention back to her potential business partner.

"Now that we have discussed the idea, location, and design," said Amber, "are there other topics you want to review today?"

Eva smiled. She pulled out an attractive leather-bound binder from her bag. Removing the strap, she handed Amber a sizeable document. The words "Business Plan for Gaia Port House" were embedded on the front cover. The entire package had a highly professional feel.

"I had help putting together all the financials. Ethan is pretty good with numbers. Although I have never been an owner, I have a fairly good idea of the resources needed to make this a success. You are the person with the best experience, but I thought it would make sense to start from a base. I detailed opening costs, renovations, overhead, staff, and the investment required. We already met with our bank and financial advisor. I obviously have no understanding of your way of working, but my assumption was a fifty-fifty partnership," Eva said this as more of a question than a statement.

Amber was taken off guard. The vision, commitment, and thorough preparation blew her away. She could see how serious Eva was taking this project. And Amber believed in it. She could see this had great potential, and she knew in her heart it could work. Their partnership made complete sense.

"I would like to take a few days to review the business plan. I see you have put in great time and effort. Everything you have presented today has gone well beyond my expectations. I am very impressed, Eva."

Water engulfed Eva's eyes. She got up, went over to Amber, and hugged her ferociously. A new chapter had begun.

EMPOWERMENT

Whether you think you can, or you think you can't—you're right.
—Henry Ford, entrepreneur

$\mathcal{T}$he crisp morning air entered Ethan's lungs as he jogged home. He had run solo. He no longer questioned whether he should get out there. The only variable was distance. This morning included ten miles with a sprinkle of sprints. After stretching out key muscles, he walked through the front door.

Luca catapulted into his father's arms with incredible energy. Kayla joined them and hung onto his left leg. Ethan carried and dragged his children to the kitchen with mock screams of agony. Eva stood, preparing breakfast for all of them. The smell of basil, eggs, and maple syrup filled the air. He kissed her, thanking her for being her.

The moment itself meant the world to Ethan. After realizing months earlier how his negative attitude had impacted his loved ones, change had been his only choice. He had Ravi to thank for that. It had brought his family to this place. Eva seemed happy and very motivated. The business plan she worked on for weeks made the desired impression on Amber. They were deep into financial discussions and already negotiating locations. The project was well on its way.

Ethan felt physically unstoppable. He had never been in this type of shape before. Months earlier, he couldn't make it up the stairs without panting. Now he could fly up steep hills. He felt younger and stronger and motivated to continue improving his well-being. His mind was clear. He had maintained his daily meditation practice. After several months, he had mastered the ability to accept his mind's chatter and simply breathe in peace. Ravi had explained the myth that meditation meant clearing the mind of all thoughts. This was impossible, according to him. Instead, one must acknowledge when the brain wandered and bring focus back to the breath. Ravi called this a mental bicep curl. It had worked wonders for Ethan, greatly increasing his level of patience and understanding. He now took time before making any irrational decisions or reacting impulsively. Just a few seconds of reflection and he could positively change most outcomes. Ravi's self-cleansing process had worked wonders.

He had a meeting this morning with his friend and unofficial mentor. Ravi had called a few days earlier requesting Ethan come to the Elevation Leadership Institute. He needed to work out a few details at Premier to make it happen, but given the fact he no longer had much support there and he now ran his department, he could make those types of decisions on his own. He tried to stay positive about his job, but he knew his days were limited at the marketing firm. It no longer fit with his values. He had already begun preparing his resume. Ethan realized Ravi had once again left him in the dark about the reason for their meeting. It did not bother him as he always looked forward to seeing him.

Ethan finished his breakfast, complimenting Eva after every bite. He quickly showered and got ready to leave. Kissing his family goodbye, he made his way downtown in a spectacular mood.

***

Julia Everhart, as Ethan had come to know her through his various communications with Ravi's office, exuded a joyful confidence in everything she undertook. She considered herself the Chief Happiness Officer and treated every guest at the Elevation Leadership Institute as one of her own. None of this surprised Ethan, given she spent significant time with the Happy King. Ethan had decided to give Ravi the nickname a few weeks earlier. He had discovered Ravi's middle name was Raj, which meant king in his native Hindi. Given his incredible attitude and passion for life, it seemed most fitting.

Another benefit Ethan had earned was the right to enter those thick frosted glass doors without supervision. Free to roam to his heart's desire. It felt good having access to what he considered one of the most innovative work environments he had ever experienced. He still found himself in awe whenever he came upon the dream facilitation rooms. *I should make one of those at home.*

Coming through the entrance to the office, he stood in front of the main glass-paneled conference room. The sight confused him. At the table sat four women and three men passionately discussing a certain topic. Hands were waving wildly, while expressions varied from amusement to disbelief. Curiously, one woman stood in the far corner of the room. She faced away from the group, seemingly in some form of punishment. Ethan knew enough about Ravi to understand this could not be a coincidence. It baffled him. *What is this person doing?* As if on cue, a dark-haired woman appeared right next to him. "Wondering what you're seeing?" she asked.

It startled Ethan, as he thought he was alone. "Oh, um, yes, I am very much trying to understand what is going on in there," he replied hesitantly.

"It's called the *indirect brainstorm*. Quite fascinating, really. Basically, the woman in the corner brought an important subject to the meeting. Perhaps a business conflict or an innovative idea. She presents and explains where she stands on the matter. Then the other members ask certain questions to clarify the situation. Next is the kicker. The presenter goes into the corner of the room, facing away from the group, and listens."

Ethan still did not get it. "Listens to what?"

"A free-form brainstorming session. Her colleagues come up with as many solutions, ideas, and experiences as they can. They throw them out in no particular order, but always coherently and professionally."

"But why does the person have to stand in punishment?"

"It is definitely not punishment," laughed the woman. "It serves a highly important purpose. You see, when we share ideas face-to-face, it is almost impossible for us to be perfectly honest."

"How so?" asked Ethan, unconvinced.

"Because our natural tendency is to let ourselves be guided by another person's reaction. We will watch for facial cues of approval or disappointment, and this will affect what we learn from the experience."

"Can you give me an example?"

"Let's say we are talking about your desire to open a clothing store. You tell us your dilemma and challenges. Then each one of us, looking straight at you, gives certain solutions or thoughts. If we see you are reacting negatively or not agreeing with us, it will make it very difficult for us to continue giving feedback in an objective manner. But if we are not seeing your reaction, everything we say becomes information your brain can choose to hear and process. There is no animosity, no obligation. We are left with an indirect brainstorming session. And trust me when I say it is very powerful. You would be amazed how many cool ideas can make their way into the airwaves when everyone is feeling loose and completely open-minded."

Ethan nodded as he mulled over the information. It made sense. In fact, he suddenly felt a desire to try the exercise. "I'm Ethan, by the way."

"I know." The woman smiled. "I've heard more about you than you would expect. And we will be seeing each other often enough in the coming weeks." Her face showed a hint of amusement. "They call me Farah in this neck of the woods." She turned and walked away without waiting for his reaction.

Before Ethan could attempt to understand her cryptic words, Ravi grabbed him by the arm, surprising him once again.

"My dear friend, I am so happy to see you! Thanks for coming this morning." The man looked straight out of a Bollywood movie. His hair perfectly waving to one side, his tall figure draped in a designer suit. And that British Indian voice still reminded Ethan of a James Bond movie character.

"Of course, I wouldn't miss it for the world," said Ethan.

"Come, let's walk to my office." They made their way to the lush chairs Ethan remembered enjoying so much the last time he had visited.

"You look good, Ethan. I would even say great, but then you wouldn't have anything left to strive for."

Ethan chuckled. "Well, thank you. More running, trying to stay at the top of my game. Still have work to do."

"Have you thought about running any more races?"

"I would like to do the half marathon taking place in June with Eva. She has been very passionate about running since she picked up the sport."

"That is fantastic! And the kids are doing well?"

"Couldn't be better. Continuing to grow faster than the eye can see."

"Wonderful. And Eva? How is the Gaia project coming along?"

"It is moving at a fast pace. Amber and Eva have met three times now, and they are planning the logistics. They are visiting a number of locations this week, hoping to make their final decision by the end of the month!"

Ravi nodded, clearly impressed. "That is a team made in heaven. I am sure they will have success together. Talking of success, there is a reason I asked you here this morning. Catching up is important, but so too are those unique opportunities awaiting us."

"More mysterious words for me," said Ethan, smiling.

"What do you mean?"

"I met a new person earlier—Farah. She said something that I couldn't quite figure out. That seems to happen a lot here. In a good way, of course."

Ravi laughed. "Yes, I agree many of us here have a tendency to use vague, almost prophetic words." He poured them both a glass of water. Ethan gulped it down. He had forgotten how thirsty he was after his morning run.

Ethan couldn't hold back any longer. He needed to tell Ravi about the encounter with his father. Ravi had been so frank and honest when relating his own paternal story months earlier that it gave Ethan courage. He described every moment in great detail, trying hard to fight back the emotions. Hearing himself speak flooded his entire being with repressed memories from his childhood. He felt in danger of losing control. His heart beat at a rapid pace and thudded deeply into his chest, almost trying to jump out.

Ravi listened with calm intrigue, never once interrupting the story. When Ethan finished, Ravi asked a simple, yet loaded question. "Having made such drastic changes over the past months, how will the new Ethan handle this?" No questions about the fantastical nature of the account. No advice being given. A simple inquiry and nothing more.

Ethan thought for several seconds. Many scenarios were playing in his mind. He didn't have the answer. Having been able to tell his story made a world of difference. A great weight had been lifted. "You know, I have no idea. But thank you for listening. I truly needed that." It had been enough. He realized at that moment he wasn't seeking advice. He wanted a sounding board. And Ravi had provided exactly that.

Ravi smiled sympathetically. "I am always available when you need to talk. I can certainly understand where you are coming from, given my personal history. I look forward to hearing the outcome in the coming weeks." A few seconds passed in comfortable silence.

Ravi broke the spell. "I had another reason for asking you here. I wanted to speak to you about a conference we are holding in two months. We have been asked by Innovation Enterprises, a very large manufacturing conglomerate, to run a 'Leadership and Change' summit for two hundred of their brightest team members from all over North America and Europe. It will be held right here in Montreal."

"That sounds very interesting."

"I'm hoping we will be able to make it a memorable event. We are putting together the agenda to ensure our audience is constantly engaged by the speakers and material we present. I thought about you, and I would like you to attend."

Ethan was confused. "I appreciate the invitation, but won't it be strange for me to participate with people from another company?"

"I'm not quite looking for you to be in the crowd," said Ravi. "I am asking you to be the first speaker."

Ethan stared at Ravi, bewildered. He had no idea what was happening. "Ravi, I'm not sure I understand what you are saying here. I heard you utter certain words in English, but my brain is clearly not processing it the right way. Could you explain the meaning of that last sentence?"

Ravi held back his laughter. "What a reaction! I could not have asked for better. You heard me correctly. I want you to give a talk describing the past months of your life. From the man you were to the man you have become. The journey you have undertaken, the changes in attitude, mental health, fitness, and familial presence. The actions that led you here today. It is a very personal piece. You exemplify the ability one has in choosing a new path. The ability to change. Wouldn't you agree the past months have brought you to a place of harmony and happiness?"

Ethan fumbled his words. "Yes, well, yes, but that doesn't make me fit to teach others."

"In fact, it does, Ethan. It gives you an obligation to tell your story. People want to be inspired. Business theory and strategic planning can only do so much. There is a personal side that is so much stronger and more powerful—one that must come first, before all else. That is why I want you to get on stage. Nothing fancy. No frills or props, but rather an honest recounting of your efforts to be a better person. It is that simple. I'm asking you to speak from the heart and let others see what can transpire when the mind pursues a meaningful goal."

A tingling sensation overtook his body. He felt nervous but very excited. Ethan recognized this as an incredible opportunity. He had given presentations throughout his years, but only to small groups consisting mostly of clients or colleagues. To be asked to stand in front of successful executives and tell them about his life was a true privilege. He had many questions, mostly concerning his lack of experience. Ravi read his mind.

"There are a million reasons you could find to question this decision," said Ravi. "I want you to ignore them all. There are a few important facts to consider. First, what you have accomplished in the past year is exceptional. Second, you are a humble person and therefore don't see or realize how well you speak in public settings. Third, and most importantly, I see in you infinite potential as a leader. This quality is extremely rare and sought after by many. It takes years to develop. By taking on this project, the doors to a brighter future will open wide because it will fill you with a confidence only achieved through action."

Ethan had never been spoken to this way. His father could hardly pat him on the back, let alone inspire him to strive for greatness the way Ravi did. He couldn't comprehend what stroke of luck he had come by to meet such an exceptional person.

"I am grateful beyond words," said Ethan after a few moments of reflection. "Everything you have done for my family and me has changed my entire outlook on life. I can breathe now. I always see the positive outcome, even in negative circumstances. But I have to ask you again, as I have in the past, why have you done so much for me? I remember your answer from our previous discussion, and I suspect now is the time to come clean!"

Ravi shook his head, smiling. "In time, Ethan, in time. I will say this. There is a very specific reason you and I met. It is not a fluke that I called Premier Marketing asking you to come and visit me. But I cannot explain the rest at this moment. One day soon, but not today."

Ethan shook his head. "Talk about leaving a man on a ledge!"

"I know," said Ravi, laughing. "But you will find out the truth sooner than later, I promise."

They shook hands, and Ethan made his way to the lobby. He bid Julia farewell, thanking her for the excellent hospitality. Walking outside, he felt the energy of new possibilities course through his body.

REDEMPTION

Whatever wrong turns you've taken in life, you can always start over and find your way back to happiness.
—Marty Rubin, author of *The Boiled Frog Syndrome*

S unshine shimmered through the kitchen window, bringing in warmth and a new beginning. Kayla and Luca were laughing in the garden, running around with a careless joy only found in children. For her part, Eva could feel butterflies all over.

She had been speechless when Ethan had told her about the reunion with his father. She had only known Francis Stone for a short time. They had never been close, but then again, no one had been close to Francis. When that awful day of his betrayal had occurred, she hadn't realized how deep the pain would cut through their family. It could have turned out in many different ways had he shown some remorse. But the man was lost, and Ethan hadn't been able or willing to salvage their already tumultuous relationship. Eva remembered when Nora, Ethan's mother, had passed. No one could find Francis. They tried for weeks on end, but the man had disappeared. It was at that moment Ethan had vowed to never speak to his father again. Ever.

Things had changed. Ethan had changed. His frustration and anger had been replaced by a softer, reasonable perspective. The unbelievable story told by Francis did not make any sense to Eva, but she could see it had affected Ethan to the core. Regardless of its lack of realism, Ethan decided to accept his father back into his life and try to forgive him for his many failures. Eva was going to support her husband through thick and thin. She knew Ethan would do the same. And she acknowledged that her own support system was irreproachable. She owed it to Ethan.

The tricky part had been their talk with the children. How to explain to their eight-year-old and six-year-old children that they suddenly had a new grandfather who would be having dinner with them?

It made little sense. In the end, they had agreed to introduce Francis as a family friend. Take things slowly.

Ethan was on his way with his father. He had offered to pick him up. Taking public transportation across the city would not have been feasible for Francis. They had also invited her parents to help with the children and provide another layer of much-needed support. This was, after all, a very important day. She wasn't sure how it would all go down. Would Ethan be able to maintain his composure? Could she manage to hold a conversation with her father-in-law—a man with whom she had absolutely no connection?

The children were very hyper in anticipation of meeting the new "family friend." Any time a new person entered their home, it caused a ruckus. They would have a million questions for Francis. She hoped he could handle it. In the end, she tried to stop overthinking and focused her attention on making their home a welcoming place.

A few minutes later, everyone arrived at the same time in the driveway. She heard voices outside and hurried to the window to witness the awkward introductions. Eva almost hit the floor when she saw Francis. For all his faults, he had always been a strong, well-built man. Now, he stooped over his cane and had difficulty making his way up the stairs. His hair had taken on a bright whiteness. Thick glasses covered his face. He looked tired and worn out. She should have expected as much with the current state of his health, but it still caught her off guard.

She tried regaining her composure as she opened the door. Her parents entered first. She hugged them anxiously and moved on to Francis. He spoke quietly:

"Hello, Eva. What a pleasure to see you. You have actually grown more beautiful since we last met." His Irish accent still carried through the weak voice.

"It is good to see you too, Francis." She moved forward, unsure how to greet him. Hesitating, she finally decided on a simple handshake. "Please come in."

The children had made their way inside, as if magically sensing the new presence. They had special intuition when it came to visitors. They rushed toward Francis. Luca stopped short, but Kayla went straight to the grandfather she had never met. "What's your name?"

"It is Francis, my dear."

"I have a friend at school, and her name is Francesca."

"That is a beautiful name," answered Francis.

"She has a Dora backpack with Cinderella stickers on it."

"I'm sure she must be a good friend."

"Sometimes, we trade backpacks. Sometimes we even change stickers together. Yesterday, I wore her shoes at school, and she wore mine. It was a secret."

Francis laughed. "I'm sure that must have been very funny."

Ethan jumped in nervously. "Okay, sweetie, let Francis come in and get settled down." He directed them toward the living room. Luca still kept his distance, holding on to Eva's hand. He seemed quieter than usual. Eva wondered if he knew something, maybe having heard them speak about this meeting. Luca always seemed to figure out their secrets.

Eva's father followed her to the kitchen to help serve tea and cookies. Her mother, always the social bee, wasted no time in getting familiar with Francis.

"It's nice to see you after all these years, Francis. Ethan told us you are back in the city."

"Indeed, I am. Trying to feel young again."

"You look full of energy today," said Robin. The comments were a clear embellishment.

"Thank you, Robin," said Francis in his hoarse yet melodic tone. "Being here brings warmth to my heart."

"Ethan mentioned you have not been feeling too well." They hadn't told Eva's parents all the details yet. It had not felt right. They had kept it simple and explained that Francis was undergoing tests.

"I could be in better health," answered Francis. "But I have a special opportunity to be around those I care most about. That is something I took for granted many years ago. Never again."

Ethan felt a sharp stab of anxiety, listening to his father. Part of him desperately wanted to forgive him, but he couldn't help feeling pain. Memories came flooding back—the unacceptable behavior, the lack of parenting, missing the birth of his two grandchildren, and worst of all, the terrible betrayal that broke his mother's heart. He felt justified in his anger. But his father looked vulnerable and in need of support.

Lingering on the past could only cause more pain. He knew this yet still needed more time—time he didn't have.

Eva walked in with the refreshments. Everyone enjoyed the snacks while mingling, keeping the small talk light.

After a few minutes, Kayla insisted Eva take her on the swings in the backyard. Luca now clung to Ethan, continuing to stare at Francis. He stared with such relentlessness that Ethan felt he may have to ask Luca to stop. But before he had the chance, Luca brought the room to a dead silence the way only a child can.

"You're my grandfather."

The room went still. No one moved. Ethan thought they had done a good job keeping this information secret. *How had Luca figured this out?* Ethan had no idea how to react. He just stared as he felt the room getting very hot.

Without the slightest hesitation, Luca walked around the table and hugged Francis. In that embrace, Ethan sensed Luca was forgiving his grandfather for all his flaws and mistakes. Such was the tenderness of his action that tears came flowing down Francis' face. He could not hold them back. He returned the affection, realizing what a privilege it was to be hugging his only grandson.

After a few precious seconds, Luca grabbed his grandfather's hand and walked him outside without saying a word. Ethan stared through the patio door as they went to the backyard together. Kayla ran to them and following her brother's example, took hold of Francis's free hand. They led him to the bench near the flower garden and sat down. Eva watched with a smile, completely unaware of the circumstances.

Inside, everyone shared confused stares. Ethan could only admire Luca's maturity. The boy had somehow alleviated a lifetime of pain in a single, precious moment. Ethan had to hold back his emotions lest tears get the better of him also.

Late afternoon turned into an evening of eating and talking. A chance to get to know each other. For all the tension Ethan had built up inside, it passed without incident. He was having a good time despite the many personal defense systems he had put up. His children were getting to know a grandfather they had never met before. They were still young enough for a fresh start. Ethan hadn't expected them to become so comfortable after a few short hours, although he could have suspected as much. Their loving nature could not be held back.

He realized the issue lay more with his past. He never wanted to open his home and his heart to the father he never knew. A year ago, the idea would have seemed absurd. He would never have accepted Francis back into their lives. Now, with his new outlook, he was able to let life take its course and observe the result. But he was still on guard, waiting to see where all of this was going.

After dessert, everyone said their farewells. Ethan walked Francis to the car. He had already offered to drive him back and forth this evening. He led them on their way.

They spent the first few minutes in silence. Much had happened during this first family encounter in nine years. Following almost a decade of anger and frustration, this moment represented a deep acceptance. A positive line had been crossed. This fact swirled in Ethan's brain, making it hard to concentrate. He felt good, yet there was still much to process.

He glanced over. Tears engulfed Francis's eyes and streamed down his face. His father, a man never able to express the slightest sliver of emotion, had become the exact opposite. Time had played a trick on him.

"I've done wrong by you, my son. Mistake after mistake, my days have been filled with regret and remorse. I realize now, in my old age, how my actions caused such great pain. I was beyond selfish. It is inexcusable. And yet, you have somehow found the strength in your heart and soul to open up and let me back into your life. Your attitude has been exceptional and thanking you cannot begin to repay this kindness. Spending time with my grandchildren, with Eva, her family, and with you has been an undeserved privilege. I am not taking even one second for granted."

Ethan gazed upon the open road. It was a quiet evening in the city at this hour. He let his father's comments sink in as he drove. There were many ways he could respond. He had every right to criticize his father for all his terrible actions. He wasn't exactly sure where he stood at this very moment. But he knew the anger had passed and been replaced by a need for resolution.

"What we experienced tonight should have happened a long time ago. My children must have the chance to know their grandfather." Ethan paused, gathering his thoughts. "I will not pretend I haven't been hurt. I have spent countless days wishing life could have been different. And I blamed you. I felt deserted in the deepest way. I was still a young man trying to figure out my place in the world when it fell apart. It has been a struggle that has challenged my every waking moment."

More silence.

"I'm so sorry," whispered Francis.

They arrived at his father's apartment complex in NDG. It was located just off the main hub of action on Sherbrooke Street. Ethan parked. "You don't need to help, son, I can manage."

Ethan ignored the comment and made his way to the passenger door. Supporting his father's arm, he walked him to the door and further insisted following him up to his apartment. No words were spoken in the elevator.

As they arrived at apartment 309, they stared at each other, each waiting for the other to speak. Instead, Francis suddenly dropped his cane and hugged Ethan as ferociously as his fragile condition would allow. He wept openly and fully. It caused Ethan to react in the same way, reciprocating the affection he had waited a lifetime to receive. In that moment, he forgave his father for all his mistakes. He decided to give him another chance, to appreciate and enjoy the time they had left together. He did not know what the coming months held in store for them, but he would be by his father's side. For his children, for his family, and for himself. Ethan knew, in that moment, it was the only choice he could make. The right decision.

LOCATION, LOCATION, LOCATION

The sun doesn't just hang on one family's tree.
—Anchee Min, author of *Empress Orchid*

E va arrived at the corner of Fairmount Street and Park Avenue early and full of excitement. Amber had called her two days earlier with great news. She had stumbled upon a great location for their port house through a friend in commercial real estate. She hadn't seen the place yet as she wanted Eva to be there. They did not want to get their hopes up too high as this was the first place they were visiting. But Amber believed that often the first place held a special appeal that stayed in the back of one's mind. And from the description, it sounded perfect. Perhaps too good to be true.

Amber arrived a few minutes later with an infectious smile stretching ear to ear. They hugged and shared the traditional double cheek kisses before heading toward their destination.

The neighborhood itself could not have been more attractive. The area was beautified by several high-end condos and townhouses. Outremont was known for its diverse community, from high-level businesspeople to artists and professors alike. All of whom could potentially enjoy a relaxing glass of port paired with the finest cheeses and desserts from around the world. Both Amber and Eva had only wanted one of two Montreal locations, the other being Westmount. It was obvious this location fit their vision perfectly.

By the entrance stood a woman in a grey business suit holding a tan leather briefcase. She introduced herself in a charming French accent. "Hello, Eva, I am Elyse Montpellier. It is a pleasure to make your acquaintance." She held out her hand.

Eva grasped it with both of her own. "The pleasure is all mine. Amber speaks very highly of you."

Elyse shook her head, smiling. "This girl always exaggerates with the compliments. She is just too nice."

"Elyse," said Amber, "you are so modest. You know very well how your talent for scouting great locations has played a monumental role in my life. It can't be denied."

Elyse laughed. "See, there you go again. Please follow me in. I think you will be quite impressed."

Before they walked in, Eva immediately noticed the majestic windows. Sunlight reflected onto the street, adding a warm glow to the sidewalk in front of the building. They entered the space and found themselves in an old bookstore. Many oakwood shelves lined the walls. A few hundred books still lingered, as if they had been left behind to ensure no one forgot the importance of printed text. A large desk took up the front area. Three rolling ladders, clearly used to reach the highest sections, confirmed the impressive height of the room. The ceiling extended at least fourteen feet, something rather rare in this part of town. A few tables and chairs made up the second half of the space. In the back, the room opened to a wider veranda. Suddenly, the true beauty of the location came to life.

Exquisite panels of glass formed the back wall, bringing in impressive amounts of natural light. As she approached, Eva had to adjust her eyes to see through them. The sight left her in awe. A gorgeous flower garden had been created with the utmost care. Pebbled rock paths curved through to the white fences on each side and the rear. Small cast-iron tables with outdoor chairs were positioned every few feet. The entire space had the look and feel of a European café. Eva knew they could not possibly find a more attractive terrace.

Amber walked over to Eva's side. "I didn't want to tell you over the phone as I hadn't seen it for myself. We didn't discuss the outdoor experience in our previous meetings, but I think you will agree, this gives us some great options."

Eva smiled, keeping her gaze straight ahead. "This is perfect. I could not have imagined a better location. And I definitely could not have envisioned such an amazing outdoor area. The potential is unlimited."

She turned and looked at Elyse. "I suppose I am ruining our negotiating position with the abundance of compliments?"

Elyse and Amber both laughed. "In fact, you have nothing to worry about," said Elyse. "The owner of the building is retiring. He closed down the bookstore only weeks ago. He owns several businesses and many real estate holdings. He has decided to move back to Italy and spend his days in the Tuscan sun. The decision happened quite suddenly, and he does not want to waste time leasing the space. I have been working with Amber for years, and the one thing she can count on with me is complete transparency. The deal on this space is very good. I know it is the first place you are visiting, but I can say with certainty it will go fast. This is not a pitch. That isn't the way I do business. With your idea in mind, it seems to be perfect timing."

Eva was having difficulty holding back her excitement. Luckily, Amber's face showed the same enthusiasm. They spent a few more minutes reviewing the leasing details and requirements.

Exiting the store, they bid farewell to Elyse and discussed the pros and cons in private. They had found a great spot—that could not be denied. Eva relied heavily on Amber's experience throughout the conversation. But she knew they had stumbled upon the perfect place. They agreed to give it twenty-four hours to sink in.

The next morning, only eighteen hours later, Amber and Eva agreed to sign the lease and begin work on the Port House, Gaia. Eva's dream was becoming a reality.

THE TIME HAS COME

It takes courage to grow up and become who you really are.
—E. E. Cummings, poet and playwright

S urroundings no longer mattered. Noises disappeared completely. Distractions melted away, consumed by the fire of focus. Life took on a different meaning in this state of mind. Thoughts of frustration and anxiety were overpowered by the flow of concentrated breathing. A refreshing wave of calm spread from head to toe. A sudden pang of joy followed by deeper inhalations. Air coming in through the nose, air imagined as bright white light cleansing the system. More air exiting, pushing away the black cloud of anger and negativity. Ethan felt alive as he opened his eyes.

His daily meditation sessions had increased in length over the past weeks. Twenty minutes were common both morning and night. Sometimes he made it to thirty. It had become a wonderful routine he could no longer live without. Everything felt right, as if it rebooted his entire system.

He had been working tirelessly on his speech every evening after work. His days at Premier were still being filled with mediocrity regardless of how hard he tried. Being alone with several interns made it impossible to succeed. A massive hole had been left by Robert's and Sasha's departures. He had spoken to Sasha a day earlier. She was now thriving at H&M, the large clothing retailer, as their head of marketing. Ethan never doubted her abilities.

He had chosen to throw himself into this Ravi-inspired journey and had now arrived at a new junction point. Tomorrow, he would be giving a keynote speech to over two hundred executives—none of whom had any clue who he was. He had expressed his anxiety to Ravi, but he had laughed off his concerns, telling him over and over to speak from the heart. The man certainly knew how to encourage and motivate. He had followed Ravi's advice and looked deep into his soul as he wrote line after line. After his initial reflection, the words began appearing effortlessly on his computer screen. And the more he wrote, the better it sounded.

Ravi had given him another piece of advice. He suggested Ethan watch YouTube clips of the world's greatest stand-up comedians. Not for him to bring the crowd to tears of laughter, but specifically for him to see their body language and confidence. This proved to be a wildly entertaining opportunity as Ethan absolutely loved watching stand-up artists do their thing. But he also realized after some footage that these individuals knew exactly how to play on the mood of the audience. Skillfully, they maneuvered their way through stories, often bringing back punch lines later in the segment and drawing the crowd back in.

Not wanting to limit himself to comedy only, Ethan also explored TED Talk videos where several of the world's best speakers presented various subjects of interest. Again, he could see common themes in the way these individuals interacted with their audience. It gave him much to think about. He had spent years presenting marketing ideas and business case studies, which could be considered public speaking. Yet the largest group he had ever spoken to was twenty. He knew on this occasion, he needed to be at the top of his game in a much different way.

After perfecting the entire speech to his liking, he proceeded with shortening each point or story to specific words and images. He knew the importance of entertaining the executives as much as getting his ideas across. It took several more hours of preparation, but in the end, he felt satisfied he had arrived at the best presentation he could create.

Ethan spent the balance of the evening practicing over and over. He videotaped himself to ensure any flaws could be corrected. He used the mirror as an audience, acting as if he were speaking to an actual person. Even Luca and Kayla were asked to give their opinions. They mostly laughed at their father, not able to take him seriously.

Putting away his notes, he spent another thirty minutes meditating, wanting large amounts of focus and energy for the big day. He planned on seizing the opportunity with every ounce of courage his body could summon.

***

Montreal's show district served as home to a famed location—Place Des Arts. A scene where the likes of Jerry Seinfeld had been welcomed on stage. The conference was taking place in a newly renovated room where everyone could interact freely and casually. Being given this privilege meant more to him than Ravi could know. Nothing had been accomplished yet. At this very moment, Ethan's name was simply text on paper. His legs could very well buckle. His throat could constrict and block any air from entering his body. He could faint. The negative thoughts crossed his mind only briefly. He worked on regaining his composure.

Arriving at 7:30 a.m., he was surprised to see the room already half full. Scores of well-dressed businesspeople were talking over eggs and orange juice. The clatter of waiters offering coffee and busboys clearing plates made him think of a bustling breakfast joint. Before he could observe any further, Julia greeted him, grabbing his hands with both of hers. "My dear Ethan, how nice to see you. Wow, you look very sharp."

He blushed. He had made a spectacular effort, going out and purchasing a new suit. Not to mention the shiny shoes. He wanted his appearance to compliment his speech. Or better yet, distract the audience. *If I look good, maybe they will remember I was that spiffy-looking fellow.*

"Thank you, Julia, it means a great deal to me. You seem to have this place rocking and rolling."

She smiled, looking at the crowd. "The turnout should be fantastic. And I hear you are giving an important talk."

"I am expected to say a few words. But I won't classify it as groundbreaking neuroscience. Just sharing some of the changes I have gone through as a person."

"Stop devaluing your experiences. People love success stories."

Ethan shook his head. "You are too kind Julia. But calling me an example of success is similar to comparing a person learning to skate with Sidney Crosby."

She looked at him with confusion. "I know nothing about this Sidney person. I am sure he is a tremendous figure skater. But don't sell yourself short. Think of what has happened over the past year." She still held his hands closely. "Come, I will get you seated. You must eat and build up some energy!"

She grabbed his arm and brought him to a table with one seat left. Then she left him.

The other seven individuals seated around him quickly made him feel comfortable. They were a talkative group. Each person introduced him or herself and explained what they did at Innovation Enterprises. Ethan immediately realized that these were sharp businesspeople from all over the world. Kimberly Strath ran sales for the entire European division. Carlos Martinez managed operations for Brazil and Argentina. Tobias Enroth was the human resources manager for the southwest U.S., the company's biggest territory. And on it went.

Although the friendliness helped, being surrounded by such high-achieving executives made Ethan feel very nervous. *What can I actually offer these people? They have accomplished more than I ever have. They can't learn from me.*

Ethan politely excused himself and headed for the restroom. Alone, he splashed cold water on his face and neck. He was sweating. Looking in the mirror, he questioned his ability to go through with the talk. A moment later, as if on cue, Ravi entered.

He stood next to him in the bathroom, not saying a word. He carried the slightest of smiles that did not reflect amusement but rather understanding. "My dear friend," Ravi whispered, "is something bothering you?"

Ethan nodded frantically. "I can't do this, Ravi! This is way over my head. I have never been on stage with hundreds of people looking at me. And I certainly did not know how important everyone in this room would be."

"Important how?"

"They are all top-level executives from around the globe. They have done great things in their careers I could only dream of!"

"This makes them superior or more significant than you?"

Ethan shrugged, shaking his head. "In a way, I do see it that way. I don't understand what they can gain from me."

Ravi nodded, his gaze transfixed on Ethan. "Let me ask you, have your children ever taught you anything powerful?"

Ethan just stared.

"Have you ever learned a lesson from a neighbour or friend? Do you remember gaining life experience by watching a complete stranger do the right thing? Was there ever a time when a colleague or coworker brought great insight to a project?"

Ethan stared.

"All of us can learn from each other, Ethan. That is the beauty of the world. If we open our eyes and hearts, knowledge will flow from anywhere and everywhere. We must be willing to listen. We must open our minds."

Ethan felt his shoulders relax.

"Last question," said Ravi. "Do you trust me?"

There was only one answer to that question. This man had opened a world of possibilities for Ethan. He owed him everything. "Of course, I do."

"Then have faith that your purpose today has true meaning, and you will make a difference in the lives of those wonderful people out there."

The tension eased. Nervousness still inhabited his body, but so did inspiration and belief. He needed to go out there and express his new way of thinking. Ravi had always given him the best advice. Why would that change now? He knew he could trust him. And the fact that Ravi was willing to put such faith in him gave him the necessary courage.

"Ethan, let's go outside." Ravi led the way, taking Ethan through a side exit. The sunlight blinded them for a few seconds, cool air filling their lungs. "Close your eyes and put your hands together. Feel the sensation of your fingertips gently touching each other. Lower your shoulders, listen to the sounds. Become mindful of the space you are in, understanding you are living an important moment in your life. Let go of any fear, any doubt you may foster. Simply believe. And breathe deeply."

Ethan sensed a calmness surround his being. His body tingled. After a few minutes, he opened his eyes. He knew he was ready.

As they entered the hall, Julia announced to the group they should make their way to the main conference area. The crowd hummed their approval and jostled their way to the adjacent room. Ravi directed Ethan to the side of the stage where the speakers for the day would share a table.

From where he sat, Ethan could comfortably see both the stage and the audience. The two hundred executives made quite an impression. The last few people made their way into the room, taking seats near the back. They were ready for the Leadership Summit.

As the crowd finally settled down, Ravi made his way to the stage. This was his zone, his element. He began speaking, and the audience immediately fell silent, mesmerized by his voice:

"What an honour it is for us to be hosting the Leadership Conference for the Executives of Innovation Enterprises. I have had the privilege in the past hour of meeting individuals from Peru, Holland, India, and even the ever-popular tourist destination of Little Rock, Arkansas."

The crowd laughed, undoubtedly enjoying the joke combined with Ravi's engaging speaking style.

"I believe there are many ways into a person's heart. You can shower them with love. Offering compliments also helps. But let us not forget another powerful strategy—that of giving. Under each chair is a book that in some way profoundly affected our team at the Leadership Institute. Have a look, and if you find yourself with something you have already read, please exchange it with one of your colleagues."

Everyone reached under their seats to retrieve the hidden token. Even Ethan put his hands under the chair and grasped the book from its position. He had in front of him Nelson Mandela's biography, *Long Walk to Freedom*. He had heard of the book and now felt excited to read it. He looked at the others to see what they had found. There was a mix of leadership books, novels, classics, and even spiritual guides. The woman sitting next to him had received Deepak Chopra's *Seven Spiritual Laws of Success*. To her left, a young man held *The Catcher in the Rye*. Across from Ethan, the executive from Holland leafed through Malcolm Gladwell's acclaimed book *Blink*.

Ethan peered over to the adjacent tables. It seemed almost every single person held a different type of book. It took him by surprise. He wondered if Ravi had actually read all of these books. But he knew the answer. What really impressed Ethan was the fact that Ravi and his team had procured so many different books for this event. Had the same book been given to everyone, it would have been easier to manage, but clearly not as exciting. Now, the executives from Innovation Enterprises were comparing their books and laughing in awe at the fact they all had a different one. A few people exchanged books, but not many given the originality of several titles.

"Our goal over the next two days is to refresh your minds and provide all of you with a new outlook on work-life balance. We do recognize that this can sometimes be interpreted as reducing one's work hours, taking more time off or going shopping for new shoes—my personal favorite. Strict directives have been sent from the big cheeses that we can have as much fun as we like, but in the end, each of you has to learn at least one valuable insight. And preferably it involves improving profitability by two hundred percent.

"It is a true honour to be spending this time with you. And we plan on making the most of it. As you have seen from the agenda, there are a number of incredible speakers that will stand up here and impress you over the next forty-eight hours. We have John Maxwell, author of *The 21 Laws of Leadership*. You will hear from Jack Daly, a man who could sell chocolate to Willy Wonka. And for inspiration purposes, we asked Cindy Klassen, winner of five Olympic medals to give us some words of wisdom. An impressive lineup, I must say. Would you agree?"

The crowd showed great enthusiasm and applauded wholeheartedly.

"To kick off the festivities, I have invited a personal friend to speak this morning. Some of you may have had a bite with him at breakfast. The man you will meet has not written any famous books. He isn't a professional speaker. He does not carry around a PhD. This person has done something rare and courageous. A thing some people dread and avoid at all costs. Something so difficult you must use every ounce of will power to accomplish. He *learned* to change.

"We have learned many things from each other. And he has confirmed the faith I have in people being able to accomplish great things. Please welcome him with the highest level of enthusiasm possible. Ethan Stone!"

The audience offered a thunderous round of applause. Ethan could feel his shoulders tense. His legs felt weak. The time had finally arrived. He had been preparing for this very moment for weeks. He had practiced with intensity and determination. He knew what he would speak about and the way he wanted to deliver his message. He still had doubts. *Why me?* The question he so often asked himself. But he also trusted Ravi. Completely. And with that in mind, he closed his eyes, took one final deep breath, and willed himself out of his seat.

He walked to the podium. Bright lights shone onto his face. He felt relieved he had been here the day before to practice. It made him feel less nervous. The first slide of his presentation was projected on the two large screens positioned on either side of the stage. Only four words: *The Power of Change.*

"It is an absolute privilege for me to be standing here today. I had the opportunity of meeting some wonderful people this morning at breakfast. A warmhearted and bright-minded team, to say the least. I was welcomed and treated like one of your own. I truly appreciate it.

"We all have a story. Every one of us has made decisions leading up to this day. Some we may regret. And that's okay. If we are lucky, we make more good ones than bad ones. In the end, what matters is how we learn to live our lives and how we treat those around us. That will be our legacy. Money is great, success is wonderful, but I don't believe these things will matter if we are not able to appreciate the people who love us day in, day out. That was my first lesson."

Ethan pressed the button on the clicker and pulled up the second slide. A picture of Luca and Kayla swimming in the ocean with Eva right behind them. The sun is shining, the sky is blue as can be, and the sand is golden.

"This is my family—a dream come true. I could not have asked for better. In fact, I would venture to say that most of you are thinking one thing right now: *boy, did he marry up.*

"Don't worry, I know. I have come to realize this shrine you see here does not compare to the model in the photo. But I swear that is my wife and children. I did not take that photo out of a magazine or photoshop it. I did pick one of the best family shots we have. Except for one problem. I am not in the picture. And that would be fine if I was taking the shot. But I wasn't. I was at work that entire weekend preparing for a pitch that never had a chance. But I made my decision and must live with it.

"That is not the point of this story, although it could be. What is much worse and hard to believe now is that, when I got home that Sunday night and my children came running to me with excitement and joy, wanting to tell me about the incredible weekend they had with their mom at the beach, I immediately brushed them off and eventually ordered them to bed because they were making too much noise.

"I would like you to imagine this scenario for just a second: Two children have spent a weekend away from their father. With their mother acting as a single parent during that time, they make the most of it by enjoying the weather and the shore. They come home and have a million things to tell Daddy. And as they try, their father grunts angrily and tells them to stop the racket, instantaneously ruining the entire mood and essentially ending the evening on the worst possible note. And by natural consequence, losing the opportunity to speak with his wife because now she is quite understandably frustrated and tired too. Sadly, that is how I spent most of my time.

"Then one day, I met a man of great wisdom. He may or may not be in this room. I was meant to offer this man the services of the company I work for. In a reversal of roles, it is I who became the willing student of his life philosophy. Knowing him now for over a year, I can surmise he does not want me to spend time complimenting him. Let me instead explain to you what he suggested."

The next slide showed the word *Breathe*.

"By a show of hands, how many people here meditate regularly?"

Only a dozen hands in the room went up.

"Meditation saved my life. It changed the way I act, the way I speak, and most importantly, the way I treat those around me. When stress rears its ugly head, it is very difficult to ignore it. We become mad, angry, and this will in some way be expressed outwardly. But when we learn to meditate, we achieve something deeper. Our mind begins to understand the root cause of the possible trigger. And then certain questions arise. We ask ourselves why a certain situation would cause tension. We can feel our emotions and wonder how something could spiral out of control when it is not life-threatening or dangerous. Essentially, we learn how to differentiate the important from the mundane. In this separation lies the key to happiness.

"Learning to meditate is, in itself, another presentation we won't have time for today. And let's be honest, there are much better teachers or books out there that will serve you better than I ever could in understanding the process. My message is simple: Please try it. Just take ten minutes every morning and every night for the next week and meditate. I promise you it will change everything. Stressful situations will become small obstacles easily surmounted. Anger and frustration will be replaced by patience and acceptance. The realization that life is too short and must be appreciated to its fullest will surface above all else. In essence, it will change your entire outlook in a wonderfully positive way."

Pressing the clicker, Ethan brought forth the next slide to the screens. It showed a photograph of two women at a table. The first seemed to be talking quite animatedly. She sat at the edge of her seat, and her hands were in a busy position in the air. The second woman had her eyes glued to a smartphone, her mouth wide open in a yawn.

"Growing up, my mother was always a wonderful listener. Whether I wanted to talk about sports, spaceships, or video games, she took the time to truly listen to every word I had to say, always showing great patience. She also took the time to explain to me how important the act of listening is. It is one of the few ways to gain complete trust from those around us. It seems like the easiest thing to do. But I think most of us here know how difficult it really is. There are distractions all around us. Those times when we are at our desk and a colleague wants to talk to us. They come in and start describing an issue. But our screen is open with several emails needing attention. We try to listen, but we are constantly glancing back at the computer. And we think the person doesn't notice!

"One experience that has always stayed with me happened during my days at Concordia University. I was working on a project with a classmate. After a few hours, we went to lunch to take a short break. I was having a rough week. I had found out that very morning that my cousin was diagnosed with lung cancer. It was obviously on my mind.

"Eventually, my classmate asked me if all was good because she may have sensed my distress. I began telling her the story. We were suddenly interrupted by a waiter. After explaining the specials and taking our orders, the waiter left. I was ready to continue my story when this class-mate moved on to discuss their upcoming weekend plans.

"I was floored. Had she even been hearing me? I was describing a deeply personal and important issue. I couldn't believe it. I felt hurt and frustrated. That lesson taught me the true importance of listen-ing. It requires effort with tons of practice. I encourage you to be very conscious the next time you are speaking with someone. Are you giving this person the attention they deserve? Are you focused on their every word, oblivious to the things happening around you? Take a moment, and you will be surprised how much difference this will make in earning the trust of those you spend time with. And from my experience, time is worth much more than we realize."

Ethan brought forward the next slide that summarized the ideas he had learned from Ravi:

"Self-renewal → Self-acceptance → Self-confidence."

"In essence, the words you see before you express the way I learned to change and be a better person. Meditation allowed me to renew my inner being. It cleansed the negativity, the judgment, and made room for much-needed clarity. Once I made this realization, I began to accept my flaws, understand my frustrations, and move past them. No one is perfect. Accepting—embracing who we are—is such a crucial step to achieving our potential. And when we accomplish this, we are filled with self-confidence and belief. Nothing can stop us. Time to step up and become a highly productive member of society. No longer being afraid of taking the high road. Treating others with such refreshing warmth that their only response can be positive reciprocity, or Circular Reciprocation, as Ravi taught me. These small changes made my life exponentially better, and I think it can work for everyone without exception.

"Having cleared my mind and created a fresh slate to work with, I needed to take my physical situation to a whole new level. I am describing pushing our bodies to a place they have not been before. Not overnight, but quickly enough because it is infinitely important. Without the body at full speed, the mind can only go so far. By conditioning the body to become stronger and full of endurance, the mental tasks we take on become easier. Stamina is both emotional and physical. One without the other is not enough. I started running in the morning. One or two days a week. Not long distances at first. I was sucking wind, gasping for air, questioning the reason for torturing myself. But then, after a few weeks, it got better. Things turned in the right direction. I could cover more ground. Still nothing to put in the record books, but certainly a solid improvement.

"Eventually, I got to ten miles without flinching. It felt great. I was going at a steady pace and had achieved what could be described as a respectable fitness level. I was working toward a goal, toward a challenge that had been thrown my way."

Then *26.2 miles* appeared on the screen.

"Most of you recognize this number or have heard about it. I am also sure some of you have attained this elusive distance. I congratulate every one of you. For those not as familiar, this number represents a full marathon distance. When I was first encouraged to run a marathon, I laughed. I laughed hard. In fact, I truly thought it was a joke. And yet, once I reviewed the training, I decided it could be achieved. Every week, you cover a little more ground. No crazy jumps, rather a steady buildup. It made sense. And I started to believe I could do it.

"I was also promised that completing a marathon would change me. It would bring me confidence. It would take me out of my comfort zone by pushing me to a new place of perseverance and determination I never knew I could achieve. I was promised a deep sense of accomplishment that would create an ever-lasting memory that I would carry with me for life. Today, I can say with absolute certainty, it did exactly that.

"What I can tell you is this. Whether you enjoy running, biking, swimming, snow-shoeing, or mountain climbing, the goal remains the same. Take on a physical challenge you honestly don't think you can accomplish today. Break self-imposed barriers. Triathlon, Spartan Race, conquering a mountain, all are relevant. But it must be quite difficult to achieve, where the only option is to seriously dedicate yourself to the challenge. Today, it must seem almost unattainable. Something you may scoff at or explain how it is for other people, not you.

"Once you pick this challenge, you research it. Look it up, get the details, and begin to understand what it would take for you to succeed. You will quickly discover that many people just like you have taken a similar journey. You will learn that the training is not that crazy. It won't be easy, but it won't be the end of you. It will require a certain number of hours a week—which typically translates to about an hour a day.

"Let's think about that for a second. In a wonderful twenty-four-hour day, it will take four percent of your time. I spend at least that amount of time on Facebook or reviewing my fantasy football team. It does not equate to a very large time commitment. Once you start, you won't look back. Your body will transform, as will your mind. Slowly but surely, your energy will rise to teenage-like levels. And best of all, you will forget life before training. That is my suggestion, one that I can honestly state will have a huge impact on your life.

"When running my marathon last year, I had the incredible privilege of accomplishing the entire training and race with my wife, Eva. She wanted to take on the same challenge, and it brought us so much closer together in a time we needed it most. I can stand here today and say with absolute certainty that running a marathon saved my marriage."

He had not planned on saying the last sentence. It meant the world to him, but it was also a deeply private thought. Somehow, he felt caught up in the moment. It came out naturally, and now he was happy being able to share his personal experience with such a diverse and attentive audience. Several heads in the room were nodding, as if most people understood that the ability to find common ground during a difficult time in a relationship could often work magic. Ethan did not feel judged in the least. He would not have cared either way. He had spoken the truth. By acknowledging the power of the commitment, he and Eva had made to accomplish a lofty goal together, and they had essentially gone all in. And they had succeeded.

He brought up a picture on the screen. It depicted a stylishly renovated façade of a trendy bar.

"I learned a very interesting philosophy during my time at the Elevation Leadership Institute. Their team has been using a concept made popular by author Matthew Kelly. It consists of helping employees achieve their dreams. The idea is simple yet powerful. You put a Dream Manager in place who will take the time with you to figure out what you want to achieve. Maybe it is saving for a family vacation. Perhaps you want to buy a new car. Or you want to become better at public speaking. It can be anything you need help in attaining. The Dream Manager helps you discover the best way to accomplish this goal. The mission is to assist you in making your dreams a reality.

"I was offered another way of looking at this amazing concept. Changing the format, the aim, was to help someone in my personal entourage in pursuing their dream. I decided to try it. You see, Eva is an incredible chef. I have the privilege of tasting truly wonderful dishes on a daily basis at home. I know, I can see the jealousy on your faces. It is a rare opportunity to have access to such amazing cuisine at any given moment. I am blessed.

"As Eva was preparing to pursue a career in her field of expertise, an accident happened—our son Luca. A spectacular moment in our lives. Eva didn't see much choice at that time. She wanted to dedicate herself to our son. Next thing you know, little Kayla arrives. All of a sudden, we are young parents with two very active children running around. I am working to make ends meet, and Eva has given herself entirely to our family. Sacrificed her career with no regrets. She enjoyed it. Everything but the sleepless nights. The children have since grown up. They are more independent. Not paying rent or anything but entertaining themselves a few minutes here and there and going to school. All of it led to Eva wanting to start something of her own. Seeing and knowing her talent, I wanted to help her in making this possible. We used some resources, and we had tons of help along the way."

He looked again at Ravi and nodded in thanks.

"The next thing you know, Eva is preparing a business plan and meeting with a successful restaurateur. They meticulously planned the details, found a great location as you can see on the screen, and pursued the opportunity. They plan on opening their 'port house' within a month. *Gaia* is the name they chose.

"Throughout the process, I tried to provide Eva with unconditional support. When she questioned herself, I reinforced her ability to make it happen. When she worried about the financial details, we took a few hours and broke down the numbers to ensure they made sense. I knew how badly she wanted this. But I also understood that her selflessness may work against her in this situation. She didn't want to put her family at risk, financially or emotionally, by taking on a new venture. It is, after all, a demanding proposition to launch a new business. But after discussing together, she came to realize that waiting any longer would only delay the inevitable. 'When will the time be right?' we asked ourselves?

"This is how dream facilitation works. I am confident everyone in this room is close to someone with a vision, an idea. Most of the time, this is labelled as unattainable. Imagine a different scenario where you could help your brother save up for the car he always wanted. Think of the look on your best friend's face when you get her an interview for that perfect job. Picture the conversation with your father when you travel to Europe with him for the first time.

"All of us have the power to facilitate a loved one's dream. The real question is if we are willing to put in the time and effort. It is about personal dedication and the ability to put someone else ahead of your own agenda. Easier said than done, but very much possible with the right state of mind."

Ethan pressed the clicker, sending the next slide on the screens. The following word appeared, *Forgiveness.*

"To forgive. To offer a person a second chance when they have hurt you so badly it seems nothing will be right again. I have often been too stubborn to accept another's mistake if it had affected me negatively. By holding on to resentment, we are only punishing ourselves. My inability to forgive has caused serious problems in my life. I am only now understanding this and trying to follow a new path.

"I am currently living through the deepest family challenge of my life. I would like to share this story with you before I leave the stage.

"You see, my father, Francis Stone, never knew how to be a father. We had food in our bellies and a roof over our heads. But he didn't acknowledge us in any way. No affection of any sort. Never a word of encouragement. He would almost flinch when I tried showing him my love, the innocent way kids do. Living through this as a boy brought about a world of confusion. It eliminated an important bond I believe a father and child must share. We had no connection whatsoever. My amazing mother did what she could, but she worked long hours at the hospital and could only do so much for our family. She also had to deal with my father and his many mistakes.

"As the years went by, my father developed a bad drinking habit. He needed the alcohol on a daily basis, and this made our situation even worse. My mother tried helping him fight the addiction, but he wanted nothing of it. On the day of my wedding engagement, my father arrived at the brunch with another woman on his arm. He had done the unthinkable. He cheated on my mother, completely severing any trust they had left. He was completely intoxicated. I was utterly disgusted. I will never forget the pain I witnessed in my mother's eyes that day. She looked…defeated. Her world had crumbled. She asked my father to leave. And he did. He left, and we never saw him again. I was relieved in many ways. I knew I couldn't stand the sight of seeing him after his betrayal. I had no idea where he had gone.

"My mother died not long after that episode. She passed away much before her time. I believe my father broke her heart. It played heavily on her soul. She was never able to truly move on. Unfortunately, she never met her grandchildren. I always speak to them about this wonderful woman who cared for me with all her heart. I want her spirit to be remembered.

"A few months ago, by complete fluke, my friend Robert met my father at a local hospital. I know it sounds crazy, but it happened. Robert then proceeded to call me and tell me about this chance encounter. Please keep in mind Robert had no idea of the complexity of the relationship and the history behind it all.

"After contemplating for a few days, I decided to meet my father. I had incredible anger built up. Truthfully speaking, I went to this meeting with the goal of lambasting this man who had caused so much pain to our family. I was determined to call him by his first name, not wanting to give him undue respect. I thought of the many horrible words I would use, the specific examples I would bring up to hurt him. I wanted him to acknowledge his unforgivable actions.

"When we met face-to-face, most of my frustration disappeared. There sat a lonely, sick man, who had paid for his sins many times over. I realized at that moment how forgiveness would be the only way for both of us to move on. I have, little by little, let my father back into our lives. He has now met his grandchildren. I have spent quality time with him. We have started creating a bond that never existed in the past. I could still blame him for all the hurt. But to what end? There was an opportunity to forgive, and it allowed us to start again. It is never too late. He apologized profusely, knowing and understanding the consequences of his actions. He has shown remorse. It took many years for this to happen, but I am happy it has come to be. We are taking the next step in our journey together.

"The past few minutes took you through my journey. Things have changed. I have changed. I have grown as a person, thanks to the selfless support of people without any agenda. True givers. In the end, it isn't about money, fame, or success. It is about happiness. Being happy is not a consequence of another person's actions. It isn't the by-product of gaining material goods or getting a promotion. Happiness is a choice. We have the privilege of being here, of being alive. This incredible privilege is taken for granted. We owe it to ourselves and those around us to take the path less travelled, to strive for more. It will make a difference in your life. And I know all of you can make a difference in this world.

"Thank you for being here, listening to my story. I can only hope it has given you some learning, some inspiration to follow your heart and know you deserve to *grow plus lead plus be happy.*"

The audience applauded thunderously, shouting warm words of encouragement and praise.

He realized then and there that this was one of the best moments of his entire life. He would never forget this day. He would never forget all that Ravi had done for him. Somehow, he would find a way to pay it back. He walked off the stage to more applause. Something important had changed. He felt a level of gratitude he had never experienced before. He recognized what it meant to be accomplishing his goals. He wanted to share this moment with his loved ones. He couldn't wait to get home to celebrate with his family.

KARMA

Life will give you whatever experience is most helpful for the evolution of your consciousness. How do you know this is the experience you need? Because this is the experience you are having at the moment.
—Eckhart Tolle, spiritual teacher and author

⌒

*H*e lay in bed smiling. Eva slept peacefully next to him. He softly kissed her cheek, not wanting to wake her. Going to his favorite corner in the bedroom, he started stretching peacefully.

His thoughts returned to two days earlier. Speaking in front of a large crowd had always been a dream. It had now come true. He had no idea if his message had come across the right way, but getting up there and showing vulnerability had been the true goal. He had achieved another important milestone with Ravi's help. The man never ran out of ways to help Ethan grow. They had a meeting scheduled later that morning. Ethan had now used up every one of his vacation days, and the workload back at Premier Marketing was piling up. He would need to get back there soon. But his level of motivation at his current job couldn't be any lower. His entire life had changed in a wonderful way, except for his work life. That daunting obstacle remained. He wanted to move on but didn't know where to start. His entire career had been spent at Premier.

He ate with his family, showering them with love. While the children played, he listened attentively to Eva and her update on the Gaia Port House. They would visit on the weekend to review the project's progress. Shockingly, their contractor was ahead of schedule and close to completing the entire project. After another few weeks, they would be ready to open. They were now fully focused on logistics, with Amber's experience leading the way in the recruiting department.

Finishing up, he got ready and left for the Elevation Leadership Institute in the best of moods.

***

Ethan no longer needed to wait at the front desk. He still took the time to speak with Julia. He had developed a wonderful relationship with the warmhearted woman.

The Elevation Leadership Institute was buzzing this morning. People filled all the glass-walled offices and conference rooms. Ethan recognized many faces and realized several executives from Innovation Enterprises had stayed an extra day to run through some creative exercises, no doubt wanting to better themselves. It always impressed him how the best companies invested in their people. He secretly wished his employer felt the same way. He didn't dwell on the thought.

Walking over to Ravi's office, he found him speaking on the phone. He smiled, waving Ethan in. "The theory is based on hiring only the very best players in the industry. It will become significantly longer to find the right people, but once in place, these new team members will have such a major impact on your business, they will be worth every penny and then some. When you are ready to review your hiring practices, just give me a call. I am always available. I look forward to hearing from you. Say hi to the team for me." He put down the receiver. "Sorry to keep you waiting, my good man. How are you on this fine morning?"

"I must say, I am feeling refreshed," said Ethan. "I truly enjoyed every moment of that speech. I want to thank you. I know it sounds cheesy, but it was a dream come true. I could not have imagined I would be given such an important opportunity. I deeply appreciate your trust—well beyond my capacity to show the sincere gratitude it deserves."

"My dear Ethan, I didn't expect such a profound response to something you absolutely earned on your own. You only have yourself to thank."

"I wish that were the case. I have changed a few things in my life, but it hardly merited being put on a grand stage in front of an impressive group of people. You gifted me in a way I still cannot fully grasp."

Ravi smiled. "I trusted in your ability to convey an important message. And you did just that. In a very commendable way, I would add."

"Thank you," said Ethan. "It means a lot to hear that. But I cannot let this go. I have thought about it for weeks now, well before the conference. Ever since you asked me to speak. I took the time to recall our first meeting and the way you asked for me, by name. I thought back to the time you spent with me, sharing your philosophies, mentoring me when I needed it most. Then you introduced Eva to an inspiring entrepreneur and helped them forge a partnership where she could pursue her dreams. And finally, the conference. Throughout our relationship, you have made my life that much better and provided me with wisdom, friendship, and shared experiences. Always giving. Considering you do this for a living, I am at a loss for the reason you have dedicated your precious time in maximizing my personal growth. I am missing something here. I know I am. As a friend, because I do believe we have become friends, please tell me where all this is coming from. I need to know."

Ravi stared at Ethan for a few seconds with an almost imperceptible hint of bemusement. He then walked over to his desk and removed a thick envelope. He placed it on the desk in front of Ethan. "Before you open that envelope, let me tell you a story." He moved to his red sofa and gestured for Ethan to join him on the opposite chair.

"I came to Canada fourteen years ago. I remember the day perfectly. The long flight from India had left me tired and restless. I was coming to a new place with very few dollars and no friends or family. I struggled mightily at first. It was to be expected. But being alone in a new country was very rough. And the cold winters! My engineering degree didn't hold much weight here. I eventually found work on the assembly line in a small lighting company. Not the most motivating of jobs, but a start nonetheless. I eventually made some friends. More importantly, I met Daniella. What a vision. I still don't understand how I got her to come on that first date with me."

Ethan knew how charming Ravi could be. He let him continue, not wanting to interrupt the story.

"We became very close and moved in together rather quickly. Daniella didn't have much family, so we turned to each other for companionship. So much love but still the hardships of low-paying employment

227

and barely making a living. We lived in a tiny apartment in Verdun. It was very difficult. One day, during the holidays, something happened that changed my perspective. In fact, this event sparked a motivation that has led me here today. The answer lies in that envelope." He shifted his gaze to the mysterious package. "Open it."

Ethan felt unsure. He slowly picked up the brown envelope and opened it. Inside, he found *As a Man Thinketh* by James Allen. It looked very familiar. He himself had read the book and loved its simple yet powerful messages. But there was more to it. He opened the first page. A note was written: *Times may seem tough right now. Keep your head up and never stop believing. There is always more to come. Eva and Ethan.*

Ethan sat there, paralyzed. It was Eva's handwriting, no doubt. He looked at the cover again. After a few moments of reflection, the memory flooded his senses. "We gave this to someone a long time ago. It is coming back to me now. But how…why do you have it? I don't understand."

Ravi laughed, clasping Ethan on the shoulder. "Let me recount the story as it happened from my perspective. He sat up, facing Ethan directly.

"As I mentioned, Daniella and I were very low on resources. We worked hard but were barely making ends meet. I knew we could do so much more. That being said, we needed to survive on a day-to-day basis. I swear I never imagined myself asking for charity in this world. But the day came where we needed a helping hand. We went to the local foundation, Always Together, which you know very well. We put our name on the list to receive the Christmas grocery basket. I got home feeling embarrassed. But Daniella was already pregnant and had to take time off work for her appointments. It was difficult. I decided we must accept it for one year and then make every effort to pull ourselves out of that situation.

"I sent Daniella away on that cold day. I couldn't imagine her facing any person coming to give us charity. We didn't know what to expect. We imagined some cocky, stuck-up people showing up and making us feel small. You see, our mentality was backward. Even though we knew any person coming that day had spent hundreds of dollars for our benefit, we decided they were going to bring a bourgeois attitude. We were dead wrong." He smiled warmly at Ethan. "That is the moment you and Eva arrived at our door with six large bags of food and two wonderful gifts for both of us."

Ethan looked down at his hands in disbelief. He was thinking back to his first meeting with Ravi at the Elevation Leadership Institute. He knew he recognized him from somewhere. It now made complete sense. "I don't know what to say. You looked very different fourteen years ago."

Ravi clasped Ethan's hands. "You and Eva came that day and showed us unbelievable kindness and respect. Bringing food and gifts and even taking the time to write a personalized message. You shook my hand and wished me the best during the holiday season. Eva even asked me about my background and origins. Both of you made me feel like a human being, not a charity case. And it made a huge difference. I read the book. I recounted to friends and family what you had done. It played a huge part in getting me where I am today. It gave me faith in the world again and confidence in myself. You see, Ethan, your generosity made a massive impact in my life."

Ethan sat in stunned silence. He had no words. His mind still trying to process the information. It seemed surreal. For this story to come full circle surpassed any expectations he ever had about the way the world worked. "Why didn't you tell me?"

"I was always going to tell you eventually," answered Ravi. "I thought it important to allow our relationship to develop and find a way to repay you. What I came to realize instead is that you are a very impressive individual, and you have truly become a great friend over the past year. I know you enjoy thanking me, but the truth is that you have taught me a great deal of important things, most notably that change is possible."

Ethan still had difficulty processing their conversation. "Ravi, you have changed my life. Honestly, without your help, I may be divorced right now. You helped save my marriage. You taught me to listen to my loved ones. Through your teachings, I have learned patience and forgiveness. Both of which have allowed me to recover from a deeply painful relationship with my father. I had lost my way over the past years. I owe you my entire happiness."

"Nonsense! I showed you another way, but you walked the path and took charge of turning words into action. I will not take credit for that. In the end, let us celebrate our relationship and be happy that both of us are following our dreams. To a certain extent."

"What do you mean to a certain extent?"

"I will ask you a simple question. I do not mean to be judgmental. I am looking for an honest answer. Are you living your life's passion by working at Premier Marketing? What the company has become today?"

Ethan did not hesitate. "No, I am not. I dread going to work and use all the other good things in my life to motivate me to go in and make an honest living."

"That is what I feared. And yet I do see other interesting options for you. One that is closer than you realize."

Ethan's curiosity was piqued. "What do you mean?"

"We have arrived at a very interesting place, Ethan. I am impressed with the increase in your leadership skills over the past months. Your work ethic and loyalty are unquestionable. It has led me to identify you as the type of key executive most companies desire and search for every single day."

"Ravi," laughed Ethan, "you need to stop boosting my ego!"

"Take it as you will, it is a fact. And it is the reason I am going to make you an offer."

Ethan stared at Ravi, unsure of what he meant. "An offer? What kind of an offer?"

"It is no secret I believe in your abilities. And I have had the opportunity to witness your growth into a truly complete individual full of passion and excitement. That is why I want you to become the Vice-President of Marketing here at the Elevation Leadership Institute."

Ethan was speechless. He could not understand what was happening. The past hour seemed more hallucination than reality. A good deed he and Eva did almost fifteen years ago had brought forth Karma as he had never experienced it before. And now he was being offered his dream job.

"Ravi, I don't know what to say. I came here this morning expecting us to recap the conference and schedule a run together. Instead, I find out we have a meaningful connection, and you offer me the chance of a lifetime. I am not sure how this is even possible. I am afraid I will wake up and won't actually be living this moment."

"You made this moment happen, Ethan. It is not a gift or a way to thank you. This company needs a person with your talent and work ethic. I have a strong track record of hiring top performers. I have every expectation you will help our team in taking this business to a new level of success. And we will have fun doing it. I suggest you accept my offer, and we can start planning the next steps in your professional journey. There will be actual work to do. It's not just fun and games, you know!"

Ethan laughed. Both men got up and shook hands. Then Ethan grabbed Ravi and hugged him. "Thank you, Ravi. I appreciate everything you have done for me and my family. I will do everything in my power to prove your decision is the right one."

"I have not a doubt in my mind," said Ravi. "Just remember, I believe in you, and I know you will accomplish great things."

Ethan left in a state of mind he had rarely ever felt before in his entire life.

Complete happiness.

DELIVERANCE

I understood myself only after I destroyed myself. And only in the process of fixing myself, did I know who I really was.
—Sade Andria Zabala, author and poet

S everal bottles of vodka, rum, and gin lined the kitchen counter. A circle of close friends was in attendance. Ravi stood close by, as did Ethan and Eva. For his part, Robert Samuels had the look of a man willing to take a leap of faith.

He knew the consequences alcohol had brought into his life. Lost opportunities, mistreated loved ones, and a very close brush with death. It seemed so simple to most people. Just stop drinking. To go cold turkey. If it were that easy, he would have stopped years ago. But the addiction ate at him day and night. He had finally admitted, after so many years of abuse, that he had a serious problem. Robert confessed to Ethan he had been drinking on the clock at Premier Marketing. He had spent more time under the influence than not over the past five years. He even suspected his impatience with his mother's condition could be attributed to his own addiction, not her illness.

The past months had opened his eyes to many things, not the least of which was the need to take responsibility for his actions. Ravi had helped him realize this, although deep down, he already knew. Only he could move forward and make the right decisions. And he was prepared to do exactly that. There were many tough nights filled with cold sweats and anxiety, but in the end, he had persevered. His network of close supporters had played a massive role, one he would never forget.

He had to exorcise his demons. He took the first bottle, slowly. As a recovered alcoholic and absolutely frugal man, it pained him to see the full bottle go to waste down the drain. But he knew the power of the gesture lay in the symbolism of the act. Without this, all was pointless.

He continued until all eleven bottles were completely empty. It took several minutes as his friends watched closely. Everyone understood what this day meant to Robert. He had worked hard to get here. Alcoholics Anonymous, counseling, and sessions working with Ravi. It gave Robert such a heightened level of confidence, he now felt he could tackle anything. Which was exactly what he was doing this very evening. Changing his world and giving himself a clean slate.

He made a vow, then and there, to never touch a drop of alcohol again. And he knew at that moment, he would succeed. Addiction would not beat him again. Ever.

BELIEVE AND THEY WILL COME

The moment you doubt whether you can fly, you cease for ever to be able to do it.
—J. M. Barrie, creator of *Peter Pan*

*I*t could not have been a more beautiful day. The sun was nearing its bedtime, its rays of light shimmering over the city. People filled the streets of downtown Montreal, bringing with them a vibrancy only experienced in spring. It was difficult to walk amid such thick crowds.

A huge pack of excited customers gathered around the entrance of the highly anticipated new hotspot. Opening night had finally arrived. It had been months in the making, years in thoughtful conception. A dream becoming reality before their very eyes. The sign above the door read GAIA.

A team of well-trained staff members bustled around the Gaia Port House, ensuring everything looked perfect. Eva and Amber were busy themselves, preparing the final touches they knew would make all the difference. It still seemed impossible. Ideas were put on paper. Concepts were imagined. But to see they had arrived at the moment where their hard work would be presented to the world was hard to believe. Eva couldn't contain her excitement. Amber, being a far more seasoned restaurateur, showed a touch more composure. Tonight would be very special. It felt right. A time for celebration.

Both Kayla and Luca sat at a table close by, folding napkins. They were too young to understand the true meaning of the event, yet they were definitely caught up in the moment. They could see the joy on their mother's face, and that made them smile.

Ethan stood behind the bar, preparing the tasting samples of various port wines. He was observing the scene in awe. Eva had accomplished something wonderful. The last months had been filled with late-night meetings. He had taken a more prominent role at home with his children. This had been another positive step for him, spending time with his daughter and son. For the first time in his life, he had taken the time to truly be with them. Reading books, playing board games, pillow fights—he had done it all. Above all else, he had listened to them with unwavering patience. It made him realize how little material things such as toys or gifts mattered to them. Kayla and Luca didn't care about that. They never had. For them, spending time with their parents meant more than the world. A new bond had formed. These were moments to be cherished forever. He promised to never let work ever get in the way of his most important priority—his family.

His thoughts were interrupted by a stunningly dressed Eva approaching him. "Where is your mind at?" she asked, hugging him.

He kissed her and held her for a moment before answering. "With you, with the kids, with this incredible place. I am still trying to get my head around it. I always believed it possible. But to witness your dreams come true is beyond my imagination. I have never seen you happier. It is such an amazing feeling."

Eva looked at him, tears welling in her eyes. "Thank you. You inspired me to do this. I don't think I could have moved forward without the support you gave me. You know, for a time, I didn't think we were going to make it. I questioned our commitment to each other. Life had become so negative. But now, everything has changed. You and I have both come a long way." Eva grabbed Ethan's face softly, kissing him on the lips. The kids shouted their annoyance at the public display of affection.

It was time to open the doors and welcome their guests. The place looked perfect. An array of cheeses, cured meats, and delectable desserts filled every table. They wanted the experience on this opening night to be unique. Every person would leave with a set of two port glasses bearing the GAIA logo. Their staff members were trained for hours on end in customer experience. Both Amber and Eva cared deeply about the need to always offer exceptional treatment to their patrons. This would serve as their primary objective above all else, for they knew that even great food and port wouldn't keep annoyed customers around.

Amber had used her various contacts in attracting some very key food and wine critics. She also invited a few reporters she knew to attend the opening festivities. They had a well-known DJ playing groovy beats in the corner of the room. The atmosphere was electric.

Amber and Eva made their way to the front door. A large red ribbon was draped from end to end, waiting to be cut. They greeted the now applauding crowd from the inside.

"Thank you all for coming on this beautiful spring evening," said Amber confidently to the crowd. "We have worked hard to bring you a new type of place, somewhere you can come and experience unique culinary creations made from the heart. Montreal has never seen a port house before. We hope you will be both surprised and comforted at once. Your utmost satisfaction will always be our goal. And to guarantee this will happen, I am honored to introduce the true mastermind behind this entire idea—my business partner, Eva!"

A loud round of applause and whistles took Eva aback. She had not expected such a warm introduction from Amber or such a reaction from the crowd. It felt spectacular. Amber smiled at Eva warmly, encouraging her to address the throng of family, friends, media, and customers.

"I want to truly thank all of you for being here. Your support means more than can be said in a simple speech. I am a very privileged person. I have thought many years about different opportunities in the food industry. Many ideas scribbled down but never taken seriously. Then I met a few important people who had faith and made me realize we must follow our hearts.

"Amber, what an incredible inspiration you are! Always finding solutions and ways of getting things done. I thank you." Amber waved away the praise, shaking her head with a smile. The crowd cheered. "Ravi," said Eva, finding him towering near the back, "your belief in all that is good made this possible. Not to mention your ability to make a person feel like a million dollars. I thank you." More applause, as Ravi grinned and nodded ever so slightly. "Mom, Dad, Ethan, Luca, and Kayla," continued Eva, her voice wavering a little, "your patience and dedication have been well beyond what I could ever deserve. To be blessed with such an exceptional family will never be taken for granted."

Eva took out a large pair of scissors and pulled Amber toward her. Together, with smiles spreading cheek to cheek, they cut the red ribbon as the crowd cheered them on. Both had to work very hard to prevent letting tears of joy ruin their makeup.

They had finally done it. Together, with the help of many others. From a simple thought, they had arrived at a very unpredictable destination. A place where Eva could express her every culinary desire and truly experience that which she had searched for her entire life. She felt completely enthralled. As if the stress of the world had suddenly disappeared and all she could imagine was the brightest future ever. She knew this chance was a privilege. Eva would work her very hardest to make this a success. It was the only way to thank her loved ones for their support and sacrifices.

PERSONAL DEMONS

It is better to conquer yourself than to win a thousand battles. Then the victory is yours. It cannot be taken from you, not by angels or by demons, heaven or hell.
—Buddha

They sat quietly in the airport lounge. Ethan leafed through a *Men's Fitness* magazine. Francis stared quietly out of the window, observing the planes taxiing back and forth. Words came at a premium as both men felt the stress of their voyage on their minds.

Normally, a father-and-son trip to Ireland would be a wonderful opportunity to catch up and visit some great sites while taking in draught beer. But this was no ordinary situation. They were now only forty-eight hours away from the one-year deadline set by the infamous banshee. Ethan still had serious doubts about his father's story. Pure fantasy. But Francis had spoken with such fervor and emotion, relating precious details that rang true to Ethan's ears. Still, how to justify believing in such folklore voodoo? It didn't make sense. He would find out sooner than later.

That was the main reason for Ethan's concern. He needed there to be some truth to the story. His father expressed unwavering belief in the entire string of events, down to the very last detail. There was no doubt in his mind of what had occurred. To Ethan, this could only mean two things. Either Francis was, very unfortunately, losing his complete sense of reality. Or something strange had indeed happened twelve months ago that could not be explained by any normal thought process. Neither scenario gave him comfort. But deep down, he did hope he would meet this instigator of his father's change. He knew it wasn't possible. He didn't believe in this stuff. But he was going to support his father no matter what.

An announcement prompted them to make their way to their departure gate. Ethan gently shook his father's shoulder, waking him from his plane-staring daze. "Are you ready?"

His father looked up at him, showing a strained smile. "Yes, my son."

***

They checked into their Dublin hotel following an uneventful flight. Both men were tired from the jet lag and decided to crash for a few hours. As his head hit the pillow, Ethan felt the energy drain away from him and instantly fell asleep.

His dreams were filled with bizarre images. At first, he was running through a forest filled with headless bodies chasing him. He was barely managing to stay away from them before suddenly falling down a massive hole. It woke him suddenly for a few minutes. Later, he found himself walking up a dark, narrow staircase. Reaching the confined space at the top, he looked out upon a vast, lifeless grey tundra. Then he heard a deep growling and turned to see a massive grizzly bear standing at his full might, ready to pounce.

His nightmares made him realize that perhaps his level of anxiety was more serious than he cared to admit. His father was still sleeping, so Ethan used his best resource to calm down—meditation. He spent several minutes working through the negative thoughts. He carefully paced his breathing to achieve a very balanced rhythm. He had spent months practicing. It made everything easier, and soon he felt refreshed and relaxed. It made him think of Ravi and how much that man had changed his life. Even now, with this trip, Ravi had insisted Ethan be with his father despite only having worked for three months at the Elevation Leadership Institute. Ethan felt guilty leaving, but Ravi knew the entire story very well and reminded Ethan again of his own regrets of not having been there for his own father. To Ravi, this represented an excellent opportunity for Ethan to rebuild the bond of trust with Francis. When Ethan voiced his concerns about the possibility of the trip causing more damage than good, Ravi insisted he keep an open mind and stay positive.

"Trust in life and in the good it brings," Ravi had said. Ethan finally agreed to move forward with it, fearing what his father would have to go through if he were alone.

After getting cleaned up, Francis and Ethan stepped into the crisp autumn air. They were famished and decided to go for a late lunch. Eva had done her research and given them a list of places to eat. The top of the pub category was The Old Storehouse. Being less than ten minutes away by foot made for an easy decision.

They arrived to find a typically Irish pub located in the heart of the city. Even for lunch, they just barely managed to find a table. The atmosphere was friendly and unpretentious. A live band of three talented musicians played in one corner. Their music carried a traditional folklore vibe occasionally tinged with rock. It sounded perfect to Ethan's ears. They decided to try the Irish burger and chips, not wanting to venture too far out of their comfort zone.

It did little to calm Francis. Since landing, he had hardly spoken a word. His limp had worsened, and Ethan wondered if it was caused by physical pain or the mental strain. This experience was as real as it came for Francis. Ethan was still unsure of where he stood, but knew his father needed his son's strength.

"How are you holding up, Dad?"

Francis looked up from his glass of sparkling water. "Oh, yes, um, fine, son. I'm doing fine."

"Feeling nervous about tomorrow?"

"No, not at all. I'm ready." Francis did not seem convinced.

"Well, for what it's worth, I will be right by your side. I will stand as your witness and tell this banshee how hard you have worked to make amends and do right by your family."

Francis smiled. "Truthfully speaking, son, I am not worried about coming face-to-face with the banshee. Something else has come to mind through all this."

"What is it?"

"You have been such a good son, coming across the ocean with me, taking time out of your busy schedule. And I am just realizing I may be putting you in danger. This spirit cursed me, and it immediately affected my health. How can I be sure she won't do the same to you?

Simply out of spite for what I did." Francis looked back down at his glass, shaking slightly.

The thought hadn't even occurred to Ethan. Was he in some sort of danger? If this whole crazy story was somehow true, would he be risking his own well-being? He didn't think so. He had done enough soul-searching and had learned to trust the universe. He hadn't done anything to this being. He caught himself, realizing he was debating something he did not believe in.

"Dad, you shouldn't be thinking about that. I made the decision to come with you and help you in any way I could. We are here together. Besides, you told me what she asked you to do. She wanted you to seek forgiveness. Make amends for your mistakes. And you accomplished it. I am positive you will find redemption." Ethan leaned over and grabbed his father's shoulder affectionately. He could tell how difficult this was for Francis. At the same time, he was very proud of his father's ability to think of others now. He was never capable of that before. He was truly a new man.

As they had the whole afternoon ahead of them, they decided to take a bus out to the Blackrock Market. It boasted a maze of stalls with vendors selling their crafts to the public. It felt good for Francis to be back in Ireland, despite the unfortunate events from his previous visit. He soaked up the atmosphere, the people, wanting it to last. Ethan was amazed by the friendliness of those he met. Always greeted with a smile, he felt part of the community at once. It made him realize he should have made this trip before. But deep down, he had, unfairly, associated his frustration toward Francis with this beautiful country, making them inseparable in his mind. He had made it a point not to visit Ireland. He now understood the error of his ways and felt a pang of guilt.

They spent hours speaking with the different people manning the stalls. Often, they were the owners themselves. They leafed through authentic books, bought a few souvenirs for the family back home, and made the most of a free day together. They could still feel the tension, but the day was filled with exploration, and they managed to forget the real reason for their trip for a few hours.

After a light dinner, they headed back to the hotel. Both men were still exhausted from jet lag. A good night's sleep was indeed in order. In a few hours, Francis would have to face a very difficult challenge of his own making. And he wanted to be ready.

***

Phoenix Park in Dublin stood mere steps away from the River Liffey. It was known as the largest enclosed park in any capital city in Europe. Some of the world's greatest artists performed in the park throughout the summer.

As Ethan and Francis entered the grounds, they immediately encountered a group of fallow deer roaming freely. The beautiful sight startled Ethan. In Montreal, he was lucky to see a deer once a year. Here he was, witnessing at least twenty deer enjoying their evening. Francis did not react. He walked past, not even noticing the exquisite animals.

The famous meeting was to take place in just over an hour. Francis had insisted they go well in advance. He couldn't control his nerves. He had been a wreck all day. He hadn't slept much the night before despite the intense fatigue. His mind kept coming back to the banshee. What would she say or do? How would he prove he had done what was asked of him? Ethan tried to calm him down, reminding him how much he had changed. It helped but did not settle Francis down completely. In the end, Ethan had agreed getting to the park early would help them both prepare for the big moment.

"You know, if someone would have told me one year ago that I would be walking in an Irish park with my father, a man I hadn't seen in almost a decade, I would have scoffed. And yet here we are, spending time together in the city where you were born. It still seems surreal."

Francis stared at his son. His shoulders loosened, and he let out a sigh. "If it weren't for the present circumstances, I would surely be making more of this trip. I do apologize. I am unable to get this nerve-racking feeling to disappear. It is all-consuming."

"I completely understand, Dad. And I am here by your side. You will get through this." Ethan grabbed his father's shoulder and nodded confidently. Francis stared ahead.

They continued walking toward the infamous spot in the park where Francis had experienced the worst moment of his life. He was shaking, unable to stay calm. The only moment on his mind for exactly twelve months was here. How would he react? What would he say? What was supposed to happen? These were all questions he needed answers to.

Francis suddenly stopped, staring into a wooded area. "This is it," he whispered. He took a few steps off the main path, heading between two large oak trees. Ethan followed him. Perhaps it was the cool air, but Ethan could feel a chill run up his spine. Everything seemed darker, more mysterious. The air stood still, as if they were the only two people in the world. Ethan didn't know if his mind was playing a trick on him, given the stress of the moment, or if something otherworldly was going on. They stood frozen in place, unsure of what to do. Ethan looked at his watch. They were right on time.

They waited. And then waited some more. Nothing happened. Minutes turned into an hour, which then became two. They stood silently, not saying a word. Darkness engulfed them, making it impossible to see much of anything. For all their expectations, this was by far the worst scenario. Francis had imagined it possible, but for some reason, he didn't think it would actually happen this way. He had visualized a miraculous meeting where he would profusely apologize, introduce Ethan as his witness, and prove all was fixed. To not get the chance, to be stuck in this state of uncertainty and sickness, was too much to bear. He glanced over at his son a few times. His world was closing in. Francis knew if nothing happened, he could lose his son's trust forever. None of it made sense to him.

Ethan could see his father's despair. "Dad, let's go back to the hotel. Maybe you had the meeting place wrong. Or the date. I'm sure you will be feeling better by tomorrow."

Francis shook his head, looking down at his frail hands. "The instructions were clear. This is where it had to happen. I've lost my chance. I don't know why, but I will not have the opportunity to make things right." He started walking out of the woods, dejected, and headed toward the stone path. Ethan followed him.

Francis took a different direction. He headed toward the river without saying a word. They moved in silence. The sun was almost gone, leaving an orange hue and deep shadows. The pathway became deserted as they distanced themselves from the main area. Ethan could sense the nightfall enveloping them like a shroud. Francis didn't seem to notice, caught up in his own reflections.

They walked slowly for twenty minutes. Francis did not stop, despite the weakness in his legs. He pushed on, his cane supporting his every step. He was in his own world, looking for an answer that eluded him. Ethan was getting worried about his father's health and wanted to get them back to the hotel.

In the distance, they noticed someone coming toward them. Red hair flowed in the wind, and the individual, seemingly female, was wearing a white shawl. Francis stopped dead in his tracks. "It's her. It's the banshee!"

As she approached, Ethan experienced his own moment of disbelief. He knew this woman. This was no banshee.

"Julia Everhart? What on earth are you doing here?" asked Ethan, hugging her.

Francis stared at his son, completely confused. "You know her?"

"Yes, Dad. We work together at the Elevation Leadership Institute. We are friends. And I promise you she isn't a strange spirit here to hurt us."

Francis turned his gaze back to Julia. He took a very long pause, observing her for what seemed like minutes. "I know you are not a banshee. I'm not senile. And yet, I know we met a year ago. I cannot explain the details, but I am absolutely positive you were in that park. This isn't a coincidence, is it?"

Julia spoke for the first time. "You are correct, Francis. We did meet a year ago on that fateful night. But the circumstances were not as you remember them. Why don't we sit?" She directed both shellshocked men to a bench facing the river.

"I was born in Dublin, and most of my family is still here. I visit them every single year. You can never really leave this beautiful city. It always remains a part of your soul. A little over a year ago, Ravi asked me for a favor. He wanted me to find you, Francis. He knew a part of your story and some of the unfortunate events that happened in your family."

"How?" asked both Ethan and Francis simultaneously.

"Through Vincent Massa, the founder of Premier Marketing. Ravi and Vincent were friends. They shared ideas and spent time together in

Montreal's entrepreneurial community. Ethan, when you joined Premier, you quickly developed a strong relationship with Vincent. He respected you and saw a young leader full of potential. You shared your family history with him, the pain you had gone through. Ravi had a special interest in you, and he probed Vincent when he found out you were working there. In normal circumstances, Vincent would never have divulged confidential conversations, but Ravi explained your history together and how you supported him when he first came to Canada. Ravi was determined to help you in every way he could. He started looking for Francis a few years back, after Vincent died, with no luck. When I joined the business, Ravi realized I had deep ties to Dublin. After a few months, he asked if I could help. Within a few weeks, through local contacts, I managed to find you, Francis. That was a year ago."

Both men sat in stunned silence. Ethan could sense his father shaking ever so slightly. He put his arm around him to comfort him.

Julia continued, "Ravi sent me to Dublin to find you. I desperately wanted to speak with you, Francis. Explain how my boss Ravi knew your son. See if we could help in any way. I sat in the pub that night, mustering up the courage to speak with you. It happened so quickly. Before I knew it, you were headed outside, ready to fight this mountain of a man. I was afraid. Exiting the pub, I found you on the floor, bleeding. Before I could give you a hand, you chased after him. You were barely able to walk straight. I followed you into Phoenix Park. That is when we spoke."

Francis was nodding, mesmerized. Memories were slowly coming back to him in fragments.

"I grabbed your arm, trying to keep you upright, but you fell to your knees. You were sobbing. And then you told me everything. The pain you had caused your wife and son. The depth of the betrayal. How terribly you treated everyone in your life. You truly believed you would die alone. I listened, not knowing how to comfort you. I tried offering words of encouragement. As we spoke, you gave yourself an ultimatum. You even cursed yourself out loud. You were determined to make things right. You set a one-year deadline to make amends. And you handed me this gold ring, telling me I must meet you in one year, at the River Liffey, to see if you had indeed succeeded."

Julia produced a gold ring from her small purse. Francis took it, holding it in his palm. "This is my wedding ring. I thought I had lost it." Tears streamed down his cheek.

"You kept the ring after all of these years, Dad?"

"Yes, Ethan. I never recovered from losing your mother. I cannot blame anyone but myself. The alcohol made me a different person. I lost all control, and then I lost my entire family."

"That night, after giving me the ring, all energy seemed to drain from your being," said Julia. "I walked you to your apartment, barely understanding where we were going, and made sure you made it home safe. Ravi and I agreed I should meet you here as promised, one year later."

They sat in silence for several minutes, taking in the strange moment. There was so much to contemplate. Finally, Julia stood. "I should give you some space. I hope you have been able to find solace in all of this. You have an amazing son—you should be proud."

Francis stood and embraced Julia with all his strength. "I cannot thank you enough. You have given me back my son, my family, my life. I am forever indebted to you. I'll never be able to repay you for your kindness."

Julia smiled. "I am happy we could help." She hugged Ethan and walked into the night.

Ethan and Francis decided to walk back to the hotel despite the late hour. They needed a few more minutes to reflect on the day's events. There was no banshee, no spirit, yet Francis had indeed experienced a life-changing moment in that park one year ago. A weight had been lifted. Ethan could clearly sense it. Already, his father walked with more confidence in his stride.

"I feel foolish," said Francis. "I was so intoxicated that I lost all sense of reality. I truly thought I had been cursed by an otherworldly spirit. And all along, I had done it to myself."

"Maybe that is exactly what you needed, Dad. It did force you to face the reality of your actions. Would we be here, right now, together, had you not lived such a terrifying experience? You have your family back. I have my father again."

Francis nodded slowly, taking it all in. "But this doesn't explain my sickness. How can I know I will get better?"

Ethan paused for a few seconds. "I can't predict what will happen. But I have learned enough in the past year to understand the world is indeed full of mystery. I believe you caused this sickness—through your guilt. This may be the result of a deep sense of regret. Science has proven over and over we are able to make ourselves sick, but we are more importantly able to heal ourselves better than any medicine ever could. We are made of energy. You sent negative energy through your system. By reversing course, by showing true remorse, I absolutely believe you will find your health again. And I will be with you every step of the way. There is no doubt in my mind. I love you and won't lose you. Not now, after all we have been through."

Ethan held his father, not wanting to let him go.

A Final Farewell

*T*hey were heading back home in the afternoon. Ethan wanted to make the most of his last morning and decided to get up early, letting Francis sleep in. He headed to scenic Merrion Square to see the famed statue of Oscar Wilde. He grabbed his journal as he left the room.

Arriving before the city awoke, he found a free bench near the historic monument. He took in the fresh air, appreciating the exceptional greenery of the park. He felt inspired and also knew it was time for resolution.

Much like his father, he carried the pain of losing his mother deep in his heart. He had never addressed it, preferring to bury the emotions where they would be lost forever. But he knew this was impossible. Until he faced his true feelings, accepted the loss, he couldn't move on.

He reflected on the memories he had of this beautiful woman. He regretted not having more time with his mother. Life got in the way, and his childhood flew by in a way that can only be understood by adults. She tried her very best to provide love, to protect his innocence. He recognized the dilemma she faced by working endless hours, always helping others in need. Being a father now, he knew the challenges she faced every day.

Ethan wondered why certain moments stayed ingrained forever—even if they weren't always the most important ones. It related back to emotions, to the way it made him feel. He remembered the day he went for a bike ride in their new neighborhood and got lost. He must have been seven or eight years old. He tried endlessly to make his way back home, but couldn't figure out the streets. It felt much like a labyrinth to him at that time. He feared his father's reaction, knowing he would be punished for coming home later than expected. By a stroke of luck, after what seemed to him like days but was probably a few minutes, he recognized a large brown house and knew he was close. Tears streaming down his face, part fear and part relief, he biked home.

There sat his mother on the front stairs waiting for him. She had come home early that day. One look told her that her son had lived a scary adventure. She walked to him as he jumped off his bike, and she hugged him ferociously. Taking Ethan by the hand, she guided him toward the nearby park to sit and talk. Ethan realized she didn't want Francis seeing him cry. They sat, and she asked him how he had gotten lost. She wanted to know every detail. Listening compassionately, she took in his story, smiling the entire time. Ethan finally calmed down.

After a few minutes in silence, his mother shared a lesson he kept with him his entire life. She explained how this day was important for Ethan. He must always be courageous and try new things. Being curious would give him the opportunity to explore the world and meet wonderful people. And the fact he found his way home, without any help, meant he was a very intelligent boy. She turned a negative situation into a positive outcome. Ethan left that conversation with confidence, knowing he could always trust his mom, no matter what happened. It gave him a deep sense of joy.

Sitting in the majestic park, he took the time to thank his mother and send her the gratitude she deserved. He couldn't live in regret. He had come too far. His best path forward was to accept what life had brought him. This meant being a better version of himself to honour her memory.

He took out his journal.

Dear Mom,
I sit here today, in a beautiful place, thinking about you. I miss you, dearly. And I wish you were next to me now. You lived a tough life. Everything you did, all your hard work, was to provide for our family, to take care of me. I was never able to fully appreciate you. Only when Luca and Kayla arrived did I grasp the sacrifices you had made for us every single day. You would love the little munchkins. Full of energy and passion. Kayla makes me think of you. Her curiosity, her selflessness. I gave her your name to remember you by.

Kayla "Nora" Stone. To honour you. And Eva is the best mom ever, just like you were for me.

Your last years were painful. I tried supporting you, mending your broken heart, but it wasn't meant to be. I hope I was a good son to you, though I will never have the satisfaction of knowing if I ever truly was. You deserved more. I should have given you more. You were an exceptional person, a dedicated mother, and my close friend.

I learned many lessons from you. I could write a book with everything you have taught me. Above all else, you always insisted I live the power of forgiveness. You may have lost a part of this near the end, understandably. I remember when you told me that hanging on to anger would only poison my own soul. I have been holding this anger for a decade now.

Recently, Francis came back into my life. The man who betrayed our family. Your ex-husband. My father. I did not know how to react, if I should let him take his place by my side. Instinctively, I wanted to push him away, make him feel the might of my anger. But I have changed, Mom. I am a better person. Someone who cares for his family, who won't repeat the mistakes his own father made. I have taken a journey of self-discovery that has brought joy to my loved ones. I feel a deep sense of happiness for the first time in my life.

I forgave him, Mom. And I forgave myself for my own selfish attitude. I hope you can accept that. Your memory will live on forever in our hearts. I love you deeply. Without you, I would be nothing.

Ethan closed his journal, shut his eyes, and breathed for a few uninterrupted minutes. He had, after many years, bid farewell to his mother. In doing so, he accepted the rush of overwhelming sadness, knowing this was a necessary part of the process. He walked out of Merrion Square, head held high, understanding a new chapter of his life could begin. And he would make the most of the opportunity he had been granted.

THE HAPPINESS GUIDE

EXPERIENCE SHARING

Progress is impossible without change, and those who cannot change their minds cannot change anything.
—George Bernard Shaw, playwright

$\smile$

I wrote this book for a few simple reasons. I truly believe people can change. We can rewire our brains to think in a completely different way. It is a matter of choice and belief. Going the extra mile, taking a chance when you doubt yourself to the core. Before getting there, however, one must take certain steps to start with a clean slate. Making the decision is one thing; changing habits, thought patterns, and self-imposed limitations is another.

If we take the time to truly think about it, deep down, we know goals can be achieved. If we can only run half a mile, we understand that by running an extra few steps day after day will increase our capacity. So why is it that we settle for less when improvement is so close at hand? My experience tells me it is a question of mindset, not physical boundaries, that gets in the way of achieving great things. And by changing the way we think, we can begin the process of taking our happiness to a new level.

In the following pages I will provide a few tools that I believe can help any person accomplish more than they believe possible. It will require self-discipline and an open mind. Luckily for all of us, those two elements are quite readily available if we look in the mirror and make a commitment to be better, one day at a time.

In my family alone, I have witnessed an asthmatic non-runner train for and finish several marathons. I have watched a six-year-old complete a four-mile race without taking one break. I have beheld a heavy drinker stop cold turkey at age sixty to live a healthier lifestyle for his loved ones. Everything, anything, is possible. I believe in you and your ability to improve. I truly do.

THE FOUR LAWS OF HAPPINESS

A. The Law of Self-Awareness = Cleansing
   1. Progressive Meditation: ten minutes morning and night
   2. The Art of Listening: Observe, Reflect, Accept
   3. Circular Reciprocation: practice exceptional kindness every day

B. The Law of Self-Improvement = Motivation
   1. Barrier Breaking: commit to a "stretch goal"
   2. Habit Hacking: routines, nutrition, technology intake, time
   3. Mental Mapping: visualize your future success

C. The Law of Self-Giving = Appreciation
   1. Dream Facilitation: help people achieve their goals
   2. Gift Giving: gift someone daily in a specific way
   3. The Time-Anger Gap: master and reduce frustrations

D. The Law of Self-Belief = Achievement
   1. Spinning Positivity: eliminate negativity from your life
   2. Belief Building: grow your abilities beyond self-limitations
   3. Go Big: pursue your dreams and dare to think big

THE LAW OF
SELF-AWARENESS =
CLEANSING

Progressive meditation: ten minutes morning and night

*I*magine those special days when life seems to be in perfect balance, where everything that can go right does. You feel at your best. Happiness courses through your veins. You feel as though the world is actually trying to help you achieve your goals. Now, ask yourself if this is caused by external factors or something you create?

Meditation is the simplest of tools we all have at our disposal. It is free, easy to learn, and will change your life. Science has recently proven that meditating a mere ten minutes in the morning and at night will cause your brain cells to transform. Your heart rate will go down, stress levels will dissipate, and clarity will come through. Given these facts, it is hard to understand why we wouldn't take this minimal amount of time each day to practice meditation. It is a wonderful experience. And no, it is not only for spiritual or religious people. The benefits of meditation have changed my life. I can now take on many stressful situations with a calm and composed approach. We come to many realizations, not the least of which is the fact that life is indeed short, and we must enjoy every moment, and learn to see the beauty around us.

Stretching and yoga techniques are also very beneficial. In fact, when you learn to breathe the right way, you will be able to combine stretching with meditation at the same time! I have never been a very flexible person, but I have worked to improve this aspect of my physical ability. It has greatly helped my fitness levels, and I happily avoid injuries when I push myself physically.

Take the time to meditate morning and night! And over time, quickly enough, integrate stretching techniques into your routine. It will make a world of difference, I promise you!

The Art of Listening: observe, reflect, accept

True listening has become an underrated tool. We are bombarded by distractions and it has become more challenging to focus our attention. Science has shown that as human beings, we are very rarely able to multitask. Books such as Cal Newport's *Deep Work* are excellent for getting a better understanding of how to get back our attention. It is absolutely key that you truly listen to the person you are speaking with and give them your full, undivided attention. This is the only way to be in the present moment. Small tip: always take one to two seconds before answering any question. Process before trying to answer too quickly.

Many things happen in a day. Some great, others not so much. Commutes, happy customers, unsatisfied coworkers, birthday parties, lateness, good food, nasty waiters, promotions, screaming children, sunshine, and on and on. How we react to all these situations is truly a matter of choice. We can be content, impatient, satisfied—it all depends on what *we* decide.

Certain things are in our control; others are not. I have learned that our actions are the result of our decisions, whether they are impulsive or not. How wonderful that we are intelligent beings with the ability to make choices! Yet we don't often use this simple gift. Acceptance is very difficult, specifically in cases where we disagree with the outcome. Yet understanding that sometimes we cannot control what others do or say allows us to realize that acceptance is the best choice for us. Move on if you don't agree, be open, and learn to value diversity of opinion. Do it for yourself, for your personal growth.

I encourage you to be conscious of your surroundings, take in what you see, and refrain from reacting too quickly lest you lose the opportunity to observe, reflect, and accept. As I have seen more often than not, impulsive behavior rarely leads us on the right path. Taking a moment often does.

Circular Reciprocation: practice exceptional kindness every day

Kindness can be defined in many ways. Smiling, listening, and offering a helping hand are all forms of kindness. It is easy enough to act this way when it is convenient. When in a good mood, this comes naturally. The challenge is to be kind even when we are stressed or frustrated. It requires true effort and commitment. As we change the way we think, it becomes imperative to look beyond our four walls and consider the lives of those around us. I am talking about society as a whole, not just our loved ones.

There is a simple way to start. Take just one day and try it. Smile at strangers, give up your spot on the train. Be courteous and sympathetic. Buy a coffee for a homeless person and actually talk to them, looking them in the eye. Ask the cashier how his day is going, showing genuine interest in the answer. Take small steps and see how it goes. I can say from experience the feeling is wonderful and contagious. It will be hard to ignore the positive responses. Science has proven that smiling, even with effort, triggers physiological effects that will raise our energy levels.

In simple terms, *be crazy nice all the time*! It will become second nature and will profoundly influence your world in the best way possible. After all, why wouldn't you want to be caring, loving, and sympathetic? It can only bring good to your life. Positive energy does exist, and it is magnetic. Make the effort, step by step, and before you know it, it will add up to something much bigger and better. Karma is real, so use it in the right way by shifting your mindset and behavior. Circular reciprocation means the universe will always find a way to give you back what you put out there. Don't expect it, but understand the way our world works. Trust the process.

THE LAW OF SELF-IMPROVEMENT = MOTIVATION

Barrier Breaking: commit to a "stretch goal"

hink of the different places where we find inspiration. We see world-class professionals accomplish great feats. We witness college athletes surpassing themselves on every level. We even have the opportunity of seeing children scoring their first goal. All of it gives us excitement we long to experience more often in our lives. Let's be honest, we all cried watching *Rudy*.

We often limit ourselves in the way we perceive our own abilities. We find excuses, claiming we wouldn't be able to attain certain goals. Imagine if you were able to erase self-doubt and instead break through the negativity. There is one way to accomplish this: commit to a goal that seems almost unthinkable today. If you can run two miles, commit to a marathon. If you can swim for two hundred meters, commit to a triathlon. If you can hike for twenty minutes, commit to climbing Kilimanjaro.

I have taken on a few key goals in my life. What I learned is that it is more about dedication than physical ability. I encourage you to go and watch a marathon. It doesn't have to be Boston. Every major city now has one. Spend an hour at the finish line as the runners cross the threshold. You will notice the joy and ecstasy, but you will also see something very interesting. Many of the runners are not super athletes. They are regular people, short, tall, old, young—it doesn't matter. The point is they are individuals who dedicated themselves to following a structured program, putting in the miles, and surpassing their limits. It won't be easy, but it will be *very* exhilarating. And it will change your life. Everything will be better from that point forward. Find that challenge that both inspires and scares you, sign up, believe in yourself, and get going!

Habit Hacking: routines, nutrition, technology intake, time

Life happens. We get busy. There are so many opportunities to justify eating the wrong things. We lack time and wonder why we are tired and don't have the energy to take on challenges. And we spend countless hours on smartphones, tablets, and computers, no longer being in the present moment.

Nutrition is a massive subject. Hundreds of new books are written on the topic every year. What goes into our bodies directly determines the state of our health. When I was younger, I believed that working out was good enough. I now understand that focusing on making changes in our diet will ensure we avoid those nasty colds, feel full of vibrant energy, and are ready for any obstacle. I recommend meeting a nutritionist (holistic or scientific) and starting fresh in a new direction. Or simply research the subject and discover the endless ways you could be healthier.

It seems so obvious that we need a good night's sleep to perform in life. Yet only a few of us sleep the right number of hours in a day. This is crucial for high productivity. And resting in different ways is as important. I am referring to stress removal. Taking time to realize when life is beating us up for a few days or weeks. When it does, it is time to get a massage, take an afternoon off, or simply go hiking. The key is understanding when our mind and body need this rest and taking action immediately. It will pay incredible dividends. Change your routines, and give your mental and physical health the attention they deserve.

I will state the next point quite directly: *disconnect*. We are passing our days hooked to technological devices and missing life! We are lacking presence and must find a way to get this back. First, do not check your phone for at least thirty minutes after you wake up. Second, no phone during family time. Finally, no screen time one hour before sleep to ensure your brain can unwind and attain the perfect resting state. Please try it!

Mental Mapping: visualize your future success

Inspiration is underrated. We know it motivates us. We understand it can drive us to achieve our goals. Yet we rarely seek out this powerful tool. Professional athletes often watch films of their favorite players accomplishing great things before a big event. Coaches give powerful speeches that lead underdog teams to victories. And what better CEO is there than the one who can inspire thousands to follow a vision?

As a rule of thumb, I ensure I am inspired several times a day. I read texts, watch videos, and listen to talks that make me feel like I too can go beyond my self-imposed limitations or those boundaries society places on us. By taking a few minutes each day, this simple tool will allow you to build a positive mindset, which will in turn lead to greater achievements. It is literally how champions are made.

Many years ago, our soccer team won the provincials (equivalent to a state championship) and had the privilege of representing our province at the Canadian National Championships. Through a few gutsy performances, we made it to the final game. We were up against a powerhouse team that could beat us ninety-nine times out of one hundred. They had boatloads of skill on us. Our coach, Dean Giuliano, gave us a ten-minute speech before kickoff that had the entire team in tears. He told us we were destined to win the game. He explained the bonds we had created as a team, a strength of union so powerful it could not be broken. And with that inspiration coursing through our veins, we went out and beat a team we had no business beating. We had visualized this moment for two years. At every practice, before every game, we pictured ourselves winning a national championship. I am incredibly lucky to have learned the power of visualization at such a young age. I have used it in my life over and over with excellent results. You can do this too. Start now.

THE LAW OF
SELF-GIVING =
APPRECIATION

Dream Facilitation: help people achieve their goals

Deep down, everyone dreams. From traveling the world to spending time with a loved one we miss and don't get to see too often. Some are big dreams, others are basic in nature, but always meaningful. Imagine if you had the ability to give someone in your community the opportunity to live an experience they have always thought about but never knew how to pursue. You can make this happen for them!

It requires a high level of selflessness, to be sure. Essentially, it means putting your own desires aside and instead dedicating yourself to helping someone else. Step one is to discover what dream they wish they could achieve. Next, put a plan in place with or without them, depending on the situation. This can involve teaching them how to save money, reaching out to someone important, organizing, planning, you name it. The key is to understand their goal and help make it happen. You have to be willing to put in the time—and even more importantly put aside your own wishes—for another person.

I encourage you to read *The Dream Manager* by Matthew Kelly. This book is focused on the business world, but I can assure you this applies to your personal life also. Think of the difference you could make by helping facilitate a loved one's dream. Be prepared to think on different levels and use creativity to make it happen. In the end, life is too short, so don't wait. Act now and make someone's year!

Gift Giving: gift someone daily in a specific way

It is remarkable how people react to being praised or how they feel when they receive an unexpected compliment. All of us love the feeling. Yet how often do we actually go out of our way to show appreciation? There may be a stigma where we see "giving" as automatically falling into the materialistic realm. This is simply not true. It is nice to get that much-desired object, but those gifts wear off quickly. What has a lasting effect is when a person looks you in the eye and genuinely thanks you for being such an amazing friend. Those moments are unforgettable. As Maya Angelou once said, "I've learned that people will forget what you said, people will forget what you did, but they will *never* forget how you made them feel" (italics mine).

An easy way to start on the positive path of showing appreciation is by promising to do it once per day. In a twenty-four-hour period, promise you will make one person you connect with feel like a million dollars. It is important to make this meaningful. People can cut through the rubbish. You have to mean it, and you should. There are so many ways to express gratitude, yet we are often caught up in our own worlds. We don't take the time to do something so easy that is so powerful.

I recently coached my son's soccer team for the summer. Great fun with a great bunch of kids. At the end of the short season, a group of three parents, accompanied by their kids, offered me a thank-you card with a gift certificate. They expressed their gratitude for the time I put into helping their children learn the game they love to play. I was blown away by their act of kindness. I promised to coach them again next year because I truly felt appreciated.

It doesn't take much, but I urge you to get in the mindset of *giving* daily. Make a phone call, offer a small token of appreciation, praise others. It can change a person's day and will likely have a bigger impact than you realize.

The Time-Anger Gap: master and reduce frustrations

Part of giving to others is finding a way to reduce the anger we feel inside when something goes wrong. By finding a way to shorten the time it takes us from becoming frustrated to regaining our composure, we can efficiently go back to offering the best version of ourselves to the world.

I want you to look back and think of a random date six months ago. Chances are, something frustrating happened that day, be it tiny or maybe more significant. Unless it was absolutely earth-shattering, you probably can't remember what happened. Think about eight months ago. Same story, right? Now, think back just two months ago. Same result! Things happen, life goes on. Why do we allow anger to take over our well-being? What does this bring us? Nothing positive, I can ensure you. It is important to realize that the darkness anger brings into our lives hurts only us. We have the power to control this. It might not be easy, but it is possible.

Use this trick the next time you get mad. Think about the future when this moment will be nothing but a distant memory. Truly acknowledge that you will be moving on from this annoying driver or this upset customer, and you will find the joy of life once again. It is only by seeing the situation for what it is, *temporary*, that we can take the step in reducing the Time-Anger Gap.

Part of this strategy is using mindfulness to your advantage. Mindfulness means seeing a situation as an observer—understanding it but not letting your emotions take over. I love to use this phrase to help me reframe any situation: "Huh, that is interesting." It may very well be frustrating, but I always try changing the way I see a situation before letting myself overreact. And I convince myself this moment will pass. It most often does!

THE LAW OF SELF-BELIEF = ACHIEVEMENT

Spinning Positivity: eliminate negativity from your life

It is a very natural tendency in life to blame circumstances for our unhappiness. Someone betrayed you. You were cut off by a maniac on the road. Your job is annoying. Yet the one thing that can be controlled in all these situations is your own attitude. As intelligent human beings, we have the wonderful ability to choose how we will react to any given circumstance. That is the constant in all this. Emotions can be strong at times. Always remember what we do and how we act is a choice we are making.

Work at eliminating negative thoughts from your life. Always tell yourself there is a solution, another way. And with that mindset, it is crucial to cut off any energy-sapping relationships you live with. Take the time to think about those people around you who cause only grief or frustration. Why are you accepting that? Science has proven we are greatly influenced by those we spend the most time with. Surround yourself with positive, energetic friends and colleagues. Meet with successful members of society who are always striving for more. Be inspired by their life philosophy and use that energy to bring more positivity into your world.

Looking inward, we must realize which destructive behaviors are limiting our growth as individuals. It is easy to get caught up in judging others. In the end, this only hurts the person in the mirror. If you want to change, to be better, you must be able to admit what is going wrong.

Write down exactly what you want to change personally. Also write down the relationships that need to disappear. Take baby steps. After all, small steps in the right direction are still moving you forward. And make a commitment to turn anything negative in your life into a positive. Every day is a fresh start!

Belief Building: grow your abilities beyond self-limitations

Do you believe in yourself? Sounds like something you were asked as a child. Yet, as adults, we often underestimate our abilities. We have painted a specific image of ourselves—one that is not reality but rather perception. I have so often heard these statements: "I can't do that" or "That's for other, more successful people." What? I don't accept these answers. Sure, there are incredible entrepreneurs and talented athletes in this world. Legends. But so are you! Don't believe me? I encourage you to Google "inspiring stories." Do you want to know how many results you will get? Here is the number: 2,970,000,000. I am not kidding. That is the real number that appears! (As of this writing.)

All of us have lived in different situations, some much more difficult than others. I don't mean to diminish this in any way. It can be very challenging when we had a family member constantly putting us down or hurting us emotionally or physically. It is tough. I am asking you to be completely honest with yourself. If you look at your life, are you absolutely 100 percent sure you have maximized your talents and abilities? Have you truly reached your plateau? Are you sure about that? Did you know that the business management guru Peter Drucker wrote thirty of his thirty-nine books after the age of sixty? The world is yours to conquer!

Consider this: we can bend reality. This may sound like *The Matrix*, but it is real. We can change our belief systems and fundamentally alter the course of our lives. Science has shown us thousands of examples, ranging from the placebo effect's role in healing patients to brainwaves being altered by meditation. The power is in your hands and in your mind. You have to change the way you perceive yourself. Have confidence. Stop worrying about being judged. I know you can take your life to the next level—no question about that. Only *you* are holding yourself back. Make a decision today to break that pattern. Deep down, you know you were meant for more. Do some soul-searching, and figure out what is stopping you from living your best life.

Go Big: pursue your dreams and dare to think big

We have accomplished many great things as humans. Society has evolved, and we continue to make innovative advances once thought impossible. Yet the general consensus is that these feats are reserved for a few "exceptional" individuals. In fact, it is part of our DNA to think small. It is the way most people are wired. We can easily admit that, when we see a great athlete or creative entrepreneur, we think ourselves incapable of achieving the same level of success. We think, "*They are special.*" This is simply not true. Any one of us can make a difference. When our energy is focused on the right goal, anything is possible. What needs to change is our mindset. We need to think *bigger*. Break through the traditional bonds of acceptance, and take on a new philosophy. Write down your personal goals. Then look at them, and change them by going one level higher. This is the only way to achieve more.

One trick I use is to read biographies of the people who inspire me. We often see very normal, grounded individuals soar to new heights based on vision and determination. We can learn, grow, and achieve so much if we are able to understand the importance of believing in our dreams. Taking small steps in the right direction is very positive. Being courageous enough to reach for a gigantic leap is exhilarating. Once you get there, your life and the lives of those around you will be changed forever. Much like athletes who visualize their goals and picture themselves crossing the finish line, you can do this with your life. I sit down every month and write my short, medium, and long-term goals. It is exhilarating. As William Arthur Ward once wrote: "If you can imagine it, you can achieve it. If you can dream it, you can become it."

Ask yourself if you are truly happy with your life and what you have done to this point. Then take the time to write out your goals for the coming years. Make a plan on how you will achieve each of these goals. Then get to work!

ACKNOWLEDGEMENTS

*W*riting a book has been one of the most challenging projects I have ever undertaken. It would likely take dozens of pages to thank everyone who helped in some way. I will do my very best to keep this brief.

Sarah, you have believed in me and supported my vision in such an incredible way that is hard to express in words. I owe you so much. You are my life, my soulmate. Chloe and Tristan, two crazy kids who find a way to make me laugh every single day. Your inspiration has given me the energy to finish this book. Your passion is limitless.

Mom and Dad, you have always supported my dreams, big and small. Your hard work, courage, and dedication have given me the opportunity to be here today, writing these words. I thank you and love you dearly.

Harmeen, Rick, Alex and Corie, and my nieces and nephew, I thank the universe every morning to have such an amazing family. I can turn to any one of you at any given moment. Your support is infinitely appreciated.

Joey, Mel, and the boys, we have travelled together, ran marathons together, and shared some of the most precious moments of our lives together. I love you deeply and always will.

Aslam and Diane, you treated me like a son from the first day we met, many years ago. I am blessed to have such loving people in my life.

To my Forum Brothers, Simon M and Simon L, Jebb, Vicken, Chris, Louis, Hicham, you were among the first to read a draft of this book and helped me reframe many of the ideas. Thank you for always being available through thick and thin, lending a helping hand.

To the great mentors and peers who helped along the way, your experience sharing has been incredibly appreciated: Warren Rustand, Robert Glazer, Verne Harnish, Spencer Sheinin, Robert Murray, Parveen Dhupar, Tom Benson, Dominique Laverdure, Martin Balcome, Cleo Maheux, Pier-Luc Gaudet, Tarina W, Marina B, Stefano Faustini, Paul Simard, and Samantha Kris.

ABOUT THE AUTHOR

Shawn left a hyper-successful entrepreneurial career to pursue his passion. Today, he has one message for the world: you can be massively successful in business *without* having to sacrifice true happiness.

In 2009, Shawn co-founded DALS Lighting, a small LED Lighting business. Fueled by an obsessive need for growth and excellence, Shawn and his business partner scaled the business to three times its revenues, bringing the company well into the eight-figure range. He was nominated for awards (EY Entrepreneur of the Year), served as President for the EO (Entrepreneurs' Organization) Montreal chapter, and mentored young entrepreneurs across Canada. He was professionally successful, financially-secure, and had a beautiful family he turned to at the end of each day.

It was a life of success that others could only dream of—but he did not feel *happy*. Shawn needed something different. He spent time studying, meeting, reading, and learning from brilliant thought leaders, business coaches, and writers on personal and professional success. He knew he had to start from scratch—all over again.

In 2019, Shawn launched Elevation, a business growth coaching and consulting firm which had one mission: to help entrepreneurs build hugely successful businesses while achieving a sense of happiness.

As he kicked off his second calling, Shawn felt compelled to share with leaders everywhere all he had learned after living the real entrepreneurial experience: the bitter failures, the sweet successes, the tough conversations, the struggling relationships, the physical shutdowns and burnouts, the incredible highs, the emotional exhaustion, the self-doubt, and the constant battle of the ego on the endless quest for happiness.

As a result, Shawn wrote *The Happy Leader*. He has also been featured in numerous publications, including INC.com, *Fast Company*, *Real Leaders* magazine, *Ladders* magazine, CEO Blog Nation, the official blogs of Entrepreneurs' Organization (EO) and Atlassian, among others.

A sought-after leadership speaker, workshop leader, and business coach, Shawn also sits on the Board of "Champions for Life," a non-profit organization working with schools and communities across the country to help children develop their physical literacy. His obsession with endurance sports and physical excellence combines with his continuous journey for spiritual enlightenment through daily meditation practices.

A major voice on business growth and leadership, Shawn is on a mission to help you realize one thing: you can experience incredible business success and be a real leader—while achieving deep happiness.

Few people know that Shawn's Indian Name - Sukhraj - can be translated as "The Happy Leader." His grandmother gave him this name at birth. It always struck a chord with him. From a young age, he found himself on a quest for happiness in everything he did.

Is Shawn happy? Ask him—his journey has only just begun. Join him at shawnjohal.com!

GO BEHIND
THE SCENES WITH
20+ WORLD CLASS
LEADERSHIP EXPERTS

DISCOVER HOW TO BUILD
A BUSINESS AND LIFE YOU LOVE.

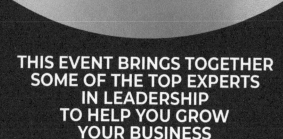

THIS EVENT BRINGS TOGETHER
SOME OF THE TOP EXPERTS
IN LEADERSHIP
TO HELP YOU GROW
YOUR BUSINESS
AND YOUR HAPPINESS AND

IT IS FREE

FOR A LIMITED TIME

WWW.HAPPYLEADERSUMMIT.COM